CHILDREN IN MORAL DANGER
AND THE PROBLEM OF GOVERNMENT
IN THIRD REPUBLIC FRANCE

EDITORS

Sherry B. Ortner, Nicholas B. Dirks, Geoff Eley

A LIST OF TITLES

IN THIS SERIES APPEARS

AT THE BACK OF

THE BOOK

PRINCETON STUDIES IN
CULTURE / POWER / HISTORY

CHILDREN IN MORAL DANGER
AND THE PROBLEM OF GOVERNMENT
IN THIRD REPUBLIC FRANCE

Sylvia Schafer

PRINCETON UNIVERSITY PRESS

PRINCETON, NEW JERSEY

Copyright © 1997 by Princeton University Press
Published by Princeton University Press, 41 William Street,
Princeton, New Jersey 08540
In the United Kingdom: Princeton University Press, Chichester, West Sussex

Library of Congress Cataloging-in-Publication Data

Schafer, Sylvia, [date]
Children in moral danger and the problem of government in Third Republic
France / Sylvia Schafer.
p.   cm. — (Princeton studies in culture/power/history)
Includes bibliographical references and index.
ISBN 0-691-01612-7 (cloth : alk. paper)
1. Child welfare—France—History—19th century.   2. Family
policy—France—History—19th century.   3. France—Moral conditions—
History—19th century.   4. Paternalism—France—History—19th
century.   5. France—Politics and government—1870–1940.   I.   Title.
II. Series.
HV761.A6S33   1997
362.7′0944′09034—dc21   97-8969   CIP

This book has been composed in Times Roman

Princeton University Press books are printed on acid-free paper
and meet the guidelines for permanence and durability of the
Committee on Production Guidelines for Book Longevity of
the Council on Library Resources

Printed in the United States of America

1   3   5   7   9   10   8   6   4   2

To my parents

Contents

Acknowledgments

THIS BOOK and I have benefited from the generosity of many individuals. First among them is Susanna Barrows, exemplary adviser and friend. Tom Laqueur and Marianne Constable both provided invaluable criticism in the early stages of writing, challenging me to argue with rigor and to make my writing accessible to a more heterogeneous audience. Thanks also to the French History Dissertation Group at Berkeley, whose members read many early drafts of these chapters and engaged in lively and useful discussions of them. Later, Lou Roberts, Joshua Cole, Katherine Kudlick, Andrew Aisenberg, and Ann-Louise Shapiro read revised versions of these chapters. Each of them offered insightful suggestions and, over the years, restorative doses of good humor and moral support. Special thanks go to Rachel Fuchs for her extraordinary generosity. Few scholars share their expertise with as much joy. In Paris the patient and helpful staff at the Archives de l'Assistance Publique and Brigitte Lainé at the Archives de la Ville de Paris et du Département de la Seine provided essential assistance in navigating the archives and the bureaucratic order that mediates research in France. Participants in the School of Social Sciences' 1991–92 seminar on "history" at the Institute for Advanced Study also contributed valuable critical readings of this work in its early form. I am also especially indebted to the members of the Pembroke Center's 1993–94 seminar, "Law, Letters, and Difference," particulary Elizabeth Weed, Ellen Rooney, and Janaki Nair, whose unsparing readings sharpened my thinking about the nexus of law, family, and history. To express fully my gratitude to Joan W. Scott would require much more than a few lines in these acknowledgments. Although I owe her much more than this, I am especially grateful to her for encouraging me to be relentless in examining the implications of my arguments and, most of all, for sharing the pleasure of reading against the grain. I also want to thank Mary Murrell, my editor at Princeton, Dalia Geffen, my copy editor, and the anonymous readers for Princeton University Press for their useful suggestions about revising the manuscript for publication.

Support in material form has similarly come from many sources. A graduate research grant from the University of California at Berkeley helped lay the foundation for this project. More extended research in France was made possible by a Bourse Chateaubriand, a grant from the International Doctoral Research Fellowship Program for Western Europe of the American Council of Learned Studies and the Social Science Research Council, with funds provided by the Ford Foundation and the Flora Hewlett Foundation, and the Mrs. Roy O'Conner Tocqueville Award for research on contemporary

France, with funds provided by the French-American Foundation. A fellowship from the Mabelle McLeod Lewis Memorial Fund provided generous support for the completion of the dissertation. A postdoctoral fellowship at Brown University's Pembroke Center for Teaching and Research on Women provided time and space for the revision of the manuscript as well as a congenial and intellectually invigorating climate. A research grant from the Graduate School at the University of Wisconsin, Milwaukee, also provided invaluable support in the later stages of revision.

These acknowledgments would not be complete without more personal thanks. In that spirit, I would like to express my gratitude to my parents, sisters, and friends, all of whom have provided essential sustenance over the years. Lucy, Willy, and Phred did their utmost to make sure that my life as a scholar could never be described as all work and no play. Although he encountered this book and its author at a relatively late stage of production, Michael Dintenfass deserves more thanks than he would ever accept. Deepest gratitude to this respected colleague and friend for all he has so freely offered.

Abbreviations Used in Notes

AAP   Archives de l'Assistance Publique
ADS   Archives de la Ville de Paris et du Département de la Seine
AGAPP   Administration Générale de l'Assistance Publique de Paris
APP   Archives de la Préfecture de Police
CGS   Conseil Général de la Seine
CMP   Conseil Municipal de Paris
_CN_   _Code Napoléon_
CSAP   Conseil Supérieur de l'Assistance Publique
_JO_   _Journal officiel_
JOS   _Journal officiel, Sénat, Débats_

Unless otherwise noted, all translations from the French are my own.

CHILDREN IN MORAL DANGER
AND THE PROBLEM OF GOVERNMENT
IN THIRD REPUBLIC FRANCE

Introduction

"HAPPY CHILDREN have no history," remarked Jacques Bonzon on the first page of his 1901 book on public assistance to children in France. "[B]ut poor children, abandoned children, they do."[1] In making this assertion the French administrator was certainly in good company. Leo Tolstoy had introduced one of his most compelling heroines almost twenty-five years earlier with a strikingly similar observation. "All happy families are like one another," he declared in the opening lines of *Anna Karenina*, "but each unhappy family is unhappy in its own way."[2]

In the regulation of the family in late-nineteenth-century France, as in Tolstoy's tale of feminine anguish in the upper reaches of Russian society, it is clear that notions of dangerous "unhappiness" have often provided a crucial impetus for constructing the plight of individual families for public consumption. In both the French report on assistance to children and the Russian novel, the beginning of "history"—and the end of "privacy"—was marked by an apparent deviation from the prescribed norms of family stability and internal cohesion. In both works, the origins of a visible, public historicity lay in a series of ruptures that tore whole families, as well as individual family members, from the moorings of apparently unremarkable conformity.

This book examines a category of dangerous unhappiness born—that is, conceptually and institutionally articulated—during the first decades of the French Third Republic, particularly the 1880s: the problem of *abandon moral*, or the "moral endangerment" of children at the hands of their own parents. In tracing the emergence and integration of abandon moral into the language, structures, and practices of French social government between the 1870s and 1914, this work explores how this new category of family unhappiness entered history and left its mark on the identity and institutional infrastructure of modern France.

What exactly did the words *abandon moral* describe? Throughout its life in the discourse and practice of family regulation in France, the term proved to be exceptionally fluid. Entering the vocabulary of administration, law, and

---

[1] Jacques Bonzon, *La Réforme du service des enfants assistés* (Paris: Berger-Levrault, 1901), 3.

[2] Leo Tolstoy, *Anna Karenina*, trans. David Magarshack (New York: Signet, 1961), 1. The novel, first published in Russian in 1877, was well known to the educated classes of late-nineteenth-century France. Beginning in 1885, the French publishing house Hachette brought out a new translated edition of *Anna Karenina* almost annually. In less than twenty years, Hachette alone produced twelve editions of the text; other publishers brought out their own versions as well.

social reform sometime around 1880, *abandon moral* was first used to denote parents' general failure to provide a proper moral upbringing, or *éducation*, for their offspring. While it drew on particular understandings of the family lives of the poor, *abandon moral* also signified moral crisis on a national scale. Stressing the dangers that would inevitably spring from a poorly developed moral character, the Third Republic's vision of abandon moral referred above all to the collapse of the domestic "civilizing process," to borrow a phrase from Norbert Elias, whereby children were inculcated with the moral standards and habits of personal conduct that distinguished them from the deviant, the marginal, and the socially dangerous.[3] From the earliest articulations of the term, notions of *abandon moral* continually invoked a primal experience of lack: the child's experience of dangerous parental "absence" from the educative process, often ironically embodied in the active presence and influence of a "morally dangerous" parent.[4]

After nearly a decade of debate and revision, French legislators attempted to ascribe a formal juridical meaning to *abandon moral* by enacting new civil legislation on the divestiture of paternal authority in July 1889.[5] Legal codification, however, was no guarantee against the term's essential elasticity. The fluid definition of *abandon moral* embedded in the law ensured that its practical meaning would remain ambiguous well after French president Sadi Carnot's signature dried on the final draft of the law. It also ensured that all future attempts to regulate abandon moral would entail a significant degree of uncertainty about establishing the practical contours of a problem so fundamentally defined by an irreducible conceptual instability. As one influential commentator admitted more than twenty years after the passage of the law, moral abandonment "does not manifest itself outwardly, as material abandonment does, through easily grasped concrete facts. . . . It is in some way a negative fact. The element that can be grasped is not the fact itself, but the practical consequences which spring from it." Abandon moral, this observer concluded, "cannot be perceived directly: it is presumed."[6]

Writing the history of a "negative fact" poses serious challenges, but it also offers exciting opportunities. The analysis of abandon moral presented here focuses on the curious relationship between power and uncertainty as it emerged in several crucial settings: the arena of legislative debate, the world of civil justice, and the domain of departmental administration. What, I will

---

[3] Norbert Elias, *The Civilizing Process: The History of Manners*, trans. Edmund Jephcott (New York: Pantheon, 1982).

[4] Psychoanalyst Leonard Shengold has suggested that child abuse can be theorized simultaneously as dangerous neglect and dangerous contact, an understanding that resonates with the uncertainty embedded in nineteenth-century notions of abandon moral (Shengold, *Soul Murder: The Effects of Childhood Abuse and Deprivation* [New Haven: Yale University Press, 1989]).

[5] The text of the law can be found in the *JO*, 25 July 1889, 3653–55.

[6] Emile Alcindor, *Les Enfants assistés* (Paris: Emile Paul, 1912), 85.

ask, were the wider implications of this multiply sited opacity and instability? What might we learn about the reading practices of public officials who had to identify abandon moral and act on it? What did the "negative fact" of moral danger in the family mean for the relationship between law, the language of moral order, and the practice of governance in late-nineteenth-century France?[7]

To fully address these questions, this book also considers the new patterns of categorizing and caring for children, patterns that emerged from within larger contemporary anxieties about the moral breakdown of family, society, and nation. In the French discussion of abandon moral, these concerns collected around the figure of the *enfant moralement abandonné*, or "morally abandoned child." Introduced by reform-minded legislators and philanthropists in the late 1870s, the category of the enfant moralement abandonné immediately challenged the coherence of the state's classification of children in need of protection or correction. Imperiled by a deficient domestic experience, these children were read both as the innocent victims of parental moral deviance and as future criminals and deviants themselves. Although the early Third Republic was not lacking for emblems of moral degeneration, moreover, the enfant moralement abandonné appears to have been invested with a unique kind of discursive potency. Defined by an imminent danger of corruption but not necessarily limited to any single path toward adult "deviance," the new category represented the pure potential of moral disorder; within the enfant moralement abandonné lay the entire cast of destructive characters—criminals, prostitutes, alcoholics, radicals, and dangerous mothers and fathers—who were so often called upon to represent the endangered moral health of the nation in this period.[8]

Fraught with internal contradictions, the new category of enfant moralement abandonné would also throw the administration of child protection and

---

[7] Many of my central questions about governance and the politics of the social in the nineteenth century arise from my reading of Michel Foucault's essay "Governmentality," in *The Foucault Effect: Studies in Governmentality*, ed. Graham Burchell, Colin Gordon, and Peter Miller (Chicago: University of Chicago Press, 1991). Giovanna Proccaci traces critical tensions in the relationship between liberalism and social government earlier in the century in *Gouverner la misère: La question sociale en France, 1789–1848* (Paris: Editions du Seuil, 1993).

[8] The prostitute, the socialist, the alcoholic, and the Communard were equally visible emblems of moral breakdown in the early Third Republic's literature of social crisis. See, for example, Susanna Barrows, "After the Commune: Alcoholism, Temperance, and Literature in the Early Third Republic," in *Consciousness and Class Experience in Nineteenth-Century Europe*, ed. John Merriman (New York: Holmes and Meier, 1979); Jill Harsin, *Policing Prostitution in Nineteenth-Century Paris* (Princeton: Princeton University Press, 1985); William Coleman, *Death Is a Social Disease: Public Health and Political Economy in Early Industrial France* (Madison: University of Wisconsin Press, 1982); Ruth Harris, *Murders and Madness: Medicine, Law, and Society in the Fin de Siècle* (Oxford: Clarendon Press, 1989); and Robert A. Nye, *Crime, Madness, and Politics in Modern France: The Medical Concept of National Decline* (Princeton: Princeton University Press, 1984).

juvenile correction into disarray. As officials worked to reorder their world, they consistently encountered difficult practical disjunctures between contemporary visions of moral pathology within and around the child and the new French republic's project of rationalizing its forms and modes of government. Through an analysis of this adminstrative disarray and the sequence of official responses to it, I shall suggest that the search to define institutional structures and practices appropriate to the new category of enfant moralement abandonné also played a significant role in fundamentally recasting the relationship between state and family in this period.

To be sure, France was not the only country to turn its sights on the question of endangered children or morally dangerous parents in this period. The last three decades of the nineteenth century witnessed an international surge in public and private action against danger within the family, against a perceived plague of domestic neglect, and against the apparent increase in the number of children roaming the city streets on their own.[9] The cross-national dimension of these questions, or at least the intersection of more particularly national versions of them, is especially evident in the staging of international conferences on these new issues, such as the International Congress on the Protection of Children, held in Paris in 1883.[10] In one recent

[9] For two brief overviews of the international arena of child protection in the late nineteeenth century, see Catherine Rollet-Echalier, *La Politique à l'égard de la petite enfance sous la IIIe République* (Paris: Editions de l'INED/Presses Universitaires de France, 1990), 139, and John R. Gillis, *Youth and History: Tradition and Change in European Age Relations 1770–Present* (New York: Academic Press, 1974), 156–70. The national literatures on the history of child endangerment have grown immensely in the past decade and cannot be cited in this space beyond a few exemplary titles. On the question of unfit parents and abuse in the United States, see Linda Gordon, *Heroes of Their Own Lives: The Politics and History of Family Violence, Boston, 1880–1960* (New York: Penguin Books, 1988), and Michael Grossberg, *Governing the Hearth: Law and the Family in Nineteenth-Century America* (Chapel Hill: University of North Carolina Press, 1985). George K. Behlmer's *Child Abuse and Moral Reform in England, 1870–1918* (Stanford: Stanford University Press, 1982) remains the cornerstone of the work on Britain. Jane Lewis's *The Politics of Motherhood: Child and Maternal Welfare in England, 1900–1939* (London: Croom Helm; Montreal: McGill-Queen's University Press, 1980) and Clark Nardinelli's *Child Labor and the Industrial Revolution* (Bloomington: Indiana University Press, 1990) are also essential reading for the British side of these questions. On Austria, see Peter Feldbauer, *Kinderelend in Wien: Von der Armenkinderpflege zur Jugendfürsorge, 17.–19. Jahrhundert* (Vienna: Gesellschaftskritik, 1980). For a broad comparative perspective, see Valerie Fildes et al., eds., *Women and Children First: International Maternal and Infant Welfare, 1870–1945* (New York: Routledge, 1993).

[10] Subsequent meetings of this congress took place in Bordeaux in 1895 and in Brussels in 1913; other international groups organized meetings focused on somewhat narrower themes, including the connections between abandon moral and juvenile criminality. See *Congrès international de la protection de l'enfance (Palais du Trocadero, 15–23 juin 1883)* (Paris: Pédone-Lauriel, 1885); *Congrès international de la protection de l'enfance (Bordeaux, 1895)* (Bordeaux: Librairie Bourlange, n.d.); and *Congrès international de la protection de l'enfance*

view, in fact, the 1880s and 1890s witnessed a "frenzy of congresses" on the topics of endangered and dangerous children, at both the national and the international level.[11] The strength of French enthusiasm for these congresses cannot be exaggerated, moreover. At the 1890 meeting in Belgium on juvenile delinquency and abandon moral, the French government sent twice as many delegates as any other participating foreign country. French members of the congress similarly outnumbered the members of every other participating nation, except the host country, by more than three to one.[12]

The confluence of national interests in child protection across borders in this period, as well as France's apparent place at the forefront of the nations studying these issues, invites much closer study than has yet been produced. At the same time, however, it is important not to reduce the primary historical significance of particular national concerns about the moral order of the family to their apparent consistency with transnational trends. Instead, as the French articulation of abandon moral and the range of possible responses to it so amply suggest, the construction of general social problems relies on situated grids of signification. The notion of abandon moral, although resonant in a developing international arena of concern about familial disorder, nonetheless derived its primary meaning from within a frame of cultural references, a pattern of social organization, and a web of political institutions and discourses that all served to mark it as a particularly French problem. That distinctive particularity in turn suffused all debate on abandon moral with the wider concerns of domestic political discourse and governmental action.

To fully understand the intersection—or coexistence—of national interests in the international arena of the late nineteenth century, it is essential to devote more scholarly attention to how social problems such as moral neglect or moral danger have been constructed, deployed, and institutionalized in the complex national contexts in which they first emerged. This approach

---

(Bruxelles) (Brussels: Imprimerie du Moniteur Belge, 1913). See also Ministère de la Justice [Belgium], Congrès international pour l'étude des questions relatives au patronage des détenus et à la protection des enfants moralement abandonnés. Anvers, 1890 (Brussels: E. Guyot, 1891).

[11] Martine Kaluszynski and Françoise Tetard, "Un Objet: L'enfant en 'danger moral.' Une expérience: La société de patronage" (1989, photocopy), 8.

[12] The French government sent six officials representatives. The next largest delegations, composed of three officials each, came from Spain and Switzerland. Fifty French members of the international body also attended the meeting in Anvers, whereas Britain was represented by the next largest group, numbering fourteen. Among the foreign members of the congress, the French also dominated with a contingent of fifty, surpassed only by the host, Belgium, with more than one hundred members. The British comprised the third largest group, with fourteen members (Ministère de la Justice [Belgium], Congrès international . . . Anvers, 1890, 26–27). Kaluszynski and Tetard note the exceptional activity of the Belgians in the areas of penal reform and child protection in "Un Objet: L'enfant en 'danger moral,'" 8.

is particularly important for France, a country whose articulations of moral danger in the family appear to have been powerful forces in international discussion. With its goal of developing an approach that fully historicizes the elaboration of social problems within overlapping arenas of discourse and governance, this work is designed to speak not only to those with a scholarly interest in France or in the politics of international reform movements but also to those with a broader methodological or theoretical stake in exploring how exactly relationships between state and family have been forged—and reforged—in the modern era.

Situating the specific case of abandon moral historically requires signaling two especially significant aspects of the French Third Republic at the outset. First, the Third Republic of the 1870s and 1880s was a regime distinctive for the political urgency of its struggle to establish the legitimate nature and foundation of moral order. Born in the crucible of devastating military defeat at the hands of Prussia in the fall of 1870, and challenged almost immediately by the outbreak of the radical Paris Commune in the spring of 1871, the Third Republic embraced moral reform as the antidote to the panoply of national travails that seemed to have led to the events of the "terrible year," 1870–71.[13] These symptoms of demoralization included radicalism, alcoholism, military weakness, and the statistical appearance of a frighteningly low birthrate.[14] During the 1870s, a period of especially great flux and uncertainty about whether France would in fact remain a republic, conservative government officials and clerics worked together to promote a "moral order"

[13] Useful general surveys of the history of the French Third Republic include Jacques Chastenet, *Histoire de la Troisième République*, 7 vols. (Paris: Hachette, 1954); Pierre Miquet, *La Troisième République* (Paris: Fayard, 1989); David Thomson, *Democracy in France Since 1870* (London: Oxford University Press, 1969); Jean-Marie Mayeur, *Les Débuts de la IIIe République, 1871–1898* (Paris: Editions du Seuil, 1973); and Jean-Marie Mayeur and Madeleine Rebérioux, *The Third Republic from Its Origins to the Great War, 1871–1914*, trans. J. R. Foster (Cambridge: Maison des Sciences de l'Homme and Cambridge University Press, 1984).

[14] On fears of moral degeneration in the early Third Republic, see, among others, Keonraad W. Swart, *The Sense of Decadence in Nineteenth-Century France* (The Hague: Martinus Nijhoff, 1964); Nye, *Crime, Madness, and Politics*; Annie Stora-Lamarre, *L'Enfer de la Troisième République: Censeurs et pornographes (1881–1914)* (Paris: Editions Imago, 1990); Barrows, "After the Commune" and *Distorting Mirrors: Visions of the Crowd in Late Nineteenth-Century France* (New Haven: Yale University Press, 1981). On the anxiety raised by the specter of France's comparatively low natality, see esp. Joshua Cole, "The Power of Large Numbers: Population and Politics in Nineteenth-Century France" (Ph.D. diss., University of California, Berkeley, 1991); John Hunter, "The Problem of the French Birth Rate on the Eve of World War I," *French Historical Studies* 11 (1962); Michael S. Teitelbaum and Jay M. Winter, *The Fear of Population Decline* (Orlando: Academic Press, 1985); Rollet-Echalier, *La Politique à l'égard de la petite enfance*; and Angus McLaren, *Sexuality and Social Order: The Debate over the Fertility of Women and Workers in France, 1770–1920* (New York: Holmes and Meier, 1983).

grounded in the authority of the Catholic Church and achieved through collective atonement and a return to "traditional" values.[15]

The year 1879 saw the defeat of the conservative monarchist republic of the 1870s and the rise of a more liberal leadership committed to domesticating France's revolutionary republican tradition in a moderate, rationally ordered regime.[16] Between 1879 and 1889, the "ten foundational years" of the republican Third Republic,[17] concern about the proper foundation of a modern moral order and the moral status of the nation intensified through the enduring sense of moral crisis as well as through the new government's efforts to create a distinctive moral identity for the republic. Devoted to the construction of a secular polity, desperate to establish a legitimate moral identity for the regime that differentiated it from both the radical egalitarianism of the revolutionary republican tradition and the conservative religiosity of the Moral Order of the 1870s, leading politicians and commentators channeled their anxiety about moral decline toward the family, appropriating it from the religious framework of conservatives and consecrating it as the basic educative and social unit of a healthy, truly republican polity.[18] As one republican legislator put it in 1900, the family was the "essential foundation of civilized societies, the source of all productive [*fécondes*] energies and all virtues."[19] In these first decades of the liberal republic, fears of collective

[15] On the monarchist republic of the 1870s and the conservative view of Moral Order voiced by its leader, Marshal MacMahon, see Mayeur and Rebérioux, *The Third Republic*, 6–9. See also Miquet, *La Troisième République*, 164, and Robert R. Locke, *French Legitimists and the Politics of Moral Order in the Early Third Republic* (Princeton: Princeton University Press, 1974), esp. 47. For an illuminating explication of moral discourse in the 1870s, see also Raymond A. Jonas, "Monument as Ex-Voto, Monument as Historiosophy: The Basilica of the Sacré-Coeur," *French Historical Studies* 18, no. 2 (fall 1993).

[16] On this shift in control of the republic, see Chastenet, *L'Enfance de la Troisième République*, vol. 1 of his *Histoire de la Troisième Republique*; Daniel Halèvy, *The End of the Notables*, trans. Alain Silvera and June Guicharnaud (Middletown, Conn.: Wesleyan University Press, 1974); Fresnette Pisani-Ferry, *Le Coup d'état manquée du 16 mai 1877* (Paris: Robert Laffont, 1965); and Mayeur, *Les Débuts de la IIIe République*, 95–133.

[17] The notion of the 1880s as the republic's foundational decade comes from Maurice Agulhon, *La République: De Jules Ferry à François Mitterrand, 1880 à nos jours* (Paris: Hachette, 1990), 22.

[18] On the republican Left's denunciation of monarchist Moral Order, see Locke, *French Legitimists*, 208–9. On the liberal republican search for middle ground in the 1880s, see Agulhon, *La République*, 22. On the secularization of morals in the nineteenth century and the importance of French positivist Auguste Comte to this trend, see Owen Chadwick, *The Secularization of the European Mind in the Nineteenth Century* (Cambridge: Cambridge University Press, 1975), 229–49. Many historians have noted the strong influence of positivist thinking among the founders of the liberal Third Republic of the 1880s. See, among others, Louis Legrand, *L'Influence du positivisme dans l'oeuvre scolaire de Jules Ferry: Les origines de la laïcité* (Paris: Librairie Marcel Rivière, 1966), and Phyllis Stock-Morton, *Moral Education for a Secular Society: The Development of "Morale Laïque" in Nineteenth Century France* (Albany: SUNY Press, 1988).

[19] Emile Rey, *Assistance aux enfants des familles indigentes* (N.p., [1900]), 7.

moral crisis clearly continued to escalate. At the same time, the family, increasingly reconceived in sentimental and educational terms, emerged in republican discourse and practice as one of the most critical sites for state action that would halt moral decline on the one hand and build a positive, secular, and morally coherent republican society on the other.[20]

The Third Republic's tendency to turn to medical science as a primary means of addressing the apparent moral and physical decline of its population has received a great deal of attention from historians in recent years.[21] Less explored, but no less important, was the new republic's deep investment in civil law as a means of institutionalizing the authority of the state and reconfiguring the moral life of the nation.[22] The turn to law in defining and regulating abandon moral also rested on the particular place law came to occupy under the Third Republic.[23] In this new political order, committed to the creation of a secular democratic nation, law emerged as a primary medium for the public regulation of individual and collective moral life. It provided a critical counterweight to the freedoms created by the regime's

[20] The work of Jean-Jacques Rousseau, particularly the ideas on family and the education of the young found in *Emile*, served as an especially important point of departure for the development of nineteenth-century views of the family as the site of affective life and character formation. See Rousseau, *Emile, ou de l'éducation*, ed. Marcel Launay (Paris: Flammarion, 1966). For the history of the changing ideals of family life, see Philippe Ariès's much debated *Centuries of Childhood: A Social History of Family Life*, trans. Robert Baldick (New York: Vintage, 1962). For influential examples of later-nineteenth-century views on the family in sentimental and moral terms, see Paul Janet, *La Famille: Leçons de philosophie morale* (Paris: n.p., 1873); Gustave Droz, *Monsieur, madame et bébé* (Paris: V. Havard, 1878); and Ernest Legouvé, *Les Pères et les enfants au XIXe siècle: La jeunesse*, 3d ed. (Paris: n.p., n.d.).

[21] See, for example, Jack D. Ellis, *The Physician-Legislators of France: Medicine and Politics in the Early Third Republic, 1870–1914* (Cambridge: Cambridge University Press, 1990); Martha Hildreth, *Doctors, Bureaucrats, and Public Health in France, 1888–1902* (New York: Garland, 1987); Harris, *Murders and Madness*; and Barrows, *Distorting Mirrors*. Robert Nye provides the most useful formulation of this tendency in his account of the Third Republic's "medical model of cultural crisis." See Nye, *Crime, Madness, and Politics*, esp. 132–70.

[22] Although historians such as Harris have also stressed the links between science and criminal justice in this period, their interest in establishing the hegemonic authority of science leads them to cast law simply as an arena of conquest. On science, especially the nascent discipline of criminal anthropology, and criminal justice under the Third Republic, see also Joëlle Guillais-Maury, *La Chair de l'autre: Le crime passionel au XIXe siècle* (Paris: Olivier Orban, 1986), esp. 253–80, and Nye, *Crime, Madness, and Politics*, 97–131. Andrew R. Aisenberg provides an important corrective to this tendency in "Contagious Disease and the Government of Paris in the Age of Pasteur" (Ph.D. diss., Yale University, 1993).

[23] On the status of law and legal reform under the Third Republic, see André-Jean Arnaud, *Les Juristes face à la société du XIXe siècle à nos jours* (Paris: Presses Universitaires de France, 1975), esp. 75–125. Arnaud suggests that civil law began to lose some of its primacy over other bodies of law, yet his work also illuminates the continuing centrality of civil law and the Code Napoléon in the Third Republic's reconsideration of the relationship between law and society. On jurists' active role in the political life of the new republic, see Yves-Henri Gaudemet, *Les Juristes et la vie politique de la IIIe République* (Paris: Presses Universitaires de France, 1970).

attempts to loosen inherited restrictions on free expression and association. Law also embodied the secular state's challenge to the church's status as the source of moral norms and sanctions. It promised rationality in the place of Catholic "superstition." And in its rationality, law appeared to express the relationship between the universal and the particular in its most perfect form, a capacity dear to republicans trained in the precepts of Comtean positivism. Finally, law appeared to republicans of the 1880s as a means of creating a society freed from the bonds of both "natural" and traditional hierarchies.

This manifest interest in law, apart from the epistemologies of science or the regulation of criminality, is the second critical characteristic of Third Republic France that needs to be highlighted at the outset.[24] Although the importance of law to the constitution of the republic seems to have been overlooked in much recent scholarship, it was apparent to comtemporaries such as Emile Durkheim. In a course offered around the turn of the twentieth century, Durkheim summed up his position on the relationship between state, law, and society. The state, he declared, "organizes the moral life of the country." For Durkheim, this process of moral organization was accomplished above all through legislative and juridical action. "Law," he proclaimed, "[is] the means by which the state enters private life."[25]

Taken together, then, the Third Republic's founding concern about reworking both the moral life of the nation and the moral identity of the state, and its deep investment in the moralizing rule of civil law, suggest that regulating the moral life of the family through the operation of civil justice was both central to stabilizing the new regime and an extremely high stake venture.[26] It is from within this historically situated intersection of the early

[24] Among those historians exploring the wider meaning of law for the Third Republic, see H. S. Jones's suggestive work on public law, *The French State in Question: Public Law and Political Argument in the Third Republic* (Cambridge: Cambridge University Press, 1993), esp. 29–54, and François Ewald's essential discussion of law, risk, and government in the late nineteenth century, *L'Etat providence* (Paris: Grasset, 1986). Stora-Lamarre's book on the Third Republic's efforts to control pornography, *L'Enfer de la Troisième République*, also points up the regime's understanding of the relationship between law, morality, and the state. On this topic see also Ian Burney, "The Obscene in Legislative Language: A Case of Moral Censorship in Late Nineteenth-Century France" (University of California, Berkeley, 1985, photocopy).

[25] Emile Durkheim, "De l'Etat," in *Textes*, ed. Victor Karady, vol. 1 (Paris: Minuit, 1975), 175. See also Steven Lukes and Andrew Scull, eds., *Durkheim and the Law* (New York: St. Martin's Press, 1983).

[26] For two useful surveys of family law and its reform under the early Third Republic, see Claudia Scheck Kselman, "The Modernization of Family Law: The Politics and Ideology of Family Reform in Third Republic France" (Ph.D. diss., University of Michigan, 1980), and Esther Sue Kanipe, "The Family, Private Property, and the State in France, 1870–1914" (Ph.D. diss., University of Wisconsin, Madison, 1976). On the evolution of women's rights under the early Third Republic, see Jules Thabaut, *L'Evolution de la législation sur la famille depuis 1804* (Toulouse: Edouard Privat, 1913). See also Claire Goldberg Moses, *French Feminism in the Nineteenth Century* (Albany: SUNY Press, 1984), 229–30.

Third Republic's particular anxieties about moral order, its particular faith in law, and its particular obsession with the family that this analysis of abandon moral attempts to illuminate the larger complexities of state building and social government in the late nineteenth century.

Making sense of the complexities of government under the early Third Republic also requires reflecting on abandon moral and the enfant moralement abandonné as problems of governance played out in local settings. Along with its focus on national-level discussions and legislative action, this book also centers on administrative debate, policy, and practice in the region largely coextensive with the city of Paris, known in this period as the department of the Seine. Abandon moral and the enfant moralement abandonné were in many respects Parisian problems, embedded in the city's complex web of historical and social representations, articulated and addressed by the capital's remarkably active administrators and local officials.[27] The Conseil Général of the Seine and the Paris Bureau of Public Assistance both played pivotal roles in the "discovery" of abandon moral and in the erection of an administrative infrastructure designed to protect and reform the enfant moralement abandonné.

The department of the Seine founded its Service des Enfants Moralement Abandonnés in 1881, the first public agency in France devoted specifically to this category of children. Even after the passage of the 1889 law stamped abandon moral as a national issue, Paris and its environs accounted for the majority of the children in France classified as moralement abandonnés by police officials and magistrates. In short, the department served as the primary laboratory in which the problem of abandon moral was distilled. Parisian experiments defined the problem. Parisian solutions served as both a potent impetus and a sturdy foundation for building the edifice of protection on a national scale. With regard to the issue of moral danger in the family, Paris officials constituted a veritable administrative avant-garde.

By focusing on Paris as both a unique and a uniquely influential administrative site, this account of the invention and institutionalization of abandon moral also permits a closer examination of the daily tasks of interpretation that gave moral danger its materiality. It is in the everyday interactions that occurred in Parisian lodging houses, neighborhoods, police stations, and courtrooms that we see the "deviance" of individual families produced for official—and popular—consumption. In these situated dialogues between popular and official interpretation, I shall argue, the state and the family manifested themselves as historically and culturally meaningful entities.

---

[27] Even in larger provincial cities such as Lyons, where the cause of child protection flourished in the nineteenth century, abandon moral remained by and large the concern of private philanthropic organizations. See Domenique Dessertine, *La Société lyonnaise pour le sauvetage de l'enfance (1890–1960): Face à l'enfance en danger, un siècle d'expérience de l'internat et du placement familial* (Toulouse: Erès, 1990).

At the same time, efforts to read abandon moral in the social fabric of Paris suggest that contemporary attempts to respond to perceived social crises were continually obstructed by the elusive nature of the problems, and that efforts to solve apparent social crises through formal action, particularly through legislation, tended to reproduce the ambiguities of the very problems they were supposed to resolve. Reading and reconstructing these problems were nevertheless essential parts of making the mechanisms of social reform run at the local level, even well after the problems and official responses to them had been formally codified. This fundamental instability of categories and meanings, so well exemplified in the enfant moralement abandonné and the issue of abandon moral, required that interpretation stand behind even the most banal gestures of protection, assistance, or regulation.

By examining the invention and institutionalization of abandon moral at both the national and the local level, this work explores the effects of intersecting efforts to delineate the contours of proper government in the late nineteenth century. Most important, in locating law, administration, and the ongoing process of interpretation that sustained them both within the contingencies of history, this book attempts to look beyond *la raison d'état* to a far more complex logic of government.[28] I call this logic—characterized as much by ambivalence and ambiguity as by clearly articulated order, as much by desire and anxiety as by the rational calculation of means and ends, and as much by the confluence of official and popular voices as by the apparently univocal expression of state interest—*l'imaginaire d'état*, or the state's imaginary.[29]

Recasting the state in these terms immediately raises several methodological issues. First, my efforts to locate and read l'imaginaire d'état in this period center on the importance of language in establishing the identity and moral nature of the state. Here I have found the insights of recent feminist and literary scholarship especially useful, for the construction of the state in ways that made official action on abandon moral possible and meaningful occurred above all in the domain of late-nineteenth-century representational practice.

[28] See the centrality of this term to the arguments about the regulation of the family presented in Philippe Meyer's *L'Enfant et la raison d'état* (Paris: Editions du Seuil, 1977).

[29] Notions of the "imaginary," or collective imagining, as part of political life have emerged most notably in recent literature on the eighteenth century and the French Revolution. Lynn Hunt, explaining her relocation of the "political unconscious" from Frederic Jameson's Marxist framework to a Freudian-inspired cultural frame of analysis, argues that in the eighteenth century "the French had a kind of collective political unconscious that was structured by narratives of family relations." Politics, Hunt argues more generally, "depend on imagination" (Hunt, *The Family Romance of the French Revolution* [Berkeley: University of California Press, 1992], xiii, xv). Georges Burdeau also notes the historical intangibility of the state, arguing for the importance of understanding the state as an imagined reality. See Burdeau, *L'Etat* (Paris: Editions du Seuil, 1970), esp. 14–18. On the politics of the social *imaginaire*, see Bronislaw Baczko, *Les Imaginaires sociaux: Mémoires et espoirs collectifs* (Paris: Payot, 1984).

Most important, these approaches both disclose and help explain the centrality of the gendered metaphors of family—and their essential indeterminacy—in the Third Republic's efforts to render the state as a new kind of moral figure in the landscape of modern republican government. On the whole, historians have tended to read the use of these tropes, and particularly the metaphorical invocation of "the father," as evidence that an increasingly "paternalist" state emerged in the later nineteenth century.[30] This history of abandon moral raises new questions about the historiographical interpretation of paternalism. It seeks a more complex understanding of the diverse relationships and patterns of discourse that have so often been identified as the stylistic signature of paternalism but that have been rarely investigated for their own historically contingent meanings and consequences. To pursue this goal of more finely textured inquiry, this book asks what the Third Republic's interests could have been, beyond the masking of an efficient apparatus of "social control," as some historians have argued, in emulating family hierarchies and deploying the metaphoric language of gendered family relations to describe the state and its various connections to the populace as a whole. What made a family model so compelling in the last quarter of the nineteenth century? How did official visions of family, fatherhood, motherhood, and childhood resonate with broader concerns about sexual difference and the family? What did those resonances signify for a regime so intent on reinventing France as a secular liberal republic? How did this familial language of sexual difference serve to articulate—and complicate—the new regime's conception of the proper relationship between government and the governed?[31]

---

[30] On the social and governmental politics of "paternalism" in the later nineteenth century, see Mary Lynn McDougall [formerly Stewart], "Protecting Infants: The French Campaign for Maternity Leaves, 1890's–1913," *French Historical Studies* 13 (1983); Mary Lynn Stewart, *Women, Work, and the French State: Labour, Protection, and Social Patriarchy, 1879–1919* (Kingston: McGill-Queen's University Press, 1989); Michelle Perrot, "On the Formation of the French Working Class," in *Working Class Formation: Nineteenth-Century Patterns in Western Europe and the United States*, ed. Ira Katznelson and Aristide R. Zolberg (Princeton: Princeton University Press, 1986), and "The Three Ages of Industrial Discipline in Nineteenth-Century France," in *Consciousness and Class Experience*, ed. Merriman. Donald Reid takes a linguistic approach to the problem of paternalism in the nineteenth century in "Industrial Paternalism: Discourse and Practice in Ninteenth-Century Mining and Metallurgy," *Comparative Studies in Society and History* 24, no. 4 (October 1985), 579–607, and in "Schools and the Paternalist Project at Le Creusot, 1850–1914," *Journal of Social History* 27, no. 1 (fall 1993): 129–43. See also the special issue of *Le Mouvement social* on paternalism, "Paternalismes d'hier et d'aujourd'hui," ed. Marianne Debouzy, *Le Mouvement social* 144 (July–September 1988).

[31] On the importance of examining how sexual difference signifies in the language of politics, see Joan Wallach Scott's seminal essay "Gender: A Useful Category of Historical Analysis," in *Gender and the Politics of History* (New York: Columbia University Press, 1988), esp. 48–50. The essay was first published in the *American Historical Review* 91, no. 5 (December 1986). See also Denise Riley, *"Am I That Name?" Feminism and the Category of "Women" in History*

The twin problems of abandon moral and the enfant moralement abandonné prove especially fertile ground for attempting to answer these questions. In identifying itself as a substitute parent for children whose own
parents had been deemed unfit by the court, the French state would confront
the confluence of its own broad use of familial tropes, its discourse on the
family, and the concrete problems of regulating and administering legal
guardianship. In this sense, the mobilization of these metaphors facilitated
more than the exercise of a naturalized state power over a population defined
as dependent and in need of authoritative protection. The use of that language was also essential, to borrow from the literary critic Stephen Greenblatt, to the state's own "self-fashioning." The Third Republic's invocation
of a parental identity in constructing and addressing the problem of abandon
moral seems to resonate in remarkably telling ways with Greenblatt's definition of the constructed "transhistorical self"; the construction of that self,
Greenblatt argues, produces "a distinctive personality, a characteristic address to the world, a consistent mode of perceiving and behaving."[32]

The image of the state as father was by no means the only component of
the Third Republic self-conscious fashioning of identity; nor were its implications always consonant with the agenda laid out by the state makers themselves. Nonetheless, the case of abandon moral suggests that the sentimen-
talized language of parenthood, and especially paternity, played an essential
part in the constitution of the state's identity as a social and political actor
during the founding years of the Third Republic.[33] No less important, it also
helped to determine the horizons of the republican imaginary as it was appropriated and reconstituted by the authors of this political regime.

Although I take up the establishment of a personality for the state in the
sense mentioned earlier, I do not wish to invoke a notion of the state as a
unitary or concrete entity. As historian Pierre Rosanvallon has warned, the

---

(Minneapolis: University of Minnesota Press, 1988). For an exemplary use of feminist and
poststructural theory in the analysis of French culture and politics, see Mary Louise Roberts,
Civilization without Sexes: Reconstructing Gender in Postwar France, 1917–1927 (Chicago:
University of Chicago Press, 1994). Feminist theorists Luce Irigaray and Barbara Johnson's
complementary discussions of language and sexual difference have also proved to be invaluable
in shaping the analysis presented here. See esp. Irigaray, *Ethique de la différence sexuelle*
(Paris: Minuit, 1984), and Johnson, *A World of Difference* (Baltimore: Johns Hopkins University
Press, 1987).

[32] Stephen Greenblatt, *Renaissance Self-Fashioning: From More to Shakespeare* (Chicago:
University of Chicago Press, 1980), 2.

[33] In his book on public law and the status of civil servants in the fin de siècle, H. S. Jones
contends that the Third Republic "was, in fact, the richest period of reflection about the state in
France at least since the Restoration" (Jones, *The French State in Question*, 52). Although Jones
bases this remark on his reading of debates from the first years of the twentieth century, it aptly
describes the earliest decades of the republic as well.

pitfall of writing the history of an overly reified and underhistoricized state, of rendering the state "a historical nonobject," is a serious one.[34] The aim here is to avoid producing yet another historical image of an intending, free-willed, and anthropomorphized state and instead to explore a state more precisely located in the history of government in France, reified only in the representation of itself and its actions by both interested partisans and more detached observers.[35] To write about the state, then, is to explore both its ongoing discursive constitution and the powerful political authority, webs of relationships, and even agency that attach to it.[36]

The organization of this book reflects my interest in exploring adjacent terrains of discourse and practices of government. Each of the three parts treats an arena crucial to the construction of abandon moral or the enfant moralement abandonné and the ranges of responses to those new social problems. Part 1 takes up the question of law, its logic, and its languages. Here I explore the discursive and ideological sinews of the 1889 law on abandon moral, its immediate antecedents, and the larger frame of Napoleonic civil law. How, I ask in this part, did the government's intercession in the ostensibly private affairs of the male-headed family become juridically thinkable in the late nineteenth century? How, in turn, did the desire to regulate moral abandonment by means of new civil legislation establish the horizons of the Third Republic's imaginaire d'état? Focusing on debates in the French legislature from the early 1870s to the late 1880s, as well as on the commentary of jurists and social critics of the era, I argue in this part that legitimating this intercession depended on a rewriting of the moral relationship between public and private paternal authority which had been established by the Napoleonic Code Civil at the beginning of the century. The debates on child protection and moral danger in this period destabilized conventional understandings of the boundaries between "public" and "private" through reformers' efforts to isolate the child's best interests. At the same time, the debates rewrote the relationship between republican government and the populace at large through an increasingly elastic language of family.

Part 2 takes the reader from the National Assembly to the local police

---

[34] Pierre Rosanvallon, *L'Etat en France de 1789 à nos jours* (Paris: Editions du Seuil, 1990), 9.

[35] As Rosanvallon has put it, "[T]he state is not only an administrative apparatus, it is equally an abstract political figure, insofar as it incarnates the principle of sovereignty. It is an efficacious form of social representation. That is why the history of the State must be the product par excellence of an articulation between the history of facts and the history of ideas and social representations" (*L'Etat en France*, 14). On the transformation of the state and its identity as a part of the history of politics, see also Foucault's "Governmentality."

[36] On the discursive constitution of the state in French political culture, see Jones, *The French State in Question*, esp. 6–28.

precincts in Paris, and from there to the city's civil tribunal. These chapters explore how individuals and local authorities instantiated the new law in their constructions—and contestations—of particular cases of abandon moral. How did the epistemological uncertainties of abandon moral, present in the earliest notions of the problem and written into the final text of the law of 1889, affect the prosecution of an individual case? How did assumptions about sexual difference, class, and morality shape the court's investigations and judgments? How was authority to speak the truth of abandon moral distributed among witnesses, the accused, the accuser, and those entitled by the state to provide "expert" opinions? Through the close reading of case dossiers from the 1890s and the early years of the 1900s, and through the analysis of a much larger number of decisions recorded in the registers of court in the same period, this part explores the operation of the juridical machine cobbled together from existing court structures, personnel, and procedures for the implementation of the new law.

Part 3 examines the fate of the "morally endangered" or "morally abandoned" children in state care. In its shift of arenas, from those of law to those of administration, it examines the ways in which public authorities attempted to enact the metaphorical parental status they had been accorded by the discourse of abandon moral through the classification and state care of the enfant moralement abandonné. How was the state to efface—or at least correct for—the early influences of a demoralizing domestic education? Could authorities fit these children into the extant system for raising the foundlings in state care, or did their unique form of abandonment require a kind of moral quarantine, not only from the other children in the care of the state but also from the provincial foster families who formed the backbone of state foundling care across France? In these chapters, I center my discussion on the experiments pursued by the Seine's Service des Enfants Moralement Abandonnés in the 1880s, experiments based on the principles of differentiation, exclusion, and moral (re)education. As a study of the place of classification in the Third Republic's art of government, part 3 also traces the internal fault lines and ambiguities running through the new category of state-assisted child. These lines and ambiguities, I will argue, rendered the enfant moralement abandonné an intrinsically unstable category, one that resisted further efforts toward rational codification and the development of equally rational institutions and policies corresponding to its particular contours.

As a whole, this book is a foray into the cultural and political work behind the articulation of social problems as such. It asks how visions of France, of national strength, of urban life, of the family as a real and abstract entity, and of moral order and disorder served as the cultural material from which both social problems and their solutions were constituted. It examines the structuring force of metaphor and languages of sexual difference, particularly where familial metaphors entered the realms of politics, law, and social policy. It attempts to discover how, to what effect, and, as much as possible, why legislators, reformers, social critics, and private individuals categorized certain conditions of family life as deviant and dangerous to children at a particular moment in France's historical trajectory.

The capacity of abandon moral to designate, simultaneously, a moral crisis of individual, social, and national dimensions demonstrates the degree to which moral discourse in late-nineteenth-century France permitted the collapse of a variety of concerns into a single issue. The history of abandon moral is thus a tale of distinctions blurred and boundaries revised. It is about suspicions of moral deviance which, in the last instance, conflated the working-class family with every family, and every family with a paradigmatic French family whose future appeared to be entwined with the future of the nation. It is about the emergence of a state defined by its desire to participate in family affairs as the impartial protector of the child's best interests and its equally powerful desire to preserve intact, as the foundation of the republic, the threshold of family privacy and the integrity of paternal authority. It is about the particular place of law in the Third Republic's efforts to stabilize and govern a modern social order. It is about the persistence of contradiction and ambivalence in the most "rationally" designed social policy.

Overall, my approach can be read as a variation on the administrative adage that opened this introduction. My aim has been to write a history of the governmental order within which poor and abandoned children and their families became knowable as objects of scorn, fear, pity, and, not least, government in the late nineteenth century. In writing this book, I have attempted to lay bare the politics, institutions, and practices that created and preserved the traces of Bonjon's "unhappy" lives, along with the state that framed those lives, as objects for future historical scrutiny.

Part I

PATERNAL AUTHORITY, PARENTAL OBLIGATION, AND THE STATE: LEGISLATING PROTECTION IN THE LATE NINETEENTH CENTURY

IN 1881 SENATOR Théophile Roussel presented his colleagues in the French National Assembly with two related proposals for a civil measure "on the protection of maltreated or morally abandoned children."[1] The senate approved a draft of the proposal in July 1883. After substantial revision by members of the cabinet, particularly the ministers of justice and of the interior, and several rounds of debate, a final version of the original bill was accepted by both the senate and the chamber of deputies and signed into law by the president of the republic on 24 July 1889. The law applied to all of metropolitan France, as well as Algeria, Guadeloupe, Martinique, and Réunion.

Also known as the law on the divestiture of paternal authority (*la loi sur la déchéance de la puissance paternelle*), the new legislation gave the civil court unprecedented power in the regulation of family affairs. By its terms, parents would automatically lose their rights if convicted for prostituting their own children or, more generally, for crimes committed against "the person or persons of their children." The law also stipulated that parents might be deprived of their legal authority if they had been sentenced to hard labor in perpetuity or solitary confinement, or if they had been convicted

---

[1] France, Assemblée nationale, Sénat, *Rapport fait au nom de la commission chargée d'examiner: 1° La Proposition de loi ayant pour objet la protection des enfants abandonnés, délaissés ou maltraités, présenté par MM. Théophile Roussel, Bérenger, Dufaure, l'amiral Fourichon, Schoelcher et Jules Simon. 2° Le Projet de loi sur la protection de l'enfance présenté par M. Cazot, Garde de Sceaux, Ministre de Justice*, Sénat session 1882, no. 451, Annexe au procès-verbal de la séance du 25 juillet 1882 (Paris: Imprimerie du Sénat, 1882). Roussel led many of the National Assembly's campaigns for new protective legislation under the early Third Republic. Trained as a physician, Roussel was elected deputy representing the Lozère in the National Assembly in 1871 and senator in 1879. On Roussel's career, see Catherine Rollet-Echalier, *La Politique à l'égard de la petite enfance sous la IIIe République* (Paris: Editions de l'INED/Presses Universitaires de France, 1990), 125–26. See also Jean Jolly, ed., *Dictionnaire des parlementaires français: Notices biographiques sur les ministres, députés et sénateurs français de 1889 à 1940*, vol. 8 (Paris: Presses Universitaires de France, 1977), 2915.

more than once for sequestering a child, for infanticide, for exposing or abandoning a child, for vagrancy, or for public inebriation. Multiple violations of an 1874 law regulating the employment of minors as traveling performers or "professional" beggars might also lead to the loss of parental rights. The 1889 law further decreed that parents who had been convicted for the prostitution of minors, whether or not the minors in question were their own offspring, and parents who had requested that the court incarcerate their allegedly unruly children—the "right of correction," as defined by article 66 of the penal code—might also be categorized as unfit and divested of all legal authority over their children.[2]

In its direct focus on the moral implications of certain crimes and actions, the new law insisted that the French justice system read adult delinquency as evidence of parental irresponsibility in a far more comprehensive manner than ever before. The truly innovative elements of the new law, however, lay elsewhere in the text. In addition to its more conventional appropriation of criminality as a sign of deviant parenthood, the law introduced new criteria for the divestiture of parental authority, which for the first time in French history superseded the bounded categories of criminal justice and relocated the issue of parental power and its misuse squarely in the realm of civil regulation.

Legislators grounded this shift in two crucial sections of the new measure. First, articles 19 and 20 of the 1889 law allowed destitute parents to yield their legal and custodial rights to the state voluntarily. To do this, they would turn their children over to a charitable institution or a third party willing to serve as guardian. After three months had passed without any attempt on the parents' part to reclaim their children, the institution or individual could petition the civil court to rule that material circumstances rendered the parents unfit to provide a child with a sound moral upbringing and so could strip them of their rights.[3] By voluntarily abandoning their parental obligations to others, in short, parents could solicit a judgment based on the notion that the exercise of parental right was contingent on the proper realization of parental duty. Although shadows of this equation had been inscribed in the Napoleonic provisions for the formal abandonment of infants, never before had it been so explicitly integrated into the logic of civil justice.[4]

[2] *JO*, 25 July 1889, 3653–55.

[3] For commentary on this aspect of the law, see Denise Bouchet, *Le Rôle de l'Assistance publique dans l'application de la loi du 24 juillet 1889 "sur la protection des enfants maltraités ou moralement abandonnés"* (Lyons: Imprimerie Grosjean-Fourgerat, 1938), 53–55. See also V. Radenac, *Du rôle de l'Etat dans la protection des enfants maltraités ou moralement abandonnés: Commentaire de la loi du 24 juillet 1889 (Titre II)* (Paris: Arthur Rousseau, 1901).

[4] On the organization of the foundling service in nineteenth-century Paris, see Alfred Dupoux, *Sur les pas de Monsieur Vincent: Trois cent ans d'histoire parisienne de l'enfance abandonnée* (Paris: Revue de l'Assistance publique à Paris, 1958). See also Rachel G. Fuchs, *Aban-

Like the provisions for the voluntary divestiture of parental rights, the second conceptual innovation embedded in the 1889 law also derived from moral norms hitherto absent from French civil law's construction of the family. According to paragraph 6, article 2, "[E]ven in the absence of any criminal conviction" the civil tribunal might divest of their rights those parents who, "by their habitual drunkenness, their notorious and scandalous misconduct, or by their physical abuse, compromise the health, the safety, or the morality of their children."[5] Here, too, in defining the grounds for divestiture through the putative effects of parents' noncriminal behavior, legislators transposed the loss of parental rights from the arena of criminal correction to a new space of civil regulation: the space between the punitive logic of the criminal code and the preventive logic of future administrative justice. One critic described the hybrid nature of the 1889 measure this way: although the law was by definition an addition to the civil regulation of the family, the nature of the articles outlining dangerous parental behavior, including the articles specifying particular criminal acts as well as noncriminal "immorality," gave half of the new law "an essentially penal character."[6]

The 1889 law on abandon moral had a powerful effect on both the practice and the perception of civil justice in France. On the practical front, the new law exploded the field within which public authorities could evaluate the quality of private family life. It armed them to act on their assessments in ways entirely unthinkable a few decades earlier. The world of opinion was no less affected. To conservative critics of the time, the law on moral abandonment represented a catastrophic transgression against both tradition and nature. To others, especially those intent on extending the terrain of government in the name of social and national health, it was the brilliant sign of the state's elevated moral sensibilities.

Across the spectrum of thought in the 1880s and early 1890s, there was nevertheless at least one point of apparent consensus: this law would radically and permanently transform relations between state and family in France. As one legal critic would remark some years later, "At the time [when Roussel introduced the first proposals in 1881], it seemed that to tamper with *la puissance paternelle* was to demolish by its very foundation the oldest, the most venerable, and the most sacred institution of the civilized world; it was to throw families into disorder, and to cast confusion and chaos everywhere."[7]

The introduction of the 1889 law on abandon moral, as well as the many efforts to explain, support, or oppose it, amplified the ironies and contradic-

---

doned *Children: Foundlings and Child Welfare in Nineteenth-Century France* (Albany: SUNY Press, 1984).

[5] *JO*, 25 July 1889, 3653–55.

[6] Radenac, *Du rôle de l'Etat*, 4.

[7] Ibid., 24.

tions of the epoch. Most important, the new measure appeared in an era when the valorization of both private life and the family was perhaps at its nineteenth-century zenith and, at the same time, anxiety about the ability of the family to function "naturally" was also reaching a new peak. Prescriptive literature lauding the essential educative, protective, and reproductive functions of the family while teaching readers how to fulfill their "natural" roles flooded the marketplace with normative counsel. Novels and serials published in the popular press similarly reinforced a social vision that foregrounded the family, the affective bonds that held it together, and the "natural" duties and rights of each family member, often in narratives that threw the orderly family into scenarios of domestic or social chaos.[8] As a new instrument for the moral regulation of the French family, the 1889 law underscored both the contemporary obsession with an ideal self-governing family, devoted to the moral formation of the young, and the growing fear of a domestic moral crisis that gave that obsession its deeper resonance.

In exposing contemporary anxieties about the family, the law on abandon moral also threw the contradictions of the liberal Third Republic, and the republican tradition itself, into high relief. How was it possible for a government that claimed to value the rights of the individual to introduce a measure restricting the rights of the individual *père de famille*? How did legislators so apparently devoted to the preservation and reproduction of the family as an autonomous institution of moral education justify this radical recasting of the state's role as regulator of private life? How did they reconcile the new law's inescapable power to destroy "natural" family ties with their valorization of the same natural ties as an essential component of a strong nation and a healthy society? How could they explain their effective erasure of masculine authority, or at least its radical destabilization, at a moment in history when the consciousness of military defeat in 1870–71 and a shockingly low birthrate produced the horrifying image of an "emasculated" France?

The three chapters in part 1 explore the historical, juridical, and discursive contingencies that shaped the Third Republic's efforts to redescribe the family and its relationship to state authority through the propagation of civil law. Chapter 1 traces the genealogy of the Third Republic's understanding of paternal power and its boundaries, focusing in particular on the legacy of the Napoleonic civil code and its gendered inscriptions of parental right.[9] Chap-

---

[8] On literary representations of the family and domestic life, see Roddy Reid, *Death of the Family: Discourse, Fiction, and Desire in France* (Stanford: Stanford University Press, 1994), and Suzanne Nash, ed., *Home and Its Dislocations in Nineteenth-Century France* (Albany: SUNY Press, 1993).

[9] Historians have recently begun to make use of Michel Foucault's notion of genealogy in a variety of ways. For a useful sample of these approaches, see Jan Goldstein, ed., *Foucault and the Writing of History* (Oxford: Basil Blackwell, 1994). Among Foucault's own writings, see especially "Nietzsche, Genealogy, History," reprinted in *Language, Counter-Memory, Practice:*

ter 2 explores the young republic's first attempts to elaborate an active parental identity for the state through the debate and enactment of three new child protection measures in 1874. The debates over these laws and the contours of the texts ultimately approved by the French legislature reveal the earliest visions of a new relationship between republican state, children, and their parents. At the same time, the laws of 1874 and the commentary surrounding them also illuminate legislators' deep ambivalence about the legitimacy of allowing the state to impose limits on a parental autonomy they saw as an essential element in the maintenance of both a healthy social order and a properly functioning polity. Chapter 3 examines legislative debates, administrative discourse, and juridical commentary on abandon moral as they emerged in the 1880s. How, this chapter asks, could reform-minded legislators and commentators of the period think themselves past the constraining borders of a Napoleonic civil order that for so long had been identified as the incarnation of natural order? By what means did they manage to reconceive the state as a protective entity more entitled to define the best interests of French children than those children's own fathers? How could they reconcile the apparent contradictions raised by the development of a parental state within their own liberal veneration of the self-regulating family ruled by the judicious and morally upright family father?

To reveal fully the historical and textual complexity of reshaping parenthood through legislative action in the late nineteenth century, the three chapters in part 1 focus in particular on the overlapping languages of paternal power and child protection, especially as they were rearticulated and deployed by the lawmakers, jurists, and social commentators of the early Third Republic. Their metaphors, narratives, frames of references, and modes of argumentation shaped both public discourse on the relationship between family and state and the policies derived from—and reinforced by—that discourse at both the local and the national level.

At the center of the republicans' new constellation of tropes and narrative strategies lay the unstable moral status of family and nation. It was here that the Third Republic's language of legislative reform drew most heavily on gendered metaphors of family identities and relationships.[10] This gendered language, centered above all on the moral authority and responsibility of the father, provided the central interpretive grids against which public authorities constructed, evaluated, affirmed, or contested allegations of moral danger within the family. In these terms as well, strategies of reform were structured and institutionalized by the officials of the Third Republic. Not least, gen-

---

Selected Essays and Interviews, ed. Donald F. Bouchard, trans. Donald F. Bouchard and Sherry Simon (Ithaca: Cornell University Press, 1977).

[10] On gender's signifying power within the matrix of political language, see Joan Wallach Scott, "Gender: A Useful Category of Historical Analysis," in *Gender and the Politics of History* (New York: Columbia University Press, 1988), esp. 44–50.

dered familial metaphors allowed legislators to speak in several registers simultaneously. In voicing their concerns about the moral regulation of individual families in a language that inscribed power, dependency, responsibility, and dangerousness within the categories of sexual difference, lawmakers were also able to articulate adjacent worries about the proper government of the social body writ large and the successful prevention of national moral decline.

In examining the Third Republic's debates on law, governmental authority, moral danger, and the family, part 1 considers France's particular version of the paradoxes inherent in liberal regimes of social governance.[11] The appearance of contradiction between the Third Republic's efforts to constitute itself as a morally and politically coherent governmental order and its efforts to justify the apparently intrusive regulation of the family signals crucial tensions in the regime's wider effort to place an apparently endangered and demoralized nation under the sign of liberal republicanism. These points of tension, and especially those that mark new constructions of the relationship betwen state and family, provide an important vantage from which to view the changing discourse, practices, and institutions of republican governance. The Third Republic's legislative regime of child protection, elaborated within and against the constraints of the Napoleonic code, speaks directly to the strained process of interpretation and self-fashioning through which a new liberal regime established a moral identity, a social agenda, and a set of governing techniques.[12]

[11] On the tensions internal to liberal constructions of the social and its proper government in France, see Giovanna Procacci's excellent book *Gouverner la misère: La question sociale en France, 1789–1848* (Paris: Editions du Seuil, 1993). See also Graham Burchell, "Peculiar Interests: Civil Society and Governing 'The System of Natural Liberty,'" in *The Foucault Effect: Studies in Governmentality*, ed. Graham Burchell, Colin Gordon, and Peter Miller (Chicago: University of Chicago Press, 1991).

[12] Foucault's schematic but suggestive essay "Governmentality" has been especially useful for framing these questions about the Third Republic's approach to the relationship between governing power and the governed. See Michel Foucault, "Governmentality," in *The Foucault Effect*, ed. Burchell, Gordon, and Miller.

CHAPTER 1

The Long History of Paternal Power

THE EARLY Third Republic's efforts to redefine the state, the family, and the relationship between them mark a decisive moment in the history of paternal power in France. To succeed, the attempts to recast these fundamental identities and essential ties had to disassemble some of the ninteenth century's most basic "truths" about the proper location and exercise of authority. What did these inherited understandings of family order look like? In what terms had they been naturalized? How and when were those understandings reproduced, strengthened, or destabilized across the social and political tumult of the nineteenth century? Outlining the nature of the task of discursive reordering facing reformers in the 1870s and 1880s requires a brief look at the genealogy of paternal power, or *la puissance paternelle*, as it initially entered into the *imaginaire* of the early Third Republic. The account provided here centers in particular on three interlocking elements that would later prove essential to the republican reimagining of family, state, and social governance: the accretion of challenges to the location of paternal authority and autonomy in a "natural" order; the gradual relocation of parenthood away from the realm of naturalized right and toward the realm of social responsibility; and, not least, the rearticulation of sexual difference within and around paternal right and parental duty. Although contests over the political implications of parenthood, particularly paternal power, were by no means original to the Third Republic, the debates and reforms in the late nineteenth century would profoundly transform both the language and the practice of authority in modern France.

The respect for male domestic authority evident in late-nineteenth-century legal and political culture had deep roots. Centuries of Roman occupation in the early part of the millennium spliced Latin visions of the family into indigenous Gallic traditions. The effects of this fusion on the traditions of French family law were far from negligible. Roman law vested an almost limitless power in the person of the family patriarch. Even after the dissolution of the empire, various regional legal traditions maintained the principle of *patria potestas* for centuries, particularly in Mediterranean and southern France.[1]

---

[1] See Yvonne Knibiehler, *Les Pères aussi ont une histoire* (Paris: Hachette, 1987), esp. chap. 1, "La Puissance paternelle." See also André Pelletier, *La Femme dans la société gallo-romaine* (Paris: Picard, 1984).

Outside France's secular legal tradition, the teachings and structure of the Catholic Church also insisted on the legitimacy of a "natural" patriarchy. Although the Catholic vision of the father's powers placed more emphasis on paternal benevolence than did the Roman model, it asserted the domestic and moral authority of the family father with equal vehemence.[2] On the political front, the practices and ideologies of absolutism, particularly in the eighteenth century, similarly underscored the legitimacy of male familial rule and added political potency to the idiom of paternal power.[3]

Although it can only gesture to the complexities of the history of paternal power and its representation, even this brief sketch points up the striking persistence with which the contours of a natural paternal authority were elaborated and affirmed in old-regime France. The ritual of rearticulation, however, also tends to betray anxiety about the stability of meaning as well as anxiety about the power relations that underpin meaning at any given point in the past.[4] The repeated appearance of paeans to paternal authority in eighteenth-century France thus may signal not only the affirmation of paternal authority but also the fear that its status might not be as stable or indisputable as could be hoped.

The principle of male domestic authority, even as it was celebrated as eternal, natural, and God-given, did in fact face overt challenges well before the reforms of the Third Republic. Popular culture of the early modern period abounded with both ritualized and improvised challenges to the authority of husbands, fathers, and masters.[5] In the texts of the eighteenth century

[2] Some scholars also point to Christianity as one of the important origins of the notion of parental duty, particularly the duty of moral protection. On this point see especially John Gilissen, *Introduction historique au droit* (Brussels: Bruylant, 1979), 548–49. See also Knibiehler's discussion of "spiritual paternity," in *Les Pères*, 39–59.

[3] On the political deployment of family metaphors in the early modern period, see Sarah Hanley, "Engendering the State: Family Formation and State Building in Early Modern France," *French Historical Studies* 16, no. 1 (1989); Jeffrey Merrick, "Fathers and Kings: Patriarchalism and Absolutism in Eighteenth-Century French Politics," *Studies on Voltaire and the Eighteenth Century* 308 (1993); and Lynn Hunt, *The Family Romance of the French Revolution* (Berkeley: University of California Press, 1992), esp. chaps. 1–2. In her critique of Merrick and Hunt, Hanley mounts a persuasive case that the metaphors of paternal authority were mobilized in the name of the crown only in the eighteenth century. By the end of the seventeenth century, Hanley argues, it became apparent that earlier visions of monarchical right as grounded in the natural authority of husbands over wives opened the way for politically dangerous critiques of "marital" despotism. See Hanley, "The Monarchic State in Early Modern France: Marital Regime Government and Male Right," in *Politics, Ideology, and the Law in Early Modern Europe*, ed. Adrianna E. Bakos (Rochester: University of Rochester Press, 1994), esp. 123–24.

[4] Hanley's reading of the monarchy's abandonment of the marriage metaphor in the eighteenth century speaks directly to the epistemolgical anxieties embedded in articulating the metaphors of power (ibid., 123).

[5] See, for example, the essays in Natalie Zemon Davis's *Society and Culture in Early Modern France* (Stanford: Stanford University Press, 1975), and Robert Darnton's *Great Cat Massacre and Other Episodes in French Cultural History* (New York: Basic Books, 1984).

as well, critiques of "domestic" tyranny implicated monarchical authority in their arguments against contemporary structures of family life.[6] Finally, the use of the courts to adjudicate family struggles, especially those related to marriage, separation, and inheritance, suggests that the juridical refusal of men's marital and, later, paternal power was increasingly common practice in the seventeenth and eighteenth centuries.[7]

Challenges once limited to local contexts and individual court cases or confined to the discursive universe of Enlightenment opinion took more concrete form in 1789 when the Revolution launched a vigorous crusade against all things marked by the signs of patriarchal despotism. As one historian summarizes the Revolution's campaign, "[T]he monarchy of the family, like the royal monarchy, became null and void."[8] The Revolution's insistence on the political power of representational linkages meant that symbolic paternal power was frequently conflated with more concrete incarnations of fatherhood. In the revolutionary agenda, disempowering—and eventually decapitating—the monarch was of a piece with the legal curbing of fathers' rights within the family order.[9]

The legal limits of la puissance paternelle underwent an unprecedented contraction in the first years of the Revolution. The right to incarcerate one's dependents on demand, the infamous lettre de cachet, or warrant of imprisonment, was abrogated in 1790, and the liberal divorce law of 1792 further loosened the grip of the *chef de famille* on his household.[10] The sub-

[6] Among Enlightenment texts on this point, see especially Montesquieu's *Persian Letters*, trans. C. J. Betts (Harmondsworth, England: Penguin Books, 1973). Hanley argues that a critique of the "tyrannical" rule of husbands over wives appears in print as early as the late sixteenth century ("The Monarchic State," 121). On educated women's critique of marriage in the seventeenth century, see Carolyn C. Lougee, *Le Paradis des femmes: Women, Salons, and Social Stratification in Seventeenth-Century France* (Princeton: Princeton University Press, 1976), 23–24.

[7] Hanley, "The Monarchic State," 121, 124. On the use of the lawsuit to challenge the privileged status of the husband, see also Hanley, "Social Sites of Political Practice in France: Lawsuits, Civil Rights, and the Separation of Powers in Domestic and State Government," *American Historical Review* 102, no. 1 (February 1997). Special thanks to Sarah Hanley for allowing me access to this material before its publication.

[8] Knibiehler, *Les Pères*, 157. For a survey of the debate on women before and during the Revolution, see Joan B. Landes, *Women and the Public Sphere in the Age of the French Revolution* (Ithaca: Cornell University Press, 1988). For an incisive critique of Landes's use of *public* and *private*, see Dena Goodman, "Public Sphere and Private Life: Toward a Synthesis of Current Historiographical Approaches to the Old Regime," *History and Theory* 31, no. 1 (1992): 1–20.

[9] On the question of generational conflict during the French Revolution, see David G. Troyansky, "Generational Discourse in the French Revolution," in *The French Revolution in Culture and Society*, ed. David G. Troyansky, Alfred Cismaru, and Norwood Andrews Jr. (Westport, Conn.: Greenwood Press, 1991). On the king as metaphorical father, see Hunt, *The Family Romance*, esp. 17–52.

[10] See Arlette Farge and Michel Foucault's commentary on the state's interest in honoring the

ordination of adult children to la puissance paternelle was also suppressed by the legislation of 1792. No rational adult, the Revolution's legal reformers insisted, could be held to the demands of arbitrary paternal rule.

No less momentous than these particular legal reforms was the general enthusiasm with which the Revolution proclaimed itself the protector of children's "best interests."[11] In this radical reformulation of power within and around the family, duty to the nation superseded allegiance to one's own family. The family's duty, moreover, was not simply to control its members as a governing body subordinated to the authority of state. It was also to educate and prepare children for virtuous adulthood in the new society created by the Revolution. For boys, this meant preparation for revolutionary citizenship and military service; for girls, it meant education in the duties of patriotic maternity.[12]

The authors of the revolutionary state also claimed a more direct governing role in the new family order. As the unselfish protector of national interest, the state would oversee the functioning of the individual family and, if necessary, defend children against the "egoism" of their parents' corrupt or antirevolutionary private interests. This new alignment, one historian has convincingly argued, sprang from the Revolution's insistence on seeing the French nation as a population of individuals, each with a direct relationship to the state, rather than as an agglomerate of families with separable interests.[13] The tendency to minimize the family's status as an independent collectivity and to posit instead an unmediated connection between child and nation would also prove to be a crucial precedent for the historically self-conscious republicans of the late nineteenth century.

---

lettre de cachet in *Le Désordre des familles: Lettres de cachet des Archives de la Bastille au XVIIIe siècle*, ed. Arlette Farge and Michel Foucault (Paris: Gallimard, 1982).

[11] See Bernard Schnapper, "Liberté et égalité dans la famille: L'autorité maritale et la puissance paternelle vues par les hommes de la Révolution," in *L'Enfant, la famille, et la Révolution française*, ed. Marie-Françoise Lévy (Paris: Olivier Orban, 1990).

[12] On the education of boys for masculine adult citizenship under the Revolution, see Dominique Julia, "L'Institution du citoyen: Instruction publique et éducation nationale dans les projets de la période révolutionnaire," in *L'Enfant*, ed. Lévy, 123–70. Julia, following the lead of his revolutionary documents, treats the child as an undifferentiated category whose male identity is nonetheless a given. For a more nuanced consideration of sexual difference and treatment of children in revolutionary France, see, for example, Christian-Marc Bosséno, "L'Enfant et la jeunesse dans les fêtes révolutionnaires," in *L'Enfant*, ed. Lévy, 207–17. See also Linda L. Clark, *Schooling the Daughters of Marianne: Textbooks and the Socialization of Girls in Modern French Primary Schools* (Albany: SUNY Press, 1984), 7–8; Ernest Allain, *L'Oeuvre scolaire de la Révolution, 1789–1802* (New York: Burt Frank, 1969); and Pierre Chevallier and B. Grosperrin, eds., *L'Enseignement français de la Révolution à nos jours*, vol. 2, *Documents* (Paris: Mouton et Cie, 1971).

[13] On this theme in revolutionary discourses, see André Burguière, "Demande d'état et aspirations individualistes: Les attentes contradictoires des familles à la veille de la Révolution," in *L'Enfant*, ed. Lévy, 25–32.

For the most part, the Revolution's revision of the family and its legal foundation did not survive into the nineteenth century. Ironically, however, its campaign for a standardized family code would later be realized, in formal terms if not in terms of substance, in Napoleon's Civil Code of 1804.[14] The Revolution's effort to contain what it saw as the despotic exercise of paternal power through a systematic recodification of family law was thus supplanted by the far more conservative vision that shaped the Code Napoléon.[15] The only exception was the retention of *partage égal*, or the equal distribution of property among all heirs, male and female.[16] Later in the nineteenth century, social critics such as Frédéric Le Play would complain that this provision alone ensured that French society would have to live under the Revolution's radical assault on the family. The state's enforcement of the principle of equal partition, Le Play argued, was a "fatal error." It "throw[s] the authority of the father, the most natural and the most fruitful of autonomies, that which preserves the best of the social bond in restraining primal corruption, in training young generations in the ways of respect and obedience, into disarray."[17]

When weighed against the many articles of the Napoleonic Code that affirmed paternal authority, Le Play's rhetoric of fear might be considered hyperbolic. The political, juridical, and symbolic ruptures wrought by the Revolution ultimately did little to undercut the faith that paternal power was an essential element in a well-ordered society. Those ruptures may even have stimulated conservatives to shore up paternal authority as part of their efforts to restore order after the fall of the Jacobins in 1794. Following Tocqueville's vision of governmental continuity across the divide of the Revolution, it seems that official respect for the father's "natural right" to rule his family passed into the nineteenth century virtually unscathed by the blows it had taken in the revolutionary era.[18] As a reinscription of "natural" paternal power, Napoleonic law crystallized the nexus of natural right and apparent social exigency into enforceable and culturally viable statutes for the nineteenth century.

[14] All citations from the code are in *Codes Napoléon*, 7th ed. (Paris: Auguste Durand, 1852). This volume contains all of the original Napoleonic legal codes, including the civil, penal, and commercial codes. See also *Les Cinq codes de l'empire français* (Paris: E. Guitel, 1812).

[15] On the drafting of the Code Napoléon, see François Ewald, ed., *Naissance du Code civil: La raison du législateur* (Paris: Flammarion, 1989).

[16] For an excellent discussion of the Revolution's impact on inheritance and the family in the early nineteenth century, see Margaret H. Darrow, *Revolution in the House: Family, Class, and Inheritance in Southern France, 1775–1825* (Princeton: Princeton University Press, 1989).

[17] Frédéric Le Play, *L'Organisation de la famille selon le vrai modèle signalé par l'histoire de toutes les races et de tous les temps* (Paris: Saint Michel, 1871), xvi.

[18] For Tocqueville's account of continuity across the turbulence of revolution, see Alexis de Tocqueville, *The Old Regime and the French Revolution*, trans. Stuart Gilbert (Garden City, N.Y.: Doubleday, 1955).

The Code Napoléon, probably the single most influential text on the family produced in nineteenth-century Europe, stood firmly on the side of all patriarchs. It left to them the governance of children and, through a series of articles outlining the "civil death" of women upon marriage, the governance of wives.[19] The code's domain ranged far beyond the national boundaries of France, moreover. Among the countries that had experienced Napoleonic rule in the first decades of the century, the Civil Code served as one of the cornerstones of exported French "civilization." It left permanent imprints on the legal traditions of those nations even after Napoleon's empire crumbled.[20]

Throughout the cycles of revolution, reaction, social change, and reform that refashioned France between 1804 and 1871, Napoleon's domestic law remained virtually untouched. At the same time, however, the cultural and ideological icon of the family increasingly appeared at the center of political, social, and cultural debate. Over the course of the century, the family was claimed simultaneously by the Right and the Left, its demise pronounced by conservative Catholics and ardent republicans, and its educative and moralizing mission likewise trumpeted by social observers of all creeds.[21] During revolutionary moments it was mourned as the victim of industrial and political upheaval and, at the same time, celebrated as the bulwark against those very same forces of disruption. Only among feminists and utopian socialists did the family of the Napoleonic Code come under direct and radical assault.[22]

---

[19] *CN*, bk. 1, title 5, chap. 6, "Des droits et devoirs respectifs des époux," describes the legal subordination of a woman to the authority of her husband, including the obligation to "obey" and to reside in her husband's house. She was also denied the right to appear in court or to dispose of goods and property without her husband's permission. During the Third Republic, the legal foundation of marriage underwent a series of important reforms, including the legalization of divorce. In particular, the Third Republic's reforms initiated the gradual erosion of the "civil death" of married women. On family law in the nineteenth century, see Jules Thabaut, *L'Evolution de la législation sur la famille depuis 1804* (Toulouse: Edouard Privat, 1913), and Charles Lefebvre, *La Famille en France dans le droit et dans les moeurs* (Paris: Marcel Giard et Cie, 1920).

[20] On the exportation of the Napoleonic law codes, see Owen Connelly, *Napoleon's Satellite Kingdoms* (New York: Free Press, 1965), 101.

[21] Limited space permits only a few examples from the extensive literature on appropriations of the family in the social and political discourses of the nineteenth century. On the family and Catholic discourse during the Restoration, see Raymond Deniel, *Une Image de la famille et de la société sous la Restauration* (Paris: Editions ouvrières, 1965). On the status of the family in nineteenth-century liberal discourse, see Katherine A. Lynch, *Family, Class, and Ideology in Early Industrial France: Social Policy and the Working-Class Family, 1825–1848* (Madison: University of Wisconsin Press, 1988). For a useful survey of the utopian socialist constructions of the family, see Claire Goldberg Moses, "Difference in Historical Perspective: Saint-Simonian Feminism," in *Feminism, Socialism, and French Romanticism*, ed. Claire Goldberg Moses and Leslie Wahl Rabine (Bloomington: Indiana University Press, 1993), esp. 35–40.

[22] The literature on French feminism and the Civil Code is far too extensive to cover here beyond a few titles. For the Saint-Simonian feminist critique of marriage, see Claire Goldberg

More often than not these critiques provoked even more vigorous assertions of the "natural" foundation of paternal authority, assertions that often served as the foundation of antifeminist discourse as well.[23]

The enduring power of the Napoleonic Code and its naturalization of paternal authority meant that any effort to recast the legal foundation of paternal power would have to be structured against—and within—the dicta of the Civil Code. How, then, did the code of 1804 actually define the exercise of parental authority in the family? Where and how did these definitions find support or draw meaning from the wider cultural context?

In its initial prescriptions on relations between parents and children, the code immediately counterpoised the principle of lifelong filial obedience to the temporal limitation of parental authority. All children, both minors and adults, owed their parents "honor and respect" for the duration of their lives. At the same time, however, the code imposed a strict end to the term of parental rule. Sons and daughters remained subject to parental authority until the age of twenty-one, except when parents voluntarily emancipated them earlier in life, for example, when parents approved a child's early marriage.[24]

As the Code Napoléon discriminated between the condition of childhood and legal majority, and between affective and legal subordination, so too did it create important distinctions in other aspects of its construction of familial

---

Moses, *French Feminism in the Nineteenth Century* (Albany: SUNY Press, 1984). Jonathan Beecher examines another facet of utopian socialism's repudiation of the Napoleonic family order in *Charles Fourier: The Visionary and His World* (Berkeley: University of California, 1987). See also Beecher's collection of Fourier's writings, *The Utopian Vision of Charles Fourier: Selected Texts on Work, Love, and Passionate Attraction* (Boston: Beacon Press, 1971). For late-nineteenth-century feminist criticism of the code, see Steven C. Hause, with Anne R. Kenney, *Women's Suffrage and Social Politics in the French Third Republic* (Princeton: Princeton University Press, 1984).

[23] After 1848, for example, Pauline Roland and Jeanne Deroin were prosecuted, among other charges, for their open criticism of marriage. An arrest order charged that Roland, "[a]n unmarried mother[,] . . . is the enemy of marriage, maintaining that subjecting the woman to the control of the husband sanctifies inequality" (as cited in Moses, *French Feminism*, 147–48). See also Moses's chap. 7, "*La Querelle des Femmes* of the Second Empire," for a useful survey of antifeminist discourses in the 1850s and 1860s, notably those of the renowned republican historian Jules Michelet and the socialist Pierre-Joseph Proudhon. For antifeminism in the Third Republic, see Karen Offen, "Depopulation, Nationalism, and Feminism in *Fin-de-Siècle* France," *American Historical Review* 89 (June 1984); Hause with Kenney, *Women's Suffrage*; and James C. MacMillan, *Housewife or Harlot: The Place of Women in French Society, 1870–1940* (New York: St. Martin's Press, 1981).

[24] *CN*, bk. 1, title 9, "De la puissance paternelle," arts. 371–72. Bk. 1, title 10, chap. 3 of the code described the conditions for "emancipation": minors are automatically emancipated upon their marriage, and they may be voluntarily emancipated by their parents, before a justice of the peace, at the age of fifteen, even when not married. Although emancipated minors were no longer subject to their parents' authority, the code did not permit them to exercise the full rights of adulthood until majority at the age of twenty-one.

relations. Thus, although the articles mentioned earlier spoke of the child's relation to the unit of "father and mother," subsequent articles of the code reveal that "parental" in fact had a more complex and highly gendered meaning.[25] If obedience was owed to both parents, it was not because fathers and mothers were equal in the exercise of authority; the parental powers vested in married couples were in practice to be wielded by the father and the father alone.[26]

Hence the code forbade minors to leave their father's household without his exclusive permission. In the case of a child's "extreme insubordination," the father of the family could invoke his "right of correction," that is, the right to have his progeny incarcerated for a fixed period of time upon "simple demand" to the local justice. The father also maintained control of his children's property, excepting wages and goods earned independently of the family or those given to the child under the express condition that they not be subject to paternal control. In exchange for the juridical guarantee of his natural paternal rights, the father was obliged to support his children and to provide an upbringing (*éducation*) appropriate to the family's estate. He also had to accept legal responsibility for the debts his children incurred while underage and for expenses resulting from their illness or death.[27] Last, and perhaps most telling, the articles defining the legal relations between parents and their children were grouped together in title 9 of the Civil Code's first book, "On Paternal Authority" ("De la puissance paternelle").

Other measures underscored the code's retooling of the institutions of paternal authority for the nineteenth century even further. The lettre de cachet, for example, banned under the Revolution, was reinvented with the 1804 code's elaboration of the paternal *droit de correction*. Once again, as under the old regime, fathers could incarcerate their children with minimal formal procedure. The most significant change seemed to be in the object of supplication: instead of addressing requests for incarceration to the king, fathers would henceforth appeal to the civil magistrate.[28] Napoleonic reformers also severely limited the terms of the Revolution's liberal divorce law, making

[25] In French, *parent* has a much broader sense than in English, and is often translated as "relative" or "kin." The primary meaning of *parent*, however, conforms more closely to our definition of "father or mother."

[26] *CN*, art. 373.

[27] Ibid., arts. 374–87.

[28] See Bernard Schnapper, "La Correction paternelle et le mouvement des idées au dix-neuvième siècle (1789–1935)," *Revue historique* 263 (1980). Farge and Foucault argue that the nineteenth-century droit de correction served to undermine paternal autonomy by extending the reach of the state into the private exercise of power within the family and by making correction an instrument of social rather than domestic control. This seems to have been true only in the latter half of the century, when requests for incarceration underwent increasingly rigorous investigation. See Farge and Foucault, *Le Désordre*, esp. 357–63. Although it fell into disuse, the droit de correction was not eliminated from civil law until 1958.

the request for divorce an exclusively masculine privilege.[29] In a similar vein, the code also proscribed paternity suits, thus freeing men from any legal responsibility for unrecognized illegitimate children. If paternal authority was to be revered, it could not be forced on men; nor could illegitimate paternity be permitted to threaten the legally protected household.

In general, the Civil Code explicitly ascribed the powers of domestic authority to the male head of household whenever and wherever possible. Thus the authors of the code shifted between the term "parental authority" (*l'autorité parentale*)—more ambiguous as to the gendered location of familial power—and "paternal authority"(*la puissance paternelle*)—which left no doubt as to the site and source of parental authority—in a pattern attesting to their essential equivalence. This conflation of the generic "parental" with the gendered "paternal" encapsulated the legal understanding of the postrevolutionary family. By the terms of Napoleonic civil law, parental power was, in the final analysis, coterminous with paternal power.

At the same time, the use of *l'autorité parentale* and *la puissance paternelle* as synonyms introduced a curious contradiction into French civil law. The mother's appearance as a parent endowed with rights, however fleeting, would also bring her under the regulating power of the law. If it tended to exclude her from the legitimate exercise of parental authority, the code nonetheless provided the means for holding her legally responsible as an authoritative parent. As her occasional inclusion under the terms of parenthood suggests, in fact, the legal elucidation of *la puissance paternelle* did not wholly efface the possibility of identifying the mother as a legal parent. For example, the Civil Code provided for the temporary delegation of la puissance paternelle to a wife in the case of a husband's prolonged absence from home. In the instance of a father's legally declared disappearance, the code permitted the mother to exercise "all the husband's rights in child rearing and in the management of their [the children's] property."[30]

In the section of the code devoted directly to la puissance paternelle, however, there are surprisingly few explicit references to mothers. Besides the exhortation to honor both father and mother, the section refers to the mother only twice more, both times in ways that circumscribed the rights of parenthood within the limits of sexual difference. First, widows who had not remarried were prohibited from invoking the droit de correction without the concurrence of two near relations from their husband's family. Second, although the code explicitly granted widows the right to manage their children's property, *la jouissance des biens*, it conferred on them that right alone

---

[29] See Roderick Phillips, *Untying the Knot: A Short History of Divorce* (Cambridge: Cambridge University Press, 1991), esp. chap. 6, "The Nineteenth Century: Liberalization and Reaction."

[30] *CN*, art. 141.

from among the many rights delineated under the title "La puissance pater-nelle."[31]

The code did in fact address the rights of the mother, but it did so in the section devoted to guardianship (*tutelle*) rather than the section on parental authority. According to this portion of the Civil Code, a mother's claim to the exercise of la puissance paternelle was legitimate only when her ties to her husband had been broken "by natural or civil death."[32] By defining the essence of a mother's parental authority in terms of guardianship, moreover, the code ascribed both a derivative and a contingent quality to her power. In these terms, a husband could specify in his will or in an official public declaration that in the case of his death or permanent absence his wife was not to exercise the authority vested in her as sole legal guardian of her children without the approval of a family council. This council would be composed of the local justice of the peace and six relatives—three from each side of the family, or some equivalent distribution of relatives and family friends.[33] If a woman was pregnant at the time of her husband's death, moreover, the family council could name *un curateur au ventre*, literally a "guardian" or "trustee of the womb," who would serve as a second guardian upon the birth of the child.[34]

Already subject to strict limitations, a widowed or abandoned mother's right to stand in loco parentis was even further restricted in the event that she remarried. Whether or not she had been left with full rights of tutelle by her first husband, the code required the convocation of a family council to determine whether she should retain parental rights at the time of marriage. If she failed to ensure that the council met to consider this question, she would automatically lose her independence as her children's legal guardian; in that case, the code stipulated, "[H]er new husband will become jointly and severally responsible for all the consequences of the tutelle which she had unrightfully maintained." Even when she was allowed to remain her children's guardian, the council "would name as coguardian her second husband, who would become jointly and severally responsible, along with his wife, for its execution as of their marriage." If the family council refused her the guardianship of her children, she would not, on the occasion of the death of their first legal guardian, be able to name a new one herself. If she wanted to choose a guardian other than herself for the children from her first marriage, she would once again have to seek the approval of the family council.[35]

In the sum of its parts, the code consistently implied that a woman's enti-

---

[31] Ibid., arts. 381 and 384.

[32] Ibid., art. 390. The code defines civil death (*la mort civile*) as the consequence of any judicial decision that deprives a citizen of his full civil rights (art. 22).

[33] Ibid., art. 407.

[34] Ibid., arts. 390–93.

[35] Ibid., arts. 395–400.

tlement to guardianship, and to the attached exercise of la puissance paternelle, was a matter of masculine power deferred. Her own parental authority,
almost entirely inadmissible while the father of her children was present,
could take only a diluted form when he was not. The weight of her decisions
was often contingent upon the concurrence of men from her husband's family who had been tapped for the family council by the local justice of the
peace. La puissance paternelle for men appeared in the code as a natural
right incarnated in law, even for stepfathers, whose claim to paternal authority over his wife's children appeared to derive not from blood ties but from
his naturalized authority as the new male head of household. In contrast, a
woman could stand in only as a provisional substitute for the male. Her
authority constituted an "unnatural" but unavoidable alternative to proper
male-centered domestic administration.[36] With the enactment of the 1889 law
on the divestiture of parental authority, the edges of this contradictory posi-
tioning of mothers as disempowered but responsible subjects of law would
become all the more acute.

To be sure, faith in the masculine essence of la puissance paternelle extended beyond the pages of Napoleon's legal texts. Indeed, that wider certainty may well have provided the materials, historical and cultural, from
which the authors of the code fashioned their text and legitimated its authority. Many early-nineteenth-century observers agreed that a strong père de
famille was both naturally empowered and socially necessary. Those conservative thinkers who defined postrevolutionary reaction, such as Chateaubriand, Joseph de Maistre, and Louis de Bonald, pronounced the intact,
patriarchal family to be one of the fundamental defenses against social disorder.[37] Enthusiasm for a stable, father-ruled family was evident in more liberal
strains of thought as well.[38] These proponents of paternal authority framed it
as an aspect of family life that should be respected for its higher natural
sanctity and therefore insulated against external intervention. As the chosen
intermediary between the newly defined public space of politics and marketplace and the private space of home and family, the strong père de famille
seemed to guarantee social and cultural stability in a capitalist world.[39] Even

[36] Mothers would not be granted full parental authority—alone over illegitimate children or
together with their children's father—until 1907 (Moses, *French Feminism*, 229–30).

[37] Deniel, *Une Image de la famille*, 95–114.

[38] On liberal visions of the family, see Michelle Perrot, "The Family Triumphant," in *A History of Private Life*, ed. Philippe Ariès and Georges Duby, vol. 4, *From the Fires of Revolution
to the Great War*, ed. Michelle Perrot (Cambridge: Belknap Press of Harvard University Press,
1990), esp. 102–4. On the wide range of philosophers' rethinking of sexual difference in the
nineteenth century, see Geneviève Fraisse, "A Philosophical History of Sexual Difference," in *A
History of Women in the West*, ed. Georges Duby and Michelle Perrot, vol. 4, *Emerging Feminism from Revolution to World War*, ed. Geneviève Fraisse and Michelle Perrot (Cambridge:
Belknap Press of Harvard University Press, 1993), 48–79.

[39] Perrot, "Roles and Characters," in *A History of Private Life* 4:167–80. See also Leonore

some of the most "radical" midcentury thinkers, such as Pierre-Joseph Proudhon, counted themselves among the proud defenders of male prerogative in overlapping terrains of society, politics, and the family.[40]

Despite the proliferation of discourses in the nineteenth century describing the "domestic" sphere as women's domain, the code's insistence on the legal authority of the père de famille suggests that the properly organized household had to be defined as much by the exercise of male power as by the expression of feminine influence. Those popular and prescriptive texts that celebrated women's rule in the home generally described their role in terms of moralizing exemplarity and the proper fulfillment of educational or nurturing responsibilities.[41] In the final instance, however, the exercise of familial power belonged, in principle at least, to the male head of household.[42] The definition of the home in nineteenth-century France rested on a particular kind of gendered irony; the "domestic sphere," particularly given the patriarchal underpinnings of the Napoleonic Code, was as much about the authoritative presence of men as it was about the maternal responsibilities of women.

As in the case of any vision of the correct distribution of power, no matter how thickly it has been swathed in legal, cultural, or ideological validation, the everyday exercise of la puissance paternelle did not necessarily live up to the prescriptions of the Napoleonic Code, even in intact legitimate families. The more historians have investigated the internal workings of the household, be it aristocratic, bourgeois, laboring, or peasant, the more they have revealed the complexities of family relations in the past. Love, respect, envy, desire, hatred, greed, and necessity conspired then, as they do now, to unmask the fiction of the family as an unproblematic social hierarchy, bound together by ties of affection and property, to which individual members happily and gratefully submit.[43] Death and remarriage unmade and redirected

Davidoff and Catherine Hall's *Family Fortunes: Men and Women of the English Middle Class, 1780–1850* (Chicago: University of Chicago Press, 1987) for a provocative analysis of the role of the father in the construction of public and private spheres in nineteenth-century England.

[40] See Perrot's discussion of the family and the ideological cleavages of the nineteenth century in her essay "The Family Triumphant." Perrot contends that although many socialist and feminist theorists advocated a reformed family in which there would be greater equality between men and women, only the most radical fringe, such as Fourier, proposed the total abolition of the nuclear family (Perrot, "The Family Triumphant," esp. 108–13).

[41] On women's educative duties as defined by contemporary ideologies of domesticity, see Bonnie G. Smith, *Ladies of the Leisure Class: The Bourgeoises of Northern France in the Nineteenth Century* (Princeton: Princeton University Press, 1981), esp. 53–92. On the reproduction of domesticity and its deep links to Catholicism in nineteenth-century France, see Marie-Françoise Lévy, *De mères en filles: L'éducation des Françaises, 1850/1880* (Paris: Calmann-Lévy, 1984).

[42] Deniel notes the importance of this notion in Catholic representations of the stable family during the Restoration (Deniel, *Une Image de la famille*, 108–9).

[43] The question of intrafamily conflict has interested a wide variety of researchers, but the works they have produced are too numerous to list here in full. Some of the most influential

affection and legal commitments. Families often existed in truncated form, particularly those in which women outlived their spouses, and many families among the urban poor and working classes, already less legitimate in the eyes of public authority when they lacked the bond of legal marriage, experienced the loss of a parent through hospitalization, incarceration, and the high rate of death associated with poverty and dismal occupational conditions. Looking at the national census, one historian has asserted that one out of fourteen children was illegitimate in 1875. In 1900 more than one-third of French households were headed by single parents. In the same year, 45 percent of adolescents had already lost at least one parent.[44] The chances of living in an intact family for the duration of one's legal minority, in short, were slim.

Observers intent on describing the effects of the industrial transformation of France in the middle and late nineteenth century facilitated the contemporary appreciation of these apparent and disturbing social facts in their narratives of the modern decline of the family. Thus some critics of the industrial age argued that skills and craft expertise once passed from fathers to sons were being lost as the changing market for labor and goods eroded family cohesion. They saw in the concentration of industry the destruction of more "moral" home-based labor in which production was inscribed in a regime of familial discipline.[45] The waves of migration that swept adults and children far from the parental hearth and their regions of birth during the nineteenth century were also presented as evidence of the destruction of the familial and moral base of national life.[46] Oppositions between city and country, between the rooted and the rootless, were crucial structuring features of contemporary moral commentary.

---

studies on the history of the internal dynamics of the French family include Philippe Ariès, *Centuries of Childhood: A Social History of Family Life*, trans. Robert Baldick (New York: Vintage, 1962); David Hunt, *Parents and Children in History: The Psychology of Family Life in Early Modern France* (New York: Basic Books, 1970); Theodore Zeldin, *France, 1848–1945: Ambition and Love* (Oxford: Oxford University Press, 1979); and the multivolume *History of Private Life*, ed. Ariès and Duby.

[44] See Zeldin, *France . . . Ambition and Love*, 315.

[45] On the question of the family and the French experience of industrialization, see Louise A. Tilly and Joan Wallach Scott, *Women, Work, and Family*, 2d ed. (New York: Methuen, 1987). See also Alain Cottereau, "The Distinctiveness of Working-Class Cultures in France, 1848–1900," and Michelle Perrot, "On the Formation of the French Working Class," both in *Working Class Formation: Nineteenth-Century Patterns in Western Europe and the United States*, ed. Ira Katznelson and Aristide R. Zolberg (Princeton: Princeton University Press, 1986).

[46] See Leslie Page Moch, *Paths to the City: Rural Migration in Nineteenth-Century France* (Beverly Hills: Sage, 1983); Philip E. Ogden and Paul E. White, eds., *Migrants in Modern France: Population Mobility in the Later Nineteenth and Twentieth Centuries* (London: Unwin Hyman, 1989); and Etienne Juillard, ed., *Apogé et crise de la civilisation paysanne, 1789–1914*, vol. 3 of *Histoire de la France rurale*, ed. Georges Duby and Armand Wallon (Paris: Editions du Seuil, 1976).

The omnipresent element in almost all of these critiques of modern life was the question of father and his domestic power. Le Play's writing again provides an important example of this textual phenomenon. In *L'Organisation de la famille* Le Play interwove a mournful account of the moral decay of the nation with an even more somber lament on the decline of paternal authority. In his view, a healthy society stood on a foundation of virtuous family units. Morally sound families were those "subjected by tradition to the strict discipline of respect and labor. Harmony is preserved in these families, through the acceptance of God and the moral order, under the control of the father."[47] Again, identifying family moral health with the relative strength or weakness of paternal authority, particularly as measured against the force of industrial change, was not unique to conservative opinion.[48] The demise of paternal authority was decried in the social criticism of the Left and in the discourses of the laboring classes as well, most of all where the Left opposed itself to feminist social criticism and action.[49]

The pessimistic vision of modern life and its material transformation was not the only set of ideas that gave rise to questions about the proper exercise of paternal authority in the French family. Although the authority of the male head of household had been challenged by other family members over the course of centuries, the nineteenth century brought a new form of opposition in its cultural validation of individuality and self-expression. Drawing on evolving currents of thought about individual autonomy and selfhood, sons, daughters, and wives struggled to assert some kind of individual freedom beyond the confines of family hierarchy. Evidence of social fracture and conflict of interest within the home was corralled by contemporary alarmists, such as Le Play and his followers, who used it to further underscore their warnings of cataclysmic social and moral breakdown as the inevitable consequence of modern individualism for all families.[50] Reconciling individualism

[47] Le Play, *L'Organisation de la famille*, 6–7.

[48] An alternative analysis of the deterioration of male authority in the working-class family, produced for the most part by male labor activists and socialists, argued that the corrosive effects of industrial capitalism, and particularly the exploitation of women and children in the labor force, resulted in the destabilization of the working-class home. See, for example, Friedrich Engels's influential text *The Origins of the Family, Private Property, and the State* (New York: International Publishers, 1972). Left-wing thinkers also applied the metaphor of paternal despotism to nineteenth-century relations of class, as in Jules Vallès's 1879 work *L'Enfant* (Paris: Flammarion, 1968), in which the story of a child abused by unloving parents doubled as a parable of the inhumanity of an insufficiently benevolent bourgeoisie.

[49] For a survey of left-wing antifeminist views in the nineteenth century, see Moses, *French Feminism*, esp. 152–61.

[50] The literature on the history of the family and the rise of liberal individualism in the West is enormous, particularly in the historiographies of the United States and Great Britain. Among the best-known works on this subject are Lawrence Stone's *Family, Sex, and Marriage in England, 1500–1800* (New York: Harper and Row, 1977); Edward Shorter's *The Making of the Modern Family* (New York: Basic, 1977); Carl Degler's *At Odds: Women and the Family in*

to the moral order maintained by the "healthy" family was a task for both critics and supporters of change.

In the discussions of the moral health of the family, social difference served as useful ground for the more global discourse of domestic moral critique. Observers in this period noted and read failures in the exercise of parental authority through a grid of increasingly acute social distinctions.[51] It was thus a truism of the age that the patterns of working-class domestic life, made visible through the new techniques of social inquiry, testified to the accelerating process of working-class demoralization.

This position easily gained purchase among middle-class social critics, whose views tended to be tempered by the increasingly stringent norms that governed their own familial lives. Their insistent defense of a father's natural and universal right to rule his family most often appeared entwined in the tendrils of pessimistic social analysis. The forces eroding the working-class French family—the waged labor of women and children, sexual promiscuity, the corrupting "urban spectacle," unemployment, socialism, feminism, and alcoholism—also were brought in to explain the weakening of paternal authority in the laboring classes. Such lines of argument were not without force on the Left, moreover. Socialists and other radical social observers signaled the same symptoms of decline as their more conservative interlocutors. The left-wing theory of causation, however, took quite a different turn. Where the more conservative script produced a narrative of individual moral collapse, the Left condemned capitalism and its effects. Hence the apparent weakness of the family, according to the dominant strains in the Left critique, derived from industrial capitalism's emasculation of the male worker and from its persistent degradation of working wives and daughters.[52]

The proliferation of these sorts of accounts of the family and its pathologies meant that reformers of the Third Republic could not avoid reading the problem of paternal authority through the lens of the "social problem."

America from the Revolution to the Present (New York: Oxford University Press, 1980); and Christopher Lasch's *Haven in a Heartless World: The Family Besieged* (New York: Basic Books, 1977). See also Burguière, "Demande d'état et aspirations individualistes," in *L'Enfant*, ed. Lévy.

[51] See Lynch, *Family, Class, and Ideology*.

[52] Some historians have reiterated the critique of liberal individualism in their own writings and hence have been complicit, intentionally or not, in perpetuating many of its more misogynistic characteristics. For a history of the disempowerment of male heads of household through social transformation and the "liberation" of women, see Shorter, *The Making of the Modern Family*. For the same disempowerment achieved via working-class women's collaboration with the agents of bourgeois power, see Jacques Donzelot, *The Policing of Families*, trans. Robert Hurley (New York: Pantheon, 1979). For a feminist reading of these discourses in the nineteenth century, see Joan Wallach Scott, "Work Identities for Men and Women: The Politics of Work and the Family in the Parisian Garment Trades in 1848," in *Gender and the Politics of History* (New York: Columbia University Press, 1988).

The Revolution had found all fathers suspect, and most particularly those whose domestic powers were derived from property and privilege. For the nineteenth-century social critic, however, the prime exemplars of degraded paternal authority were the dispossessed. In the century between the late eighteenth and the late nineteenth century, then, the definition of problematic fatherhood came to lose its implications of tyrannical and excessive power; instead, the improper fulfillment of the paternal role tended to be characterized by inadequacy, weakness, and indifference.

The reversal of poles in the critique of paternal right—from strong to weak, from socially powerful to socially disempowered—was not absolute. In a curious and politically powerful play of contradiction, absence, weakness, and inadequacy came also to signify excess, tyranny, and abuse. As Roussel would put it in 1882, "In those social milieus where poverty, drunkenness, ignorance, [and] the absence of a moral culture necessarily efface family sentiment and spirit, children are vulnerable . . . to all the weaknesses, all the abuses, [and] all the excesses of la puissance paternelle."[53] In the place of the propertied despots who peopled the eighteenth-century critique of the family, reformers such as Roussel discovered the tyrannical "deficient" fathers of the working classes.

In the hands of Third Republic reformers, however, the lens of the social also yielded a far more general critique of the family, one that produced a surprising and influential inversion of social valences. In the particularity of malfunctioning working-class fatherhood, lawmakers would read the problem of paternal authority more generally. On the basis of a set of representations of the working-class family in its modern urban and industrial context, they would produce legislation recasting the rights of fatherhood and the state in far more generalized and politically fundamental terms.

Finally, the increasingly fine texture of nineteenth-century definitions of fatherhood, motherhood, and childhood worked to shift the accepted foundation of family life from the exercise of authority to the bonds of mutual love and nurturance.[54] By the advent of the Third Republic, a substantial shift in the definition of parenthood from right to obligation, a common theme in the growing literature on parenting as a form of nurturance, came to dominate

[53] France, Assemblée nationale, Sénat, *Rapport fait au nom de la commission chargée d'examiner: 1° La Proposition de loi ayant pour objet la protection des enfants abandonnés, délaissés ou maltraités, présenté par MM. Théophile Roussel, Bérenger, Dufaure, l'amiral Fourichon, Schoelcher et Jules Simon. 2° Le Projet de loi sur la protection de l'enfance présenté par M. Cazot, Garde de Sceaux, Ministre de Justice*, Sénat session 1882, no. 451, Annexe au procès-verbal de la séance du 25 juillet 1882 (Paris: Imprimerie du Sénat, 1882), 3.

[54] For an exemplary and influential work from the growing body of prescriptive literature on the affective family, see Gustave Droz, *Monsieur, madame et bébé* (Paris: V. Havard, 1878). See also Ariès, *Centuries of Childhood*; Perrot, ed., *A History of Private Life*, vol. 4; and Donzelot, *The Policing of Families*, for discussions of the growing emphasis on protection and nurturance in the nineteenth century and its implications.

public opinion and public policy.[55] By the last quarter of the century, a parent's role was defined as primarily educative and essentially altruistic. In the ideal it was shaped by the instinct to protect and nurture one's offspring through the vulnerable years of childhood, the subordination of self-interest to the greater interest of child and nation, and the acceptance of the responsibility to provide the child with a sound moral upbringing, or éducation.

These changing norms, articulated in both popular and "expert" literature, provided new standards against which the contemporary French family, again particularly but not only the working-class family, appeared deficient. The debate on the working-class family was especially evident in nineteenth-century fiction, for example, Victor Hugo's *Les Misérables*, Eugène Sue's *Les Mystères de Paris*, and later, Emile Zola's Rougon-Macquart series.[56]

In this new context, the minimal prescriptions in Napoleonic law on parents' obligations to their children—"food, support, and upbringing"—took on new meaning in a cultural milieu increasingly oriented toward the affective and educative aspects of everyday family life.[57] As obligation increasingly crowded the terrain of authority, moreover, mothers—particularly working-class mothers—became ever more visible in their parental capacities, ever more accountable for the gendered exercise of their parental influence.[58]

The reinscription of sexual difference in these new understandings of parental identity and responsibility would profoundly affect the production and interpretation of family law in the Third Republic. Despite the increasing emphasis on parental duty, however, the question of authority did not drop from the picture completely. Instead the proper exercise of masculine paternal authority in the fulfillment of parental obligation was deemed an essen-

[55] Claudia Scheck Kselman stresses this shift of emphasis from authority to obligation in her chapter "From Right to Duty: Changing Definitions of Parenthood in the Third Republic" (Kselman, "The Modernization of Family Law: The Politics and Ideology of Family Reform in Third Republic France" [Ph.D. diss., University of Michigan, 1980]).

[56] For a useful account of the problem of the family in nineteenth-century literature, see also Roddy Reid, *Death of the Family: Discourse, Fiction, and Desire in France* (Stanford: Stanford University Press, 1994).

[57] The historiography positing a profound transformation in the affective life of the family, centered on the child, begins with Ariès's book on the seventeenth and eighteenth centuries in *Centuries of Childhood*. Many historians have since argued that Ariès's groundbreaking work accurately describes relations in elite families but contend that a widespread sentimentalization of family life did not occur until well into the nineteenth century. Others submit that strong familial sentiment can be found in the early modern period, and others find its expression even in antiquity. On the reception of Ariès's work on childhood and the subsequent debate on the history of familial sentiment, see Richard T. Vann, "The Youth of *Centuries of Childhood*," *History and Theory* 21, no. 2 (1982). See also Linda Pollock, *Forgotten Children: Parent-Child Relations from 1500–1900* (Cambridge: Cambridge University Press, 1983).

[58] On shifting views of poor mothers in later-nineteenth-century France, see esp. Rachel G. Fuchs, *Poor and Pregnant in Paris: Strategies for Survival in the Nineteenth Century* (New Brunswick, N.J.: Rutgers University Press, 1992), 35–76.

tial feature of the modern moral order. In this sense, the family came increasingly to be defined through the operation of sexual as well as social difference.

By the end of the nineteenth century, la puissance paternelle came to serve as a crucial point of reference in articulating—and reconceptualizing—the relations of power that shaped both the most banal moments of everyday family life and the highest levels of political and intellectual debate. As a result, the attempts to rethink and redistribute paternal power which began to take shape in the last quarter of the century sent waves of anxiety through the world of opinion. These efforts would affect not only the legal definition of the father's authority but the entire fabric of social relations and their representations in which paternal power had been a dominant motif. Reconceptualizing la puissance paternelle and the parental identities it structured opened the door to the recasting of the identity of the state itself. With the founding of the Third Republic, the gendered metaphors of parenthood would prove a powerful discursive tool, both for establishing the new political regime and for transforming relations between government and the governed.

CHAPTER 2

Protection, the State, and the Laws of 1874

ONE OF THE MOST important elements in the early Third Republic's efforts to redraw the boundaries of social government and to rethink the limits of paternal power was the assertion that the state might have a legitimate role in the drama of family life as supplementary or alternative parent. In constructing a protective identity for the state as a parent, and particularly as a father, lawmakers of the late nineteenth century located their discourse within a constellation of partial antecedents. Danton's pronouncement during the French Revolution, for example, posed the first and most radical challenge to the ties of blood and lineage under the sign of republicanism: "Children belong to the Republic before they belong to their parents."[1] Although this position would prove far too extreme for the reformers of the late nineteenth century, its spirit tinged even the most moderate discussions of the state as a supplemental or alternative parent.

Perhaps even more than in the charged language of the Revolution, reformers found materials for the construction of the Third Republic's parental identity in the administrative institutions of state they inherited from previous regimes. Napoleon's organization of the Service des Enfants Assistés in the first decades of the nineteenth century explicitly placed the legal guardianship (la tutelle) of foundlings, abandoned children, and poor orphans in the hands of public authorities. By the provisions of the law of 15 *pluviôse*, year XIII (4 February 1805), and the decree of 19 January 1811, tutelle was to be exercised by the administrators of the regional *hospice* in each department of France. One member of the administrative commission would be named *tuteur*, or guardian, and the others would serve as members of an ad hoc family council. The tuteur and the council together were empowered with the full rights of la puissance paternelle as it was described in the Civil Code. These measures, as one legal commentator noted more than a century later, amounted to "the substitution, for the family of the children taken in by the state, of another family, this one administrative, to manage their affairs and to exercise its tutelle."[2]

Napoleonic penal law provided the courts with their own mechanism for

---

[1] As cited in Yvonne Knibiehler, *Les Pères aussi ont une histoire* (Paris: Hachette, 1987), 161–62.

[2] Geneviève Azèma, *L'Etat et les enfants abandonnés* (Bordeaux: Imprimerie de l'Université, 1930), 80.

substituting public parenthood for the authority of the biological family. According to article 335 of the penal code, magistrates might call for the forfeiture of la puissance paternelle in cases where parents had been implicated in the prostitution of their own children. In addition, article 66 of the same code stated that in the case of minors acquitted of crimes, the criminal court might remove them from the physical custody of their parents (*la garde*) when it considered the paternal household an unacceptable moral environment. Although this last provision did not strip parents of all formal legal authority over their children, it transferred the ultimate determination of the child's best interest from parent to magistrate and positioned the parent as the direct object of legal regulation. Even more important, the partial forfeiture of parental powers in such cases comprised a gesture that was both punitive and protective.

Where parents had been convicted of crimes thought to refract into the heart of the family, in short, the penal code authorized the state to substitute its own parental powers for those of the delinquent father or mother. Like the directives on the care of foundlings, these penal measures would become important elements in the collection of precedents assembled by the reformers of the Third Republic. Reference to these articles would buttress the quest to justify the seizure of authority from parents whose behavior appeared to threaten their children's lives or moral integrity.

If Napoleonic penal law provided reformers with a founding text that established the possibility of a parental state, more complex visions of the French state's protective authority emerged in the mid-nineteenth-century debates on the protection of working children. Under the July Monarchy, the assembly enacted France's first child labor law in 1841.[3] The new measure was in fact quite limited in scope, addressing only the employment of children in large-scale factory production. In 1841 this form of manufacture accounted for only a fraction of France's total industrial labor. Even where it pertained, observers noted, the new law was rarely applied with vigor.[4]

Ten years later, the legislature approved a second child labor law, requiring written contracts for all minors placed in apprenticeship.[5] In principle, the 1851 law opened the small workshop to the protective supervision of the state. Despite the efforts of contemporary lawmakers, this too proved to be a relatively impotent measure. In the laissez-faire economic climate of the

---

[3] On child labor law in the nineteenth century, see Lee Shai Weissbach, *Child Labor Reform in Nineteenth-Century France: Assuring the Future Harvest* (Baton Rouge: Louisiana State University Press, 1989), and Colin Heywood, *Childhood in Nineteenth-Century France: Work, Health, and Education among the "Classes Populaires"* (Cambridge: Cambridge University Press, 1988). Weissbach includes the translated texts of the 1841, 1851, and 1874 labor laws in his appendixes, 231–47.

[4] On efforts to implement the 1841 child labor law, see Weissbach, *Child Labor*, 84–107.

[5] Ibid., 108–22.

mid-nineteenth century, regulating labor, even the labor of "vulnerable" children, drew little support beyond the realm of philanthropy. Further, the lack of a specialized professional inspectorate meant that the state could not oversee the implementation of its protective legislation to any significant degree.[6]

The full historical significance of law, however, does not always lie in its immediate efficacy or even in its broad social impact. The appearance of these early gestures toward protection, however limited in their effects on the utilization of child labor, were crucial moments of speech in a period more remarkable for its silence on the place of the state in the lives of French children. As interventions in juridical thinking, these midcentury laws staked out important ground for subsequent reform. By the advent of the Third Republic, the theme—if not the reality—of child protection had come to be a legitimate element in the debates on the proper relationship between state and family.

If the topos of state-legislated child protection was familiar by the first decades of the Third Republic, it also was fundamentally reconfigured—and expanded—by France's changing historical circumstances. The sense of vulnerability spawned by military collapse before Bismarck's troops in 1870 and the wave of anxiety that accompanied the new public awareness of France's low natality rates forced public attention onto the issue of children's physical and moral vulnerability.[7] Cast as defenseless beings, children seemed a perfect metaphorical incarnation of France's victimization at the hands of the inhuman Prussians. As the germ of future generations, children seemed a scarce national resource to be husbanded and nurtured in preparation for future military conflicts and increasingly fierce industrial competition.[8]

[6] Ibid., 121–22.

[7] See, for example, Alexandre Mayeur, *De la mortalité excessive du premier âge considérée comme cause de dépopulation et des moyens d'y remédier* (Paris: Baillière et fils, 1873). Mayeur, founder of the Société protectrice de l'enfance in 1866, argued that the disasters of 1870–71 could be blamed in large part on a decline in national morals, particularly in familial sentiment, which placed more and more infants at risk (Mayeur, *De la mortalité*, 24).

[8] Joshua Cole, "The Power of Large Numbers: Population and Politics in Nineteenth-Century France" (Ph.D. diss., University of California, Berkeley, 1991). Like Cole, Catherine Rollet-Echalier notes that these fears had begun to be articulated in the 1860s as reformers framed recent research on fertility and infant mortality within a narrative of France's vulnerability in the increasingly hostile arena of industrial, military, and colonial competition (Rollet-Echalier, *La Politique à l'égard de la petite enfance sous la IIIe République* [Paris: Editions de l'INED/Presses Universitaires de France, 1990], 109–14). On the connections drawn between demographic crisis, the fragility of infants, and the sense that France was endangered, see also George D. Sussman, *Selling Mothers' Milk: The Wet-Nursing Business in France, 1715–1914* (Urbana: University of Illinois Press, 1982). On the association of demographic crisis with the dangerous reproductive and child-rearing practices of the urban poor, see Rachel G. Fuchs, *Poor and Pregnant in Paris: Strategies for Survival in the Nineteenth Century* (New Brunswick: Rutgers University Press, 1992), 56–76. Maurice Crubellier notes the new weight placed on

The living memory of the Commune added yet another layer to the concern about children's moral and physical development, motivating so many of the protective endeavors of the early Third Republic.[9] Baron Othenin d'Haussonville elaborated on this theme in 1876 in his series of articles for the *Revue des deux mondes* on the dangers of childhood in Paris and the need for protective action. "It suffices to know," d'Haussonville argued, "that 651 children under the age of sixteen were arrested among the defenders of the Commune with arms in hand to get an approximate idea of the vices that the future citizens of the capital cultivate [*travaillent*] from the moment of their birth."[10] Poor urban children, implicated by the disorder manifested in the Commune, appeared to need protection from themselves; they seemed to need stronger moral guidance to counteract their learned or innate impulses toward social deviancy and revolutionary action than their families had hitherto provided. By the last decades of the century, most social critics agreed that, in principle, this would best be achieved through the implementation of a two-pronged program of reform: proper moral education to shape the child's character on one hand and the elimination of "dangerous influences" from the universe of the child's daily experience on the other.[11]

Protection in this context implied nothing less than protecting the poor or working-class child, and the nation, from the destiny that he or she quite literally embodied. As historian Michelle Perrot has put it, by the 1880s, childhood had become "a political stake."[12] After 1870–71, the project of child protection required more than the regulation of industrial production. It

---

physical education for children in the immediate wake of the Franco-Prussian War (Crubellier, *L'Enfance et la jeunesse dans la société française, 1850–1950* [Paris: Armand Colin, 1979], 194–99).

[9] The apparent links between the suppression of the Commune and the Third Republic's project of child protection have inspired the "social control" interpretations of protection, most evident in Philippe Meyer's *L'Enfant et la raison d'état* (Paris: Editions du Seuil, 1977) and to a lesser degree in Jacques Donzelot's *The Policing of Families*, trans. Robert Hurley (New York: Pantheon, 1979).

[10] Othenin d'Haussonville, "L'Enfance à Paris," *Revue des deux mondes* 17 (1 October 1876): 483. In 1888 Doctor Paul Moreau de Tours, one of the Third Republic's most influential experts on child psychology, signaled the "pathogenic influence of the events of the siege of Paris and the Commune" on the moral and physiological development of children born in late 1871 (Moreau de Tours, *La Folie chez les enfants* [Paris: Librairie J.-B. Baillière et fils, 1888], 37).

[11] On post-1870 conceptions of "dangerous" working-class children and the development of new approaches to their moral reform, see Alain Faure, "Enfance ouvrière, enfance coupable," *Les Révoltes logiques* 18 (winter 1980–81): 13–35. See also Michelle Perrot, "Sur la ségrégation de l'enfance au XIXe siècle," *La Psychiatrie de l'enfant* 25, fasc. 1 (1982), esp. 183, 196, 203–4. Jean-Marie Renouard argues that in the first decades of the early Third Republic experts on juvenile criminality developed notions of childhood delinquency that increasingly tended to represent the "dangerous" child as a victim, particularly a victim of his or her own family (Renouard, *De l'enfant coupable à l'enfant inadapté: Le traitement social et politique de la déviance* [Paris: Centurion, 1990], 62–66).

[12] Perrot, "Sur la ségrégation," 204.

meant protecting children from material and moral harm in an ever-widening arena of danger. It meant, through the inauguration of a new vision of the protective state, building a national future through the correction of a compromised past.

The *Dictionnaire de la langue française*, published by republican positivist Emile Littré in 1877, codified the doubled meaning of *protection* for the new regime. In negative terms, *protection* signified an act of guarding against danger, of protecting against imminent harm. At the same time, *protection* also signified an act of cultivation or assistance.[13] These two senses of *protection*, made all the more concrete by the experiences that had brought the Third Republic into being, particularly the war with Prussia, would perfectly serve the new regime's entwined efforts to defend and cultivate the population. It would underwrite the republic's strategies to preserve the nation through the protection of the young. For the activists of the Third Republic, this meant above all that the state would have to assume the identity of the natural protector itself; it would have to become a parental figure.

Developing mechanisms of protection appropriate for the new republic proved to be more complicated, however, than simply positing their necessity. The Third Republic's protective ambitions were tempered, and at times disabled, by its profound ambivalence about assuming the role of a protective parent. To what degree could the exercise of public power in the name of protection be cast in the affective and authoritative terms of family hierarchies? How could the state, in assuming the metaphorical position of the *bon père de famille*, push aside the real but delinquent parent in order to fulfill his natural paternal functions itself? What would be the price of this intervention structured by the gendered metaphors of family and family functions?

Senator Roussel, the figure behind much of the young republic's protective legislation, was among the most confident of all the proponents of legislated state parenthood. "[P]ublic authority," he would argue in 1882, "has the duty and the right to replace or substitute itself for the ineffectual or unfit family in order to ensure the care and education of a minor."[14] Even for Roussel, however, matters grew more complicated when it came to designing policy and imagining the means of its implementation. Most important, and of greatest concern to both Roussel and his opponents, developing a regime of public protection would demand broad, even radical, revisions of

---

[13] Emile Littré, *Dictionnaire de la langue française* (Paris: Hachette, 1877).

[14] France, Assemblée nationale, Sénat, *Rapport fait au nom de la commission chargée d'examiner: 1° La Proposition de loi ayant pour objet la protection des enfants abandonnés, délaissés ou maltraités, présenté par MM. Théophile Roussel, Bérenger, Dufaure, l'amiral Fourichon, Schoelcher et Jules Simon. 2° Le Projet de loi sur la protection de l'enfance présenté par M. Cazot, Garde de Sceaux, Ministre de Justice*, Sénat session 1882, no. 451, Annexe au procès-verbal de la séance du 25 juillet 1882 (Paris: Imprimerie du Sénat, 1882), 8.

the standing relationship between state and society. Substituting the state for delinquent parents in the role of protective agent would require a redefinition and realignment of the interests running through and, indeed, defining the child in contemporary thinking. It would precipitate a profound recasting of notions of right and duty within the family. It also would require giving a literalized institutional weight to those metaphors of family increasingly invoked in the representation of social and political relations in the 1870s and 1880s.

In the early 1870s, these issues would move directly to the center of political debates with the introduction of three new child protection laws. In the course of these debates the new regime began to limn the edges of its protective identity. Also in these debates the radical implications of the parental metaphor became acutely apparent.

Eighteen seventy-four was in fact a signal year for child protection under the Third Republic. Three times that year French lawmakers reworked the boundary between paternal power exercised by the state and the rights and responsibilities attributed by civil law to natural parents. The law of 19 May 1874 imposed new restrictions on the employment of minors and adult women in industrial occupations. The second law, enacted in early December, addressed the employment of children by traveling performers and "professional" beggars.[15] Later in December the National Assembly passed its third protective law, this one regulating the structure and practice of wet-nursing.

In each instance, the debates and the laws they produced turned on protecting children in a social fabric that legislators described as increasingly rent by conflicting interests and divided spheres of authority. Crystallizing these issues in the context of the new republic's particular social, political, and cultural concerns, the laws of 1874 effectively opened a new discursive field. In particular, they provided the basis for developing a working logic of public protection for the new regime. In forging these laws, legislative reformers reworked familial metaphors through a newly malleable web of possible relations between state, family, and individual. The discussion and enactment of these laws also served as an opportunity for some of the most influential activists of the early Third Republic, such as Senator Roussel, to cut their legislative teeth, to learn the necessary strategies for developing and enacting legal reforms.

Most important for the question of regulating moral danger in the family, the legislative efforts of 1874 provided the script and the rehearsal space for

---

[15] For a more extended discussion of this law, see my article "Law, Labor, and the Spectacle of the Body: Protecting Child Street Performers in Nineteenth-Century France," *The International Journal of Children's Rights* 4 (1996). A slightly different version of this article appears in *Governing Childhood*, ed. Anne McGillivray (Aldershot, England: Dartmouth, 1997).

future, more radical state action in the protection of children. In particular, they introduced the possibility of separating children's "vulnerable interests" from the "dangerous self-interest" of their parents. The 1874 laws pointed toward the possibility that the state could protect children in the most juridically and culturally sacred of all spaces: the domestic sphere of the family.

The law of 19 May 1874, the first of the three new laws to be passed, imposed new restrictions on the labor of children and adult women in industrial production. Included among the law's provisions were limitations on the length of the workday and the workweek, the establishment of minimum ages of employment, and a prohibition against employing young children for night work, for underground work in the mining industry, and for work in dangerous industries, particularly those which required the use of toxic chemicals. Many of these restrictions were also applied to girls up to the age of twenty-one and in some cases to adult women.[16] The law also introduced new educational requirements for working children and held employers responsible for adjusting the children's hours according to their level of primary instruction.[17]

Like the less ambitious child labor law of 1841, the 1874 law was poorly enforced and made only a small dent in the hiring practices and working conditions affecting children in industry. In focusing exclusively on large-scale industrial production, the law also left entirely untouched those minors who worked in small shops and, especially, the vast majority of child laborers who worked in agriculture.[18] Again, as in the case of the 1841 labor law, the influence of this new legislation was not necessarily limited to the strength or weakness of its application. The process by which the law had been forged in parliament left an important residue in the increasingly weighted debate on the state's relation to families; the heated exchanges on the limits of state power and crumbling of "private" paternal power were perhaps more effective in transforming the crucible of parliamentary opinion than they were in changing patterns of industrial organization. In reconfiguring the discourse of legislative reform around legitimate power and the family, in clarifying the lines of cleavage and the obstacles to acceptable forms regulation, these debates would result in even bolder efforts to remake the

---

[16] On state regulation of women's labor in the late nineteenth century, see Mary Lynn Stewart's *Women, Work, and the French State: Labour, Protection, and Social Patriarchy, 1879–1919* (Kingston: McGill-Queen's University Press, 1989).

[17] For more extensive discussions of the 1874 child labor law and its impact, see Weissbach, *Child Labor Reform,* 181–226, and Heywood, *Childhood in Nineteenth-Century France,* 260–86.

[18] Although most historians agree that the majority of French children worked in agriculture, Heywood notes that nineteenth-century labor statistics, notoriously inadequate even for industry, cannot sustain a crude numerical estimate of the child agricultural labor force (Heywood, *Childhood in Nineteenth-Century France,* 21).

family through law and, in time, efforts to create a more effective apparatus of implementation.

The central purpose of the new child labor legislation, according to its sponsors, was to protect children from abuse and exploitation in the workplace. These terms had quite specific meanings. *Abuse* in the case of industrial labor meant exposure to working conditions that might threaten the bodily or spiritual well-being of a category of workers who were, by definition, weak, vulnerable, and essentially ill suited to the demands of unregulated industrial production.[19] In the early 1870s French lawmakers were also careful to redefine industrial labor as a potentially abusive experience whose effects would have serious implications for the child's successful transition to adulthood. According to one member of the legislature, for example, the proposed law would protect children against the "deplorable abuse[s]" they commonly experienced in the workplace, "to the great detriment of their health, when they are too young, as well as to their intellect, to their education, and even to their professional apprenticeship."[20]

No sooner did members of the assembly raise the question of abuse than they encountered the far more difficult question of accountability. In their final debates over the bill, lawmakers vacillated between laying the responsibility for abuse at the feet of industry and blaming working-class parents for allowing or even encouraging the exploitation of their own children. The stakes in both narratives of responsibility were high: if industry was to bear the blame, then the state's effort to protect children would challenge the principles of free enterprise. If, however, parents were found guilty of abuse by permitting their offspring to work under harmful conditions, then the state was de facto pronouncing parents incompetent judges of their children's best interests, poorly endowed with the natural desire to protect them, and ill suited to exercising their parental rights. It was suggesting that these parents were in fact not parents at all.

Despite the widespread distrust of the laboring classes in philanthropic circles, and even given the proliferation of accounts demonstrating the disintegration of the laboring family, questioning parental instinct and right in any social context was no simple matter. Tempers flared in the course of the legislative discussions on how much of the industrial abuse of children could

---

[19] Thus Deputy Charles Kolb-Bernard, responding to the first proposal for the law in 1871, contended that the justification for protective legislation was grounded in the social duty "to extend our material and moral patronage over our young generations of workers." This protection, he went on to explain in strikingly dramatic language, was a matter of "simultaneously defending their bodies and their souls against the abuses of a doubly homicidal liberty" (Kolb-Bernard, as cited in Jean-Baptiste Duvergier et al., *Collection complète des lois, décrets, ordonnances, règlements et avis du conseil d'état* 64 [Paris: Société du Recueil Sirey, 1874], 145). Kolb-Bernard's report was originally published in the *JO*, 23 August 1871.

[20] Ibid., 19 May 1874, 3351.

be blamed on their parents and on what steps could be taken to control them. The author of the 1874 bill, Deputy Ambroise Joubert, defended his project against the accusation that it infringed on natural paternal authority by claiming that it condemned only the *mis*use of familial power.[21] Although the state should in general demonstrate "the greatest respect" for paternal authority, he argued, it should not hesitate to step in when "that authority, instead of protecting the child, becomes oppressive" and when "the father, instead of being provident and good, reveals himself as uncaring, as barely human. . . . As far as I'm concerned," he added, "I believe that society has the right to set the limits."[22]

The champions of inviolable paternal authority tried for their part to deflect the debate from the issue of ultimate responsibility. Instead, they recast the question of the limits of paternal power in spatial terms. How far would the new law go, they asked, not in holding parents accountable as the source of abusive child labor practices but in entering their domain in order to subject them to the standards and forms of surveillance that the law would require? "Does the law that you would pass accept the threshold of the father's home as the absolute limit to the state's control or to that of its agents?" one deputy asked his colleagues with rhetorical flourish typical of these debates. In this remark, moreover, the gendered contradictions woven into the question of parental authority appeared in full force; in the domain of possible state regulation, the domestic sphere was defined not in terms of women's feminine influence but in terms of the rightful exercise of autonomous paternal rule.

Devoted to protecting the authority of the père de famille over his own family—even that of the working-class père de famille—some legislators agitated for revisions that would admit a distinction between the children who labored in the charge of an unrelated *patron*, or master—a situation that, according to one legislator, "breaks family ties"—and those who worked or were apprenticed in a family enterprise under their own parents' supervision.[23] The emphasis on the essential distinction between parent and patron reveals a critical shift in both the language and the logic of parenthood by the late nineteenth century. Employers could no longer be trusted to fulfill "paternal" functions where their young workers were concerned. The protective associations borne by the term *patron* no longer defined either the structure of child labor or its symbolic order.[24] Hence legislators agreed that

---

[21] Ibid., 27 June 1871, Annexe 333. Joubert was a textile manufacturer from Angers who in his political career supported MacMahon and the monarchist agenda. See Claudia Scheck Kselman, "The Modernization of Family Law: The Politics and Ideology of Family Reform in Third Republic France" (Ph.D. diss., University of Michigan, 1980), 195.

[22] *JO*, 19 May 1874, 3353–54.

[23] Ibid., 3352–53.

[24] The etymology of *patron* ties it directly to the language of protection. The term has histori-

the unrelated patron could legitimately be held to a set of formal legal prescriptions. At the same time, they were adamant that children who worked in a space and structure of production dominated by their own fathers be excluded from the law's purview. In encoding this distinction into the proposed legislation, Joubert's opponents were successful: the new law, like the child labor law of 1841, was to be applied only to industrial sites such as factories and mills where children were employed by patrons other than their own fathers.

It seemed, at least for the moment, that the most disturbing questions about the regulation of parental interests and responsibilities had been sutured over in the final draft of the bill. By the logic of the law, employers, and not parents, exposed children to risks. Employers, and not parents, were likely to exploit children to extract a maximum profit from their labor. In apportioning responsibility according to this abstract opposition between parent and employer, the new labor law endorsed a version of state protection that began only when children were clearly beyond the reach of the continuous, implicitly protective supervision of their own parents. One legislator crystallized this view in his assertion that the state had "not only the right but the duty to serve as tuteur when the father and mother are absent. [The state] has the duty to intervene when they are not there; it has the duty to understand how citizens of the future are formed or malformed."[25] The sanctity of the paternal threshold thus survived these debates.

If the law implied that employers no longer could be counted among the numbers of effective substitute or supplementary parents, it did not leave a vacuum in their place. The new legislation, along with the reports and debates from which it had been born, began to embed a new notion of the state

cally been used to refer to employers or heads of institutions, but it also has a long-standing place in the language of French Catholicism, where *patron* refers to one's patron saint. Historians of the eighteenth century tend to agree that the paternal inflections in relations between the patron and his workers had begun to erode well before the Revolution. See, for example, Robert Darnton's essay "The Great Cat Massacre," in *The Great Cat Massacre and Other Episodes in French Cultural History* (New York: Basic Books, 1984), and especially Michael Sonenscher, *Work and Wages: Natural Law, Politics, and the Eighteenth-Century French Trades* (Cambridge: Cambridge University Press, 1989). The expectation that the patron fulfill some kind of paternal function in relation to his young apprentices continued into the nineteenth century nonetheless, but the enactment of the 1851 law regulating conditions of apprenticeship signaled the disintegration of that faith as well. As Donald Reid and others have suggested, however, paternalism lived on in the late nineteenth century as both a discourse and a technique of labor management, particularly in large industrial firms. See Donald Reid, "Industrial Paternalism: Discourse and Practice in Nineteenth-Century Mining and Metallurgy," *Comparative Studies in Society and History* 24, no. 4 (October 1985): 579–607. See also Donald Reid's "Schools and the Paternalist Project at Le Creusot, 1850–1914," *Journal of Social History* 27, no. 1 (fall 1993): 129–43.

[25] *JO*, 19 May 1874, 3353.

as parent in the language and practice of child protection. At the same time as these debates redistributed parental identity, authority, and responsibility, it also significantly expanded the borders of the social terrain in which it could legitimately—that is, in terms consistent with the republic's imaginaire d'état—act "in the interest of the child."

The question of parental responsibility did not disappear from the floor of the legislature with the passage of the child labor law in May. Several sessions over the summer of 1874 were devoted to discussing a report and bill on "children in itinerant trades" (les professions ambulantes), presented by Eugène Tallon in March. Tallon, like Joubert in the debates on industrial labor, also centered the question of state protection on the problem of "abusive" or exploitative labor practices. In this case, however, the proposed legislation addressed a quite different, and far more marginal, kind of employment: children's labor as wandering musicians, acrobats, carnival performers, and "professional" beggars.

The National Assembly's debates about child labor and protection in this new context once again centered on the state's right to regulate commercial activity, on parental responsibility in the exploitation of their own children, and on the difference between an unrelated patron and a parent. Once again, legislators wrestled with the implications of a legal model that distinguished parental interests from the interests of their children. What, they asked in this second forum of debate, would be the consequences of a law that opposed parent and child and that required the state to challenge the authority of its (male) citizens out of its selfless interest in the well-being of children and the national future they represented? In the consideration of these questions, the legislators' discussion of the proposed legislation on protecting children in the itinerant trades brought important refinements to their definitions of danger and protection. In particular, the debates developed an ever more complex understanding of "abuse" as directly grounded in the child's "exposure to vice" or other moral danger. These new layers of moral concern would provide one of the crucial points of departure in the debate on the forfeiture of parental authority (la déchéance de la puissance paternelle) that would take place in the next decade.

According to Tallon's report, children in les professions ambulantes were in particular need of protection. The risks they faced were determined not by the general conditions of industrial production but by the physical and moral "perils" of "abandonment, ignorance, and demoralization" that defined traveling performance. Their lives were marked not by the persistent and debilitating exhaustion that accompanied labor in the enclosed space of the factory but by a lack of fixity in public space. They were exposed to physical and moral risk not in the name of production but in the name of entertainment; their work was to satisfy popular appetites for spectacle, or in the case of "intentionally" maimed or disfigured children who accompanied beggars, "to draw compassion"—and coins—from passersby.[26]

Although Tallon asserted that the majority of children involved in these trades were not employed by their own parents, he nevertheless blamed parents for the mistreatment their children suffered. For Tallon, employment by others signified a common and more or less accepted structure of industrial production; in the professions centered on human display, it signaled an unnatural commerce in bodies. Parents who "sold" their children into the ambulant trades, or who simply allowed them to be used as performers or as props for beggars, thus turned their own offspring into marketable commodities. They engaged in a human traffic that violated the natural law of parental concern. Tallon described it this way: "[T]he sale of children [is] the greatest abuse of paternal authority that the legislator could ever repress." To underscore his point, Tallon invoked the authority of Maxime Du Camp's accounts of the Parisian underclasses in *Paris et ses organes* and quoted Du Camp's own assessment of these practices as a "monstrous commerce."[27]

This strategy of argumentation had its significant ironies. In stressing the immoral trade in children between parent and patron, Tallon and other reformers in the assembly struggled to uncouple the proposed law from the discourse of danger and protection underlying the recently enacted law protecting children in industry. In their arguments about traveling performance, Tallon and his supporters inverted or simply ignored the arguments that had been used in the previous debates on child labor that same year. Most important, they reassigned the positive and negative valences among industrial patron, itinerant patron, and biological parent. Looking back at the industrial legislation of the 1840s, for example, one legislator argued that in factory labor "it was a matter of children entrusted to industries that constituted the glory and wealth of the country." In the itinerant trades, however, "[I]t is a matter of miserable wretches who are, in contrast, . . . the object of an odious speculation."[28] Tallon likewise differentiated between "respectable" industrial labor and labor in the service of traveling performers, even when those performers were the child's own parents. Whereas ordinary "honest" labor in industrial production would allow the child "to raise his condition through thriftiness," the child's good qualities "are lost in base occupations, where, after long years of suffering, he finds nothing but demoralization and degradation."[29]

The inversion of arguments and valuations so useful for the 1874 industrial labor law extended further still. As legislators thinking about itinerant

---

[26] See Tallon's report on the bill, ibid., 4 March 1874, 2514.
[27] Ibid., 4 March 1874, 2514.
[28] Ibid., 23 June 1874, 4260.
[29] Ibid., 24 June 1874, 4283–84.

labor and abuse recast industrial employment as the poor child's salvation, arguments that once had protected paternal territory from external regulation in matters of labor became the objects of protest and derision. When, for example, one Daniel Chévandier stated his fear that "[in the] name of freedom itself you would commit, simultaneously, a double offense against the freedom of labor and the freedom of the père de famille," an argument that had essentially won the day in the regulation of industrial labor, he was apparently booed by many of his fellow legislators.[30]

Tallon and the commission he represented, by contrast, were adamant about the importance of applying the law directly to the père de famille. "It is legitimate," Tallon wrote in his report, "to protect the child from all those who would turn him from the path of morality, utility, and hard work," even the child's own parents, if the child's interests were threatened and the good of society was at stake.[31] Initiating a child into such "immoral" professions, he added, was a violation of one of the Civil Code's most fundamental definitions of parental duty: "[T]he obligation to feed, support, and raise their children."[32] When the aforementioned M. Chévandier contended that natural "paternal feeling" would ensure that no father would do intentional harm to his own children, Tallon replied that sentiment was no longer an acceptable guarantee against abuse: "Sadly, the facts are there to prove to you that affection is not always strong enough, although I'd like to believe it exists in the hearts of all fathers."[33]

That Tallon should invoke the logic of the developing social sciences in putting the abstract and "natural" assertion of benevolent paternal instinct to the test of empirical observation suggests once again that it was through debates such as these that the transhistorical "natural" family of the 1804 Napoleonic Code was coming to be supplanted in legislative discourse—and practice—by a family far more firmly rooted in the empirically observable and mutable realm of the social. In fact, nature was becoming increasingly untenable as a general foundation for the law and social policy of the Third Republic. According to François Ewald, in his book on law, risk, and the construction of the social under the French Third Republic, by the end of the century "law referred less to nature than to society. . . . Law became social and corrective: reestablishing destroyed balances, reducing inequalities through the redistribution of social responsibilities."[34] As law itself changed, the legal regulation of the family had also to recast its objects in the historicity and the materiality of the social order.

[30] Ibid., 23 June 1874, 4262.
[31] Ibid., 4 March 1874, 2515.
[32] Here Tallon was referring directly to art. 203 of the Code Napoléon found in bk. 1, title 5, chap. 5: "Des obligations qui naissent du mariage."
[33] JO, 8 December, 1874, 8084.
[34] François Ewald, L'Etat providence (Paris: Grasset, 1986), 19.

In the early 1870s, however, these shifts had only just begun, and law-makers remained uncertain as to the natural status of paternal right. The final draft of the proposal on regulating the employment of children in the itinerant professions thus ceded parents some degree of exclusion from regulation. That exclusion was not as definitive, however, as it had been in the case of regulating children's labor in industry. In fact, where the law on the itinerant professions found parents guilty of abuse, it subjected them to punishments that struck squarely at their civil identity and rights as parents. The law as enacted in December 1874 thus prohibited the use of children under sixteen for performance in the traveling professions but allowed parents to employ their own children in the same acts once they reached the age of twelve. Parents violated the law, however, if they employed their own children when they were still underage or engaged them in the service of other performers. As possible punishment for these infractions, the law empowered the court to strip parents of all rights of la puissance paternelle at its discretion. In keeping with the increasingly important differentiation between categories of parental figures, finally, the law also stipulated that legal guardians other than the child's biological parents would automatically lose all rights of guardianship.[35]

Given the intensity of the debate on protecting paternal prerogative in the case of industrial labor, the proposed measures regulating children's work in the itinerant trades aroused surprisingly little contestation in the National Assembly. The relative lack of controversy may have been the result of a strategy of preemptive argument; in his initial report, Tallon engaged in an elaborate defense of the state's right—embodied in the court's prerogative—to evaluate the fulfillment of parental duty. According to Tallon, the legislature could treat parental authority and obligation only as legally defined attributes, assimilated into an undiscriminating system of regulated civil rights. "La puissance paternelle," he argued, "is, like all other rights, governed in modern legislation by civil law . . . law which, in consecrating parental right, also defines its duties." Tallon further stressed the legal precedents for denying parents custody of and authority over their children, stressing, for example, the provisions of article 203 of the Civil Code: "If the father neglects his duty, a verdict from the court may dispossess him of his authority." In addition, Tallon cited the child labor law of 1841 and the 1851 law on apprenticeship, as well as recent legislation in Italy on the itinerant professions, as moments when the "legislator's right to intervene" had been legitimately invoked to protect the intersecting interests of children and those of society.[36]

---

[35] The mandatory sentence called for a six-month to two-year term of imprisonment and the imposition of a fine ranging from sixteen to two hundred francs. These conditions applied to employers, legal guardians, and parents alike.

[36] *JO*, 4 March 1874, 2514–15.

Tallon's rendering of the relationship between parent and society, centered on his narrative of legislative innovation, was crucial for his justification of expanding the state's right to participate in parenthood. In his analysis, the limits of parental authority extended only so far as parents fulfilled their social duty to raise their offspring and no further. When the balance between authority and duty became skewed by parental "cupidity," or self-interest, it constituted a "criminal excess" and required external redress. "As for the deprivation of the rights of la puissance paternelle and the removal from guardianship," Tallon argued, "it would seem the appropriate sanction . . . against those who have violated the laws of nature, of affection, and of duty."[37] Thus, although Tallon accorded paternal feeling the status of a natural attribute, he suppressed the possibility of a natural origin that might imply that parental rights superseded civil law. Instead, he argued that la puissance paternelle was essentially a social attribute, and as such it was subject to socially encoded moral standards. In his reading, nature could be admitted to the discussion of paternal rights only insofar as it did not contradict the social and juridical definition of parental obligation.

Despite the relative silence of the National Assembly, the debates on the law regulating children's labor in the itinerant trades marked an important moment of transition from the 1804 Civil Code's consecration of nature to a new kind of legislative regime. In this new order, the stamp of nature would appear only as a rhetorical shadow in the articulation of a social order based on social law. Given the radical form of Tallon's conclusions about the instability of la puissance paternelle, his colleagues' apparent silence on these implications of the new law seems even more remarkable, particularly in comparison with the conflagration that was to greet similar arguments for the law of 1889 on abandon moral. It seems all the more unlikely that Tallon's arguments were so persuasive on their own that his first report preempted further discussion.

How can such a seemingly casual acceptance of what was ten years hence to be considered by some a shocking violation of the natural order of the family be explained? In part, the 1874 law's passage was facilitated by the fact that the penal code already contained provisions by which the courts could strip parents of their rights under particular circumstances, especially when the criminal conviction of a parent resulted in the loss of all other civil rights. In addition, the new law did not mandate divestiture in all cases but merely permitted the court to use it as one form of penalty when it saw fit.

The intensifying efforts to shift the ground of the family and its rights from the realm of nature to the realm of the social may also have played a critical role in disarming the critics of the proposed law. In 1874 the process of moving nature to the margins was only just beginning, but even these preliminary gestures yielded surprising results. The decade of debates sur-

[37] Ibid., 2515, and 8 December 1874, 8084.

rounding the law on abandon moral and its eventual enactment in 1889 would mark an even more decisive move in this direction. If any kind of epistemological break can be found in the Third Republic's reform of family law, it may well be in this subtle but monumental shift between these fields of reference.[38]

The political disincentives for referring to nature were perhaps as powerful as the epistemological ones. In the legislative arena, accepting the authority of nature in matters of law or social policy may have seemed dangerously close to an acceptance of some kind of divine origin of natural law, a notion that would be anathema to the anticlerical, antimonarchist republicans of the 1880s. Overall, another historian has argued, the Third Republic had little stake in finding its proper metaphysics, whether in a spiritual or a natural order.[39]

Paradoxically, then, despite their pronounced distaste for nature as referent in politics or social theory, liberal republicans continued to connect their discussions of the family, albeit at an increasingly remote level, to a notion of a natural moral order. The realm of family law, so deeply tied in the late nineteenth century to questions of population and reproduction, was perhaps the last to make the transition from the natural to the social grid. Nonetheless, the rhetorical invocations of nature should not be confused with an epistemological or discursive reliance on nature. Even as they spoke of nature, the reformers of the early Third Republic were engaged in a process of radical detachment. By working the paradox of nature as social referent for the family against itself the lawmakers were recasting the terrain of regulation. In the 1880s' debates on abandon moral, legislators would thus give voice to the last gasp of nature while carving out a wholly social frame for the distribution of familial rights and obligations in modern France.

This shift, to be sure, was neither simple nor complete. Nature continues to serve as an important rhetorical referent in debates on the family up to the present day. Uncertain in the 1870s and 1880s of whether they were actually violating natural law in subordinating paternal authority to the abstract authority of the state, legislators and critics continued their ambivalent circling of nature. Invoking it, partially, critically, obliquely, and uncomfortably, they simultaneously looked for other ways of justifying their intrusion into the natural order of the family. Given this level of paradox and the depth of this ambivalence, how did legislators of the 1870s even begin to evade or efface the constraints of nature?

---

[38] Ewald also argues for an epistemological break in the last decades of the nineteenth century, most of all in the shift from the liberal society of individuals to a vision of the social based on the acceptance and calculation of risk within an organic whole. Unfortunately, Ewald overlooks the ways in which the family has played important roles in defining the individual and the social whole in both of the epistemic moments he examines (Ewald, *L'Etat providence*).

[39] See Jacques Chastenet, *La République des républicains, 1879–1893*, vol. 2 of his *Histoire de la Troisième République*, 7 vols. (Paris: Hachette, 1954), esp. ch. 1, "La Pensée française à l'avènement de la république des républicains."

In the debate on the law on itinerant labor, the challenge to the sacred or natural rights of parenthood became most tenable where legislators delineated the populations and spaces to which it would be applied. Like the laws regulating the apprenticeship and industrial employment of minors, this law also operated only beyond "the threshold of the father's home"; that is, its authors posited it in a social space constituted by a presumed breakdown of family life. The law regulated family relations only where the state could defend itself from the accusation that it had violated the forbidden border between it and the still ideologically sacrosanct domestic life of its citizens. The abuses suffered by children in les professions ambulantes, according to lawmakers, thus sprang from the fact that they worked and lived in the unregulated spaces of public display, commodification, and the circulation of strangers.[40]

Raising questions of commodification and the public market for bodies to put to use in the creation of spectacle was not the only means of isolating a particularly problematic social space of family relations. There was also the question of itinerancy itself.[41] A widespread and historically deep-rooted fear of transience, both geographical and social, provided lawmakers with yet another cultural validation of their desire to protect children against their own parents.[42] Because there was no paternal foyer at all, because the entire life experience of the child in the itinerant trades appeared to take place in public, the highly volatile question of state-sponsored trespass could be

[40] Catherine Gallagher's study of representations of the social body in the work of the British social observer Henry Mayhew provides a suggestive account of contemporary fears of nomadic street laborers. Gallagher argues that Mayhew was particularly disturbed by the economically liminal, constantly circulating food provisioners because they so clearly embodied and escaped the workings of the competitive market. See Gallagher, "The Body versus the Social Body in the Works of Thomas Malthus and Henry Mayhew," *Representations* 14 (spring 1986).

[41] Michelle Perrot argues that "[o]f all solitary men and women, the homeless aroused the greatest suspicion in a society where residence was a condition of citizenship and the hobo was seen as one who rejected the prevailing morality" (Perrot, "On the Fringe," in *From the Fires of Revolution to the Great War*, ed. Michelle Perrot, vol. 4 of *A History of Private Life*, ed. Philippe Ariès and Georges Duby [Cambridge: Belknap Press of Harvard University Press, 1990], 302).

[42] Many studies, particularly those by—and inspired by—Michel Foucault have centered on the anxiety about the dangers embodied in unfixed populations and those hidden in the darkness of "obscure" social spaces. See especially Foucault, *Discipline and Punish: The Birth of the Prison*, trans. Alan Sheridan (New York: Vintage Books, 1979); Patricia O'Brien, *The Promise of Punishment: Prisons in Nineteenth-Century France* (Princeton: Princeton University Press, 1982); and Michelle Perrot, ed., *L'Impossible prison: Recherches sur le système pénitentiaire au XIXe siècle* (Paris: Editions du Seuil, 1980). See also Meyer, *L'Enfant*; Robert A. Nye, *Crime, Madness, and Politics in Modern France: The Medical Concept of National Decline* (Princeton: Princeton University Press, 1984); Ruth Harris, *Murders and Madness: Medicine, Law, and Society in the Fin de Siècle* (Oxford: Clarendon Press, 1989); and Louis Chevalier's discussion of the bourgeois reading of vagrancy in his *Laboring Classes and Dangerous Classes in Paris during the First Half of the Nineteenth Century*, trans. Frank Jellinek (Princeton: Princeton University Press, 1973).

avoided altogether. And as the flip side of the problem, because the parents of children employed in these professions had failed to provide them with a protected "private" life, they were already guilty of dereliction in the fulfillment of their parental role. As Tallon put it, the loss of parental right was something they called upon themselves when they "trangressed against the laws of nature, of affection, and of duty."[43]

Third, intervention in the natural order of the family was justified through reference to traveling children's overexposure to public life, its abuses, and its temptations. For these children, doubly cursed by the lack of a permanent home of their own and by a premature exposure to a public world saturated with "vice,"

> ideas of the right and the good, the lessons of an honest and hardworking father, the caresses of a good and loving mother, all these sacred ties which throughout his entire life bind man to the path of honor and duty, are replaced by coarse talk, perverse stimulation, the spectacle of drunkenness, of dishonesty, of debauchery, by the incessant expression of the most base sentiments and the perpetual negation of the most noble aspirations of human nature.[44]

Finally, the fact that the problem of the itinerant trades and circus performance was initially cast as one of foreign immigrants—Italians, Bohemians, or Gypsies—helped legislative reformers to render their distinctions between types of families and familial labor even more plausible.[45] The presumed foreign origins of the problematic population of workers denoted all that was unfixed, irregular, and beyond the pale in the cultural imagination of the late nineteenth century. By contrast, the French laboring classes, no matter how problematic or pathological when observed in a national context, seemed fully integrated into the French social order when compared with outsiders.

By addressing the question of exploitative labor in the terms of nationality and ethnicity, French legislators perhaps felt more secure in experimenting with norms of parental responsibility and state obligation, norms that would later seem applicable to the French populace as a whole.[46] Lawmakers in 1874 appear to have found it fairly easy to dissociate vagrant and possibly foreign parents from "real," "honorable" French parents. Through these layers of association and differentiation, they were able to subject the former to severe legal sanctions directed at their parental status without disturbing the state's avowed respect for France's own bon pères de famille.

Creating these patterns of linkages and exclusions, particularities and gen-

---

[43] *JO*, 4 March 1874, 2515.

[44] Ibid., 2512.

[45] On Italian child performers in the nineteenth century, see John E. Zucchi, *The Little Slaves of the Harp: Italian Child Street Musicians in Nineteenth-Century Paris, London, and New York* (Montreal: McGill-Queen's University Press, 1992).

[46] See Kselman, "The Modernization of Family Law," 183–84.

eralities, was a fundamental element in the Third Republic's approach to the legislative regulation of the family in the 1870s and 1880s. On the ground of the specific case, marked and contained by the limits of class, nationality, sex, and the occupation of a distinctive social space, lawmakers devised new measures that ultimately effaced those differences in the abstract universality of both their immediate scope and their wider implications. This too would be evident in the debates and discourses surrounding the question of abandon moral.

Parenthood came under the scrutiny of the legislature for a final time that year in the consideration of Senator Théophile Roussel's proposal for a law regulating professional wet-nursing.[47] In this instance as well, ambivalence about the reliability of natural parental sentiment figured among the primary motivations for state supervision of parental prerogatives and desires. Contradictory concerns about the regulation of the family's private affairs also appeared in the course of this third series of debates. On the one hand, lawmakers anxiously discussed the question of inappropriate state intervention in the "free exercise" of a profession. On the other hand, they once again addressed themselves to the apparent imperative to protect children from dangerous commodification, in this case, commodification produced through the market relations between unnatural parents and the exploitative nurse. In their examination of these issues, lawmakers were faced for a third time with the problem of where and how to draw the line between the paternal responsibility of biological parents and that of the state.

La loi sur la protection des enfants du premier âge was enacted on 23 December 1874. It required parents who sent their infants out to nurse to register with local municipal authorities. It further required that professional wet nurses submit to state examination and certification and that their homes be subject to periodic inspections to ensure that the modern rules of hygiene were being followed.[48] According to Roussel, who presented his full report on the subject in July of that year, the popularity of wet-nursing put an ever-increasing number of French infants at risk. Child mortality among infants put out to nurse was exceptionally high, he argued, and that mortality put the collective vitality of the nation in jeopardy.

Roussel contended that the root of the problem could be found, at least in part, in modern life's erosive effect on parental feeling. The development of industrial France, he claimed, brought "oft-repeated lamentations over the weakening of family spirit and maternal sentiment."[49] Children, exposed to poor hygiene, inadequate supervision, and minimal affection when they were

---

[47] I am especially indebted to Joshua Cole for our long hours of conversation on the relationship between the Roussel law on wet-nursing and the law of 1889 on abandon moral.

[48] On the history of wet-nursing in nineteenth-century France, see Sussman, *Selling Mothers' Milk*, 101–88.

[49] *JO*, 26 July 1874, 5152.

put out to nurse, were seen as the victims of their mothers' disinterest in her maternal duties. They were martyrs to their parents' failure to protect them against the "abuses" that arose from a system of "mercenary motherhood." Although Roussel expressed a certain amount of sympathy for mothers who put their children out to nurse because they simply could not afford to stay out of the labor market, he nevertheless expressed regret about the evident weakening of the primary, natural moral fibers that held families together.

Because they focused far more on parental responsibility than on right, the debates on the wet-nursing law were particularly sensitive to the distinctions of gender. Fathers were found guilty of failing to consider their children's "best interests," that is, of exposing them to the possibility of material privation and of death, all beyond the reach of their own protective surveillance. Mothers, however, were seen as guilty of allowing their maternal instincts to fade, thus permitting an unnatural egoism to turn them from the protection of their children's interests. The critics of wet-nursing argued that any good mother would keep and nurse her own infant on the strength of her natural sentiments. Therefore, they reasoned, any woman who did not nurse her own child had been denatured by her environment, and particularly by her exposure to urban life.[50]

The new law on wet-nursing authorized the state, for the third time that year, to step in where parents proved themselves incapable of fulfilling responsibilities dictated, now simultaneously, by nature and society. As Roussel put it, "[T]he law must provide an effective remedy for the monstrous abuses against which public morality and conscience are, in these times, sadly powerless."[51] The state's obligation to separate the interests of "helpless infants" from those of their "monstrous" parents was consistently justified as an action against the self-interest of parents concerned only with eluding their obligations, and against what came to seem an unnatural series of market relations, most of all, commercial mothering and the commodification of infants. In acting to protect children against "abuse," "deadly mistakes," "indifference and inertia," and "ignorance, often more fatal than ill will," the state could justify its move into the parental domain precisely because a space for public parenthood had been opened by the vacuum created by the confluence of paternal and maternal deficiencies.[52]

---

[50] Cole's discussion of the growing distrust of maternal instinct in the nineteenth century is especially illuminating here. See Cole, "'A Sudden and Terrible Revelation,'" in "The Power of Large Numbers." As many other historians have pointed out, this view was articulated in its most influential form by Jean-Jacques Rousseau in the eighteenth century, who was cited throughout the following century by "experts" who advocated maternal breast-feeding. See, for example, Edward Shorter, *The Making of the Modern Family* (New York: Basic Books, 1977), 175–83.

[51] *JO*, 27 July 1874, 5150.

[52] Ibid., 2 August 1874, 5207.

Like the law on children in les professions ambulantes, the law regulating wet-nursing also passed with little opposition. The proposal proved especially palatable to legislators and to the public at large because of the direct link between nursing and infant mortality that had been established by doctors and statisticians in the 1860s, a connection that served as the foundation of the state's discourse on population, infant mortality, and protection. In a climate of opinion where the ebbing size and strength of the population generated tremendous anxiety about the future of France, the validity of state protection designed to stem the deaths of future citizens and soldiers struck a solid chord with many people. As with the two other laws promulgated that year, the legal construction of a state acting out of parental solicitude turned on the strict observance of spatial distinctions; the mechanisms of regulation engaged only once the child was outside the space of the family home.

In its final form, the Roussel law addressed the issue of parental responsibility as gingerly as did the other pieces of protective legislation passed that year. Whereas the law did constrain parents to accept state limitation on their choice of nurse, the nurse herself was subject to regulation in far more global terms. First, the law was designed to regulate her desire to traffic in children as a nurse for hire. Second, and more subtle perhaps, the law was structured to control the manner in which she sold her own maternity on the open market. The new law thus displaced the greater part of its authors' concern about unnatural parenting onto the regulation of the nurses themselves. In the logic of the new law, wet nurses occupied an even more pernicious category of unnatural motherhood than the biological mother who wished to put her child out to nurse.

The similarities to nineteenth-century efforts to police prostitution are striking here.[53] Instead of regulating the anonymous sale of sexual bodies unincorporated in the webs of familial or affective ties that supposedly bound husbands and wives, the Roussel law attempted to regulate maternal bodies that were given meaning by the market rather than by the physical expression of natural motherly sentiment. It is perhaps not surprising, then, that the late-nineteenth-century debates over wet-nursing, and over the protection of children from their debased mothers more generally, coincided temporally and thematically with the debates over the regulation of prostitu-

---

[53] On the regulation of prostitution in nineteenth-century France, see Alain Corbin, *Les Filles de noce: Misère sexuelle et prostitution aux 19e et 20e siècles* (Paris: Aubier, 1978), translated by Alan Sheridan as *Women for Hire: Prostitution and Sexuality in France after 1850* (Cambridge: Harvard University Press, 1990). See also Jill Harsin, *Policing Prostitution in Nineteenth-Century Paris* (Princeton: Princeton University Press, 1985). Jann Matlock traces the emergence of enduring cultural anxieties about prostitution in the first half of the nineteenth century in *Scenes of Seduction: Prostitution, Hysteria, and Reading Difference in Nineteenth-Century France* (New York: Columbia University Press, 1994).

tion.[54] This conflation of unnatural mother and prostitute, critical in the debate on wet-nursing, would also become a central theme in the discourse on abandon moral and the forfeiture of parental authority in the next decade.

In its elaboration of standards of hygiene against which a nurse's professional legitimacy could be measured, the wet-nursing law of 1874 also participated in the logic of spatial displacement that had facilitated the passage of the two protective laws earlier that year. The home of the wet nurse rather than the domestic space of the biological family was ultimately constituted as the primary site of danger and, consequently, as the primary site of regulation.

Taken together, the three protective laws of 1874 provided republican reformers of the next decade with a set of difficult but discursively powerful contradictions, all defined by an overwhelming ambivalence about destabilizing parental authority in order to "preserve" the family. Of particular importance to considerations of danger within the family in the next decade, the new legislation posited parenthood as simultaneously grounded in nature and socially constructed. Further, all three laws raised and then evaded the question of regulating domestic life itself by addressing parental authority only when it was "not there" or when it was embodied or usurped by artificial parents, such as the industrial employer or the wet nurse. Similarly, the 1874 laws conjured and then suppressed the possibility of a direct challenge to the competence of its adult male citizens, whose identity as individuals in a collective society was grounded in their alternative identity as bon pères de famille. No less significant, the legislation of 1874 located feminine parenthood in the nexus of legal right and responsibility even as that gendered parental status was subsumed where the civil code identified parental authority uniquely in the person of the father.

By the end of 1874 all of these contradictions were firmly implanted in the discursive frame of child protection. Although suppressed in the ambivalent structures of the 1874 legislation, these critical paradoxes would explode in the course of the debates on the moral danger in the family in the next decade. The uncertainties embedded in the 1874 laws would also allow observers to place the 1889 law on abandon moral within two contradictory narratives simultaneously: one in which it was the culmination of decades of progressive reform, and the other in which it stood as a definitive and shocking break with the past.

The contradictions manifested in the debates on protection in the early 1870s would serve as crucial purchase for those seeking more radical change

---

[54] On Third Republic fears of clandestine prostitution as the unregulated circulation of vice, see Corbin, *Women for Hire*, esp. 22–24. For one of the most prominent contemporary voices of reform on the question of prostitution and its regulation in Third Republic France, see Yves Guyot, *La Prostitution* (Paris: G. Charpentier, 1882).

in the next decade. These discussions and the laws they produced opened the way for the positing of a new kind of private space to which the state did have some right of access as protector and universal parent. The more members of the National Assembly attempted to draw lines of potential conflict between parental self-interest and the overlapping interests of child and nation, the more pressure they placed on the very limits of the state's parental powers they had written into law. The more they attempted to respect the integrity of private domestic space, the more it appeared that no socially defined space—including the *maison paternelle*—offered adequate guarantee that physically vulnerable and morally impressionable young children would be naturally protected from material or moral danger.

The laws of 1874 thus served as essential antecedents for the law of 1889 on abandon moral. They should not, however, be taken as a kind of originary point. Nor should any direct causal link or inevitable trajectory be presumed between them. Instead, the forging of the 1874 protective legislation demonstrates how discursive and legislative experiments were inextricably linked. Their history suggests how the juridical and conceptual destabilization of the category of the natural began to be thinkable. In themselves, the legislative gestures of 1874 were inescapably uncertain, contorted, and disarmed by lawmakers' efforts to protect parental rights against their own line of reasoning. Although the laws of 1874 placed parents squarely within the horizon of culpability, their authors persisted in averting their eyes from the implications of their successes.

The 1874 laws thus should be considered more of a scouting expedition for the next generation of protective legislation than its progenitor. Even after the reforms of the 1870s, French lawmakers and critics were still in no way certain just how the state should or could act in regulating the world of familial relations. Indeed, it is striking that the issue was debated as much in terms of voyeurism—how to look into the heart of the family—as it was in terms of intervention and trespass. The problem of reshaping the relation of public power to private life was cast in two interlocked and competing questions: how and when the threshold of the maison paternelle could be crossed, and how and when the home and the family it contained could be rendered transparent.

In examining both of these questions, the lawmakers and reformers in the 1880s would pick up where the efforts of the 1870s had left off. They would expand on earlier efforts to define the state's rights and obligations in terms of its parental solicitude for the family and the nation. Even as they resorted to familiar metaphors, however, the theoretical and practical solutions to these problems remained far from self-evident. Nor would the final legislative product be free of the same uncertainties and ambiguities. Ironically, even as it posed a far more radical challenge to notions of the family grounded in nature, the 1889 law on abandon moral would reinscribe many of the earlier contradictions and ambivalences apparent both in the Civil Code and in the protective laws of 1874. In its rearticulations of relationships around and within the family, in its extrapolations from particular sites of moral danger to the general condition of the French family, however, it would also significantly relocate the shifting borders between public and private that shaped late-nineteenth-century social and political space.

CHAPTER 3

The Divestiture of Paternal Authority and the Law of 1889

THE 1889 LAW ON abandon moral marked a decisive moment in the history of paternal authority in France. In authorizing civil magistrates to evaluate the quality of paternal rule, and in authorizing them to strip both fathers and mothers of la puissance paternelle in order to protect the moral interests of their offspring, the law struck at some of the nineteenth century's most fundamental assumptions about the proper location and exercise of familial power. In addition to its blurring of the edges of gendered parental identities in its attribution of moral responsibility, the new legislation also signaled a radical effort to remove family order from the realm of nature consecrated by law, as the authors of the Napoleonic Civil Code had understood it, and relocate it in the realm of the social, a realm now both essentially defined and regulated by law.[1]

This effort to transform the legal construction of the family, part of the Third Republic's larger program of legislative reform, inspired anxiety, resistance, and outright hostility.[2] Even into the twentieth century, traditionalists defended the natural foundation of paternal authority in the family, and the translation of that foundation into the Napoleonic Code. Paraphrasing Jean Portalis, one of the main voices in the articulation of Napoleonic law, one legal critic remarked in 1920 that paternal authority (la puissance paternelle) was "a right founded in nature and confirmed by law."[3] For many conservatives of the Third Republic, the best form of family law would fully encode the natural, even sacred, foundation of paternal right.

During the 1880s, opponents of the new liberal republican regime consistently called upon nature to justify their devotion to the cause of paternal

---

[1] On natural law, the family, and the conceptual foundations of the Napoleonic Code, see the debates excerpted in François Ewald, ed., *Naissance du Code civil: La raison du législateur* (Paris: Flammarion, 1989).

[2] For comprehensive surveys of the Third Republic's legislative reforms regarding the family, including the Ferry laws on mandatory secular primary education and the divorce law of 1884, see Esther Sue Kanipe, "The Family, Private Property, and the State in France, 1870–1914" (Ph.D. diss., University of Wisconsin, Madison, 1976), and Claudia Scheck Kselman, "The Modernization of Family Law: The Politics and Ideology of Family Reform in Third Republic France" (Ph.D. diss., University of Michigan, 1980).

[3] Charles Lefebvre, *La Famille en France dans le droit et dans les moeurs* (Paris: Marcel Giard, 1920), 56.

right. Thus opponents of the Ferry Laws on mandatory primary education erected their barricades to defend the father's authority on the foundation of nature as well. Critics thus deemed "[f]reedom of instruction," that is, the freedom to school one's children as one wished, "a natural right of man," that is, a natural right of fathers.[4] Although the struggle over mandatory public secular education was arguably one of the most bitter events of the Third Republic, it was not the only context in which questions about the natural foundations of paternal power were raised. The distress over the republic's challenge to natural paternal authority was perhaps nowhere more evident than in the reaction to proposals for a law on abandon moral.

Discomfort with the implications of the proposed law was not wholly apportioned according to an individual's political or social conservatism, moreover. Even the most militant advocates of reform in family law had their misgivings. In the course of defending their proposals against the opposition of critics, reformers at times expressed their own anxiety over the possible consequences of such potentially profound transformations of the relationship between child, parent, and the state. Overall, the collision of radically different definitions and expectations in the realm of public discourse, along with the internal uncertainties that left deep fissures in the heart of the reformist agenda, ensured that any legislative effort to revise the family under the Third Republic would be fraught with contradiction and ambivalence.

These irreducible uncertainties led observers to weave two, often very contradictory accounts of the proposed law on abandon moral into their analyses and critiques. The first, more common among the critics of the proposal, described sudden and radical rupture with the past, the traumatic destruction of a hitherto untouchable authority. By contrast, reformers who supported the law of 1889 tended to characterize its enactment as a single— albeit dramatic—step in a more gradual redrawing of the lines between public and private authority. In this account, evolutionary progress had begun with the moderate Revolution's plans for social assistance, principally the program of assistance to the poor laid out by La Rochefoucauld-Liancourt in 1790.[5] After an interruption during the period of the Bourbon Restoration, it continued with the 1841 law on child labor and through the protective legislation of the 1870s. In this historical narrative, the new law's appearance in

---

[4] Ibid., 65.

[5] La Rochefoucauld-Liancourt, head of the Revolution's Committee on Mendicity, was perhaps the most frequently cited figure in the Third Republic's history of social welfare and the origins of its own "generous" policies. In the committee's report of 1790, La Rochefoucauld-Liancourt described the nation's role in providing assistance to the poor, and most of all to poor children, as one of duty (*devoir*). This theme would also be revivified by the Third Republic. See Albert Dupoux, *Sur les pas de Monsieur Vincent: Trois cent ans d'histoire parisienne de l'enfance abandonnée* (Paris: Revue de l'Assistance publique à Paris, 1958), 128–29.

the landscape of civil legislation was also figured as a radical challenge to tradition, but it was qualified as a challenge rich with precedent and rooted in the long-term organic evolution of law and human society that ran through the better part of the century. No doubt the story of gradual progress resonated most with those republican reformers who had fallen under the spell of Comtean positivism and who had incorporated it into their own vision of the history and ideology of progress.[6]

At the center of the hostile critics' tale, then, the 1889 law came as a violent deathblow to the rights of the family patriarch as confirmed in the Napoleonic Code. For reformers, however, it was simply the culmination, albeit a radical one, of a historically grounded logic of protecting children against danger and abuse that had been initiated decades earlier. Again, however, the separation of narratives did not always fall so purely along the divide of political positions; both lines of explanation were often mixed in the same text, if not in the same paragraph of the same text. The interweaving of these two narratives points to the deep and unresolved concern that such an assault on paternal right inspired in late-nineteenth-century France, particularly when it seemed to place the state in the heart of the family as the adjudicator of children's and parents' conflicting interests. With such a complex conceptual base, it is small wonder that knots of contradiction would later emerge to complicate the interpretation of the law and its application in the courtroom.[7]

In the debates and commentaries on the proposed law regulating abandon moral, many of the questions that had clouded the issue of state protection in the early 1870s returned to haunt both advocates and foes of the new protective legislation. Uncertainty about the limits of public authority resurfaced in every effort to ascertain how and when parents became threats to their own offspring, and how and when the state ought to act once it had determined the existence of these dangerous families. The proposed law's potential to unmake and remake families at the will of the magistrate also distressed many legislators and public officials. It seemed that the passage of such legislation would impose dramatic changes on the state's relationship to the families, changes that might threaten the legitimacy of the Republic's political and moral identity. In addressing social spaces and familial relationships that had been explicitly exempted from prior legislation, the proposed law on abandon moral posited troubling new lines of cleavage, both within the family and in the family's relation to the world at large.

The law on moral danger in the family also significantly raised the stakes

---

[6] For the influence of Comte in the educational ideology of the Third Republic, see Phyllis Stock-Morton, *Moral Education for a Secular Society: The Development of "Morale Laïque" in Nineteenth Century France* (Albany: SUNY Press, 1988).

[7] See pt. 2.

in the effort to protect children from their own parents. By the terms of the final draft of the law, the consequences of the state's disapprobation, again determined by court decision, were severe. In substantiated instances of moral endangerment, the civil court would be empowered to strip unfit parents of physical custody and all legal parental authority. In some cases, most of all where parents had already been convicted in criminal court for prostituting their children, this divestiture would ensue automatically. In most other cases, the decision would rest in the hands of the civil magistrate.

The law on abandon moral appears to have spoken directly to the moral anxieties of the age. The term used to describe the civil divestiture or rights, *la déchéance de la puissance paternelle*, resonated with moral and even ecclesiastical meaning. To be sure, *déchéance* in the secular legal lexicon of the late nineteenth century meant simply "forfeiture" or "dispossession." Derived from the verb *déchoir*, which means "to fall," the term also carried broader moral implications: *déchéance* suggested a kind of moral decline or decay; *un homme déchu*, for example, was a fallen man. Indeed, *déchéance*, *déchoir*, and *déchu* most likely appeared with greater frequency in relation to humankind's fall from grace and spiritual failing than they did in the secular vocabulary of nineteenth-century civil law, at least before the introduction of the law of 1889. *Déchéance* had more secular resonances as well; it implied a loss of ruling authority. Thus the fall of a king, for example, was a matter of déchéance. For parents accused of abandon moral, then, the term marked the intersection of two axes of concern, both critical to the legal elucidation of moral danger. Déchéance tied moral failings directly to the loss of authority.[8]

Although legislative realities cannot be reduced to the words in which they are codified, shifts in language often signify important conceptual and institutional transformations. Neither the Napoleonic penal code nor the 1874 law on children in *les professions ambulantes*, the two places where the divestiture of parental rights had ever appeared before the law of 1889, had employed the term *déchéance*. Instead, they described the consequences for convicted parents as "the loss of the rights of la puissance paternelle," or "the removal from the offices of tutelle." The shift in terminology reinforces other evidence that for the reformers of the Third Republic parents' failure to fulfill the most basic educative obligations had been accorded a far weightier moral burden than these earlier, limited precedents.

The loss of paternal rights where framed in terms of déchéance thus did not simply represent a neutral form of punishment analogous to the loss of other kinds of civil rights, a common form of punishment under the penal

---

[8] Emile Littré, republican thinker and lexicographer, codified the diverse meanings of *déchéance* in 1889 in his *Dictionnaire de la langue française*, 4 vols. (Paris: Librairie Hachette et Cie, 1889).

code. Instead, a decision calling for la déchéance de la puissance paternelle, posited here in the context of the civil regulation of the family rather than that of criminal correction, both exposed and left an indelible mark on the "fallen" individual. In this sense, the proposed law spoke far more directly to the Third Republic's moral concerns and its secularizing impulse than it did to the constraints on legislative authority imposed by the authors of the Napoleonic code.

In its emphasis on domestic morality in the context of civil rather than criminal justice, the law of 1889 broke with the Napoleonic legal tradition in other ways as well. As the range of causes for pronouncing the divestiture of parental authority suggests, the interior moral constitution of the parent—as opposed to any particular act motivated by that moral status—became a new and highly charged element in the discourse of protection. Simultaneously, a newly conceptualized interior space of the family emerged at the center of the new law's implications for the juridical construction of cases of abandon moral. As a measure addressing the problem of diffuse moral danger, the law necessarily raised questions of interiority, from the literally interior space of the home to the internal qualities of intrafamilial relations to the most abstract interior of the child's or parent's individual moral constitution.

The spatial compass of the law's application, unlike that of the three protective laws of 1874, thus lost its specificity; no particular industry or trade defined its field of operation. Legal recourse against parental abuse was no longer confined to the cases situated in a defined public sphere. The text of the 1889 law admitted no threshold dividing the world into opposing terrains. The protective laws of 1874 had defined "dangerous abuse" as exposure to a particular set of external circumstances, such as an overly long workday or the forced performances of physically dangerous stunts. The law on abandon moral forwarded a more general definition, one that made parents themselves, and especially their moral constitution, the essential feature of the child's environment and the main source of his or her possible moral endangerment. Further, the category of moral endangerment or moral neglect subsumed the question of physical danger. Where an instance of bodily harm appeared in this new discursive field, it stood primarily as the sign of the deeper moral dysfunction that was the ultimate object of protective action. The new law blurred the question of parental domain. In its formulation, danger was no longer uniquely equated with the absence of parental supervision. It now also loomed behind the presence of morally dangerous parents. Although this move had been partly presaged in the law regulating the marginal space of the itinerant professions, its generalization in the law of 1889 still had the power to shock.

If the legislators and reformers who drafted this law and pressed for its passage admitted that parents could pose a direct threat to the moral wellbeing of their offspring, they took little comfort in that position. One of the most worrisome themes in the heated debates around the proposed law was the epistemological instability embedded in the law's evisceration of familiar boundaries and identities in the terrain of state child protection. Most of all, legislators, reformers, and social critics considering the implications of the law were forced to confront the profound uncertainty embedded in the heart of the measure. How, they asked, could a state that presumed to respect the private integrity of the French family observe and assess the interior moral constitution of that family? How could it ascertain the presence of moral danger in a family's day-to-day experience without being present in that daily life? How, in short, could a liberal republican state justify and carry out any effort to regulate the domestic moral life of its citizens without jeopardizing its own larger claims to political and moral legitimacy?

To resolve, or at least attempt to resolve, the profoundly troubling conceptual problems that seemed inherent in the proposed law on abandon moral, legislators and commentators once again carefully articulated and pried apart parental interests and the best interests of children. Once again, French lawmakers had to struggle with a paradox implicit in their conceptions of family, legal regulation, and state protection: the French family could best be strengthened by providing the state with the power to disassemble and reconstitute it at will. In the eyes of reformers, "dangerous" parents constituted a threat to the lives and characters of their own offspring and to the moral health of society as a whole.

Senator Théophile Roussel made this association between danger in the family and social danger explicit in his formal presentation to the senate in 1883. France, Roussel claimed, was desperately in need of this new law protecting children "who, because they have a family, are not protected under our present laws of assistance" but for whom the family proved to be only "the nursery of young convicts and criminals."[9]

Roussel's evocation of juvenile crime in elucidating the stakes in moral protection within the family was not accidental. His initial report for the senate on les enfants moralement abandonnés and the bill he coauthored sprang from a study of crime and penal reform issued in 1879 by the Société générale des prisons. A man of many causes, Roussel was an active member of this private association, which wrote and lobbied for most of the penal reforms carried out in the first decades of the Third Republic.[10] Despite its focus on the institutions of criminal law and correction, the Société's 1879 report significantly shaped the Third Republic's conception of moral danger in the family. Most of all, the report cemented a causal connection between a

[9] *JOS*, 2 May 1883, 423.

[10] See Martine Kaluszynski, "Les Juristes en action: La Société générale des prisons (1877–1940) ou l'exercice politique d'une société savante" (1989, photocopy). Kaluszynski also stresses the ideological and structural connections between theories of penal reform and the interest in child protection.

child's early experience of abuse or neglect and an adult life of crime and "debauchery." In this formulation, one that would be seeded directly into Roussel's account of abandon moral and its perils, a child's own parents might be the primary source of the bad influences that inevitably led to the moral corruption of the young.

The connections between the civil constitution of the moral family and the question of criminality determined the genealogy of the 1889 legislation as well as its conceptual foundation. According to Roussel, the proposed law sprang from three other reform projects introduced in 1880: a revision of the penal code's provisions for prosecuting minors under the age of sixteen; a revision of the law of 5 August 1850 on the incarceration of minors; and a new proposal for the care and reform of neglected or maltreated children. All three projects, Roussel noted, stressed prophylaxis over punishment, education over correction.[11]

Because the notion of abandon moral was first fully developed in the liminal zone between penal and civil reform, it was permeated by a distinctive moral genealogy: in the past of every criminal, Roussel's report on les enfants moralement abandonnés seemed to suggest, one might find a child who had suffered some form of moral endangerment or moral neglect. In turn, Roussel argued, abandon moral enfolded the signs of two forms of crime and of two criminal moments: the past moral abuse of the child by his or her parents and the crimes that the abused child would commit in the future. This oscillation between the endangered and the dangerous, between the culpability of abusing parents and that of their abused children, and between innocent past and compromised future was an omnipresent feature of the wider discussion of the enfant moralement abandonné and la déchéance de la puissance paternelle.

If the theoretical underpinnings for the law of 1889 can be found in the debates on penal reform and juvenile crime, the practical impetus came from the experience of the department of the Seine's Service des Enfants Moralement Abandonnés.[12] The department's General Council and the Bureau of Public Assistance in Paris founded the Service in 1881 as a response to growing fears that the city was being overrun by neglected and vagrant children who threatened to swell the "army of crime" to a point where it could no longer be contained by the forces of order.

The departmental administration and the administration of the Bureau of

[11] France, Assemblée nationale, Sénat, *Rapport fait au nom de la commission chargée d'examiner: 1° La Proposition de loi ayant pour objet la protection des enfants abandonnés, délaissés ou maltraités, présenté par MM. Théophile Roussel, Bérenger, Dufaure, l'amiral Fourichon, Schoelcher et Jules Simon. 2° Le Projet de loi sur la protection de l'enfance présenté par M. Cazot, Garde de Sceaux, Ministre de Justice*, Sénat session 1882, no. 451, Annexe au procès-verbal de la séance du 25 juillet 1882 (Paris: Imprimerie du Sénat, 1882), 2.
[12] For a detailed account of this service, see pt. 3.

Public Assistance in Paris reasoned that this flood of future criminals could best be stemmed through the mechanisms of assistance. Because the children were mostly over twelve, however, the age at which the Service des Enfants Assistés would no longer accept them, and because their uncertain moral status threatened to contaminate both the other children in its care and its complement of peasant foster families, the department was compelled to set up an alternative structure by which these "morally abandoned" children could be assisted and, if need be, reformed, without recourse to the penal system. Roussel argued that by turning to the structures of assistance as part of a project of prevention, the state could realize enormous savings compared with what it would have to spend to incarcerate and rehabilitate young criminals.[13]

Progressive reformers saw the Service des Enfants Moralement Abandonnés in Paris as an innovation in the correction of children deemed marginal both in the sense of their potential criminality and in the sense that their adolescence constituted an ill-defined moral region between the innocence of childhood and the culpability that came with adulthood. After the passage of the law on abandon moral in 1889, Parisian officials described the founding of the Service as the prescient institutionalization of the law's intent. It was, however, the Service's discovery that it had no legal status in the life of its wards and that this lack of authority was a serious obstacle to its programs of placement, education, and reform that drove frustrated administrators to plead with the National Assembly for a law that could legally remove its wards from the authority of their own parents.

Administrators working in the Service des Enfants Moralement Abandonnés, as well as their analogs in the growing number of private establishments devoted to the same cause, were particularly troubled by the problem of reclamation, or the parents' legal right to withdraw their children from public or private care whenever they so desired.[14] Although the Service assumed parental responsibility for the children it found roaming in the streets of Paris or who had been brought to it by police, by neighbors, or by parents

[13] *JOS*, 2 May 1883, 425.

[14] In the last few years the role of private charity in child protection in the late nineteenth century has become a topic of increasing interest among both French and American historians of Third Republic France, although much remains to be done. Among these more recent forays see Lee Shai Weissbach, "*Oeuvre Industrielle, Oeuvre Morale*: The *Sociétés de Patronage* of Nineteenth-Century France," in *French Historical Studies* 15, no. 1 (spring 1987), and especially Domenique Dessertine, *La Société lyonnaise pour le sauvetage de l'enfance (1890–1960): Face à l'enfance en danger, un siècle d'expérience de l'internat et du placement familial* (Toulouse: Erès, 1990). For a comparative perspective, see Linda Gordon's suggestive study of women's activism and private child protection agencies in the United States, *Heroes of Their Own Lives: The Politics and History of Family Violence, Boston, 1880–1960* (New York: Penguin Books, 1988).

themselves, there was no legal means of transferring la puissance paternelle from living parents to the state except under the limited circumstances described in the penal code and in narrowly defined instances outlined in the law on les professions ambulantes.

The Service at first attempted to circumvent this problem by instituting a system of contracts. According to the terms of these contracts, parents formally renounced any future claim on the right to exercise their rights over their children, and they authorized the Service to place them in suitable foster homes or institutions. They further agreed to reimburse the Service for the cost of raising their children if, at some point in the future, they wished to take them back.[15]

French civil law, however, did not permit this sort of voluntary transfer of la puissance paternelle or the obligations that accompanied it. In fact, the code directly prohibited the abandonment of parental responsibility in its stipulation that parents were legally bound to ensure the proper rearing and education of their own children. As one official in the Bureau of Public Assistance put it later, "[P]aternal authority is not an object of commerce."[16] Administrators and philanthropists were nonetheless particularly distressed by the fact that the contracts were not legally binding under existing law. Roussel himself used the failure of the contract as an important justification for the new law: "[T]hese contracts, legally impotent, are without value and are violated with impunity by parents as lacking in scruples as they are in resources."[17] The fact that public structures of protection crumbled before the legal consecration of familial prerogative was clear to all observers, many of whom, like Roussel, were horrified by this institutional impotence whereby

---

[15] Dupoux, the official historian of public assistance to children in the Paris region, provides a sample of these contracts.

> I the undersigned . . . . [sic] without condition and of my own free will, agree to confer the child . . . . [sic] into the care of the General Administration of the Bureau of Public Assistance in Paris, and authorize the above administration to provide him with a suitable placement of the sort that will enable him to earn his own living.
>
> I agree, moreover, not to interfere with the placements procured for this child, and in the case where I request that he be returned, to fully reimburse the administration for the costs occasioned by his upkeep, placement in apprenticeship, etc.

Dupoux, *Sur les pas*, 248–49. Archival records do not reveal how many of these contracts were actually written in the 1880s.

[16] Conseil Supérieur de l'Assistance Publique [CSAP], *Projet de réglement d'administration publique pour l'exécution de la loi du 24 juillet 1889. Rapport par M. le Directeur de l'Assistance et de l'hygiène publiques; Rapport de Loys Brueyre; texte de projet de décret adopté par le Conseil supérieur; Session ordinaire de 1906*, fasc. 103, in France, *Rapports*, vol. 12 (Melun: Imprimerie administrative, [1906]), 35.

[17] *JOS*, 2 May 1883, 424, and 11 May 1883, 462.

children's best interests were trampled, in their view, by greedy and unworthy parents.[18]

One of the most audible voices in the protest against the "immoral" reclaiming of children from protective institutions was that of Henri Rousselle (no relation to the senator), a member of the Seine's General Council who had been one of the founders of the Service des Enfants Moralement Abandonnés. In a report to the council just after the law of 1889 had been passed, Rousselle described the difficulties that the Service had faced earlier in the decade.

> When [the Bureau of Public Assistance] had extracted a ward from misery, from maltreatment, or from the contagious baseness of his kin, when the child, transported to a healthier milieu, had grown, improved, and began to be practiced in a trade, his family, which had formerly mistreated or abandoned him, returned, and, law in hand, reclaiming this child, it abducted him from a moralization just begun, from a professional training not yet completed, it reimmersed him in his original environment to make use of his bit of knowledge, to exploit his youth, and often to destroy it. That led to the miscarriage of our work.

With the enactment of a law permitting la déchéance de la puissance paternelle, Rousselle asserted, the Bureau of Public Assistance "found itself armed to defend its wards against their families."[19]

Private charitable organizations devoted to child protection had also been instrumental in the passage of the law. They too had decried the way in which "dangerous" parents were empowered to interrupt protective institutions' educational mission and reclaim their children once they were old enough to contribute their earnings to the family economy. As Senator Théophile Roussel explained to his legislative colleagues in 1883, the heads of

---

[18] Many social historians now argue that working-class parents' resistance or use of the apparatus of child protection was motivated far more by economic necessity and by a different understanding of the child's role in the family than it was by corruption or greed. For the majority of poor families, the contribution young children made to the family economy in the form of wages, labor in family enterprises or workshops, and, for some, the money they begged or goods they stole made the difference in the struggle to survive. See Lee Shai Weissbach, *Child Labor Reform in Nineteenth-Century France: Assuring the Future Harvest* (Baton Rouge: Louisiana State University Press, 1989); Colin Heywood, *Childhood in Nineteenth-Century France: Work, Health, and Education among the "Classes Populaires"* (Cambridge: Cambridge University Press, 1988); Louise A. Tilly, "Women and Family Strategies in French Proletarian Families," *Michigan Occasional Paper*, no. 4 (fall 1978); Peter Mandler, ed., *The Uses of Charity: The Poor on Relief in the Nineteenth-Century Metropolis* (Philadelphia: University of Pennsylvania Press, 1990); and Rachel G. Fuchs, *Poor and Pregnant in Paris: Strategies for Survival in the Nineteenth Century* (New Brunswick: Rutgers University Press, 1992). See also Louise A. Tilly and Joan W. Scott's *Women, Work, and Family*, 2d ed. (London: Methuen, 1987) for a useful overview of labor and the family economy in the nineteenth century.

[19] Seine, Conseil Général [CGS], no. 15, *Rapport fait au nom de la 3e commission par M. Henri Rousselle sur le service des moralement abandonnés* (1889), 14.

charitable establishments who had been consulted about the proposed law had expressed tremendous enthusiasm for a law that would allow institutions to protect their charges against their own parents' cupidity: "[T]hey were almost unanimous," Roussel proclaimed, "in their demand for a *droit de garde* guaranteed against the claims of the parents and the premature withdrawal of children [from their institutions]." The number of times that these private institutions had witnessed the "premature" removal of the morally abandoned children in their care, he remarked in the course of the senate's first deliberation on the proposed law, had led many to turn away from this category of children altogether and to devote themselves exclusively to the "materially abandoned," or "children without families," where the danger of interfering parents did not exist.[20]

Both in the National Assembly and in the wider world of critical commentary, exemplary dramatic narratives were among the most powerful weapons of argument in the debate on the consequences of "immoral" reclamation. Often such narratives centered on parents' double culpability in first abandoning and then reclaiming the endangered child. Léon Lallemand, one of the Third Republic's most vocal conservative Catholics devoted to philanthropy and child protection, warned his readers in 1885 that present laws governing assistance to children invited exploitation. They permitted parents, and particularly women, to disencumber themselves of their children at the expense of the state and then to "buy" them back whenever it pleased them to do so. "Here is a mother who earns her living in debauchery," he wrote in *La Question des enfants abandonnés et delaissés au XIXe siècle*,

> she rejects her child whose presence impedes her dissolute activities; later, when her daughter has grown, this woman wants to take her back, perhaps to make her take her place, and she would have only to drop a bit of change to have the power to abduct this poor creature from the family which had raised her, from the administration which had protected her.[21]

Lallemand's story centered on the possibility of an abandonment and a reclamation equally inspired by the pleasures and profits of illicit sexual activity, activity that was the conceptual hallmark of the "unfit" working-class mother. The story similarly warned against charity's complicity in the easy commodification of children as they circulated through institutions of protection. Although Lallemand's devotion to the natural order of the family compelled him to oppose the proposed legislation on abandon moral, he nevertheless deplored the existing system as one that allowed delinquent parents to disregard their children's best interests in such a flagrant manner.

---

[20] *JOS*, 11 May 1883, 462.

[21] Léon Lallemand, *La Question des enfants abandonnés et delaissés au XIXe siècle* (Paris: Alphonse Picard/Guillaumin et Cie, 1885), 41.

Lallemand's parable of abuse is especially notable for its foundation in apparent contradiction—the simultaneous attack on and defense of parental authority—and for the way in which he negotiated a gendered resolution of that contradiction. The bad parent in this story, as well as in other sections of *La Question des enfants*, is the mother. In attacking the way in which women "exploited" parental rights, Lallemand found he could both defend children against the claims of their unnatural (female) parents and leave natural *paternal* authority intact. Lallemand's approach was in no way unique, and, after the passage of the law of 1889, such a location of unnatural sentiment and immoral exercise of parental authority in the person of the mother would reappear in the way in which Parisian magistrates defined *unfit parenthood* in their jurisprudence.

Discussions like Lallemand's, centered on the state's apparent inability to stop "dangerous" parents from reclaiming their own children, also turned the issue of inappropriate intervention inside out, thus significantly recasting the larger debate on the violence of state protection action. Instead of casting the family as violated by agents of the state, instead of arguing against the state's illegitimate trespass into the private domain of the père de famille, this line of reasoning identified the protective institution as the object of an "unjust" exercise of power. Parents—in fact, mothers—and not the agents of the state, "abducted" children from their "proper" educative milieu. In this rationale, parents' interventions in the artificial but more salutary forms of child rearing provided by the state and private philanthropy disrupted the proper moral education of their children. The boundaries between public and private were no less fluid here, and no less dependent on the attribution of relative degrees of moral integrity and altruistic concern for the child's interest, than they were in the parallel discussion of whether or not the state had the right to cross the threshold of *la maison paternelle*. This discursive strategy, displacing and then reversing the questions of violation and power, would have a powerful effect on the larger effort both to denaturalize parental right and assimilate it, metaphorically, to the responsibilities borne by the protective state.

Inversion and reversal also affected the identity of the state in these debates. The broad agitation for institutional rights against abusive parents permitted legislators and reformers to cast the state as the passive and disempowered defender of the exploited rather than a force of active intervention. Lallemand and others contended that parents would take merciless advantage of a state that proclaimed its own universal obligation to raise "morally endangered" children, particularly children over the age of ten whose parents were still alive. In that exploitation of the state's generosity, the bonds of family would be permanently broken. As Lallemand argued,

[F]rom the moment a departmental administration, a communal administration, or the state takes official charge of children over this age without their being genuinely abandoned, all families will have their children reared in this manner, and no budget could withstand such an invasion. Moreover, what will the relationship be between these thousands of parents and children, who barely know each other? There will be neither love in the former, nor affection and respect in the latter: those sentiments born in part from real sacrifices and from everyday devotion. Without that, there remain only strangers, the family is destroyed, and from a social point of view, all efforts should tend, in contrast, to strengthen it.[22]

Lallemand's remark crystallized the common concern over the inappropriate crossing of borders and an unnatural transfer of roles as the consequence of a state that allowed itself to be used by individual families. The "invasion," according to Lallemand, would not be perpetrated by agents of the state into the domain of the naturally virtuous family father. Instead, it was the act of the dangerous and overempowered parent, using the authority vested in all parents—especially fathers—to penetrate the domain of the state's proper concerns.

As the language of moral danger in the family consistently drew connections between the condition of the family and the past and future of the nation, the language of bounded domains similarly worked to locate these debates in a larger national context. The persistent use of metaphors describing borders and the possibility of violent incursion, although intrinsic to the field of family law, no doubt resonated strongly with the collective memory of literal, and deadly, border crossings in the Franco-Prussian War. Although no observer appears to have drawn this connection explicitly, the similarities in these parallel fields of anxiety attest, however indirectly, to the ways in which questions of family integrity were sewn into the very fabric of national identity at the end of the nineteenth century.

Lallemand's theme of an overly generous protective state exploited by unnatural parents emerged in governmental debates on the law as well. Most concerned with the law's potential "invitation" to parents to leave the economic and educative burden of child rearing to the state was the minister of the interior, René Waldeck-Rousseau. Because the Ministry of the Interior supervised the work of the Bureau of Public Assistance as well as the activities of the police, Waldeck-Rousseau's concern about this legislation and its consequences for the state was far from negligible. Attending the senate debate in May 1883, Waldeck-Rousseau spoke against the proposed law with great conviction. The measure on abandon moral, he argued, would simply facilitate the abandonment of older children. It would sanction parental dereliction in the care of the family and the fulfillment of what was once inalienable responsibilities. "We must avoid presenting the State as being prepared to take in all children whose parents don't care for them," Waldeck-Rousseau argued. Parents should not see the state "as opening a kind of permanent *tour* in which families who would prefer not to work to support their

---

[22] Ibid., 210–11.

children, who would rather not educate them . . . [or] give them the most basic care, would come to leave off those they considered a burden, thus forcing the State to fulfill not only their rights but also their duties."[23] For this declaration, Waldeck-Rousseau was widely applauded on the senate floor.

Self-conscious defenders of the state's interests, such as Waldeck-Rousseau, thus argued that the legislature's solution to moral abandonment risked placing an unreasonable economic burden on the state. Most important in the reasoning of these critics, the proposed law would place this unnatural and untenable economic obligation on the state by making parenthood transferable from private individuals to public authority. Again, the troubling specter of the commodified child appeared at the center of the legislative debates. In this rendition of the deeply destabilizing effects of the proposed law, a version that stressed unnatural obligation instead of unnatural power, the child was transformed from an object of solicitude into a circulated object and a quantifiable expense. Here the attribution of parenthood depended far less on questions of influence or authority than on the concern about who should ultimately be held responsible for bearing the cost of raising morally and physically healthy workers and citizens.

The anxiety about the overextension of state dominion in the name of protecting endangered children, first apparent in the debates on child protection in the 1870s, resurfaced with a vengeance in the 1880s. Observers were in fact far more worried that the law might normalize the dispossession of parental right as an ordinary part of protective governance. Hence Lallemand, despite his avowed interest in protecting the lives and moral qualities of poor French children, ultimately condemned the proposed law for granting the state a dangerous level of authority and responsibility in private family matters.[24] Waldeck-Rousseau, although speaking from an entirely different political and ideological position, also saw in Roussel's proposal the potential for pitting a legally overempowered state against the family. "It must not be said," he argued, "that society substitutes itself, violently and unfairly, for the natural and legitimate rights of the family." In this view, parental right, as much as parental obligation, was a natural consequence of procreation. Although parents who voluntarily ceded their children to the state revealed themselves as denatured, hence already forfeiting their claim to parental authority, the state that took the active initiative against parents would nevertheless have to face the moral consequences of dispossessing

---

[23] *JOS*, 11 May 1883, 464. The tour was a form of revolving depository that facilitated the anonymous abandonment of infants to the care of charitable institutions. On the debates over the morality of the tour and its implications for the state over the course of the nineteenth century, see Rachel G. Fuchs, *Abandoned Children: Foundlings and Child Welfare in Nineteenth-Century France* (Albany: SUNY Press, 1984).

[24] Lallemand, *La Question*, 92.

"children's natural protectors."[25] For Waldeck-Rousseau, in short, endorsing a measure divesting parents of their rights was not only a matter of protecting state coffers. The fundamental moral legitimacy of the state lay in the balance.

Against objections based in the consideration of parents' "natural" duties and rights, defenders of the proposed law counterpoised a critique of parenthood and the alleged problem of state intervention. This alternative vision was also grounded in the attribution of rights, the identification of dangers, and the alignment of interests. In this case, however, these attributions, identifications, and alignments called for the state to act in the name of protection. Thus advocates argued that the law's challenge to parents' natural claim to the rights of la puissance paternelle was both a necessary and a legitimate form of protection. As Councillor Rousselle put it, only by directly counteracting the existing legal consecration of paternal right could a child be protected against a harmful (*malfaisante*) puissance paternelle.[26] The evident fact that parents endangered the moral and material well-being of their own offspring, he added, required a law that could intervene to protect these children.

Proponents of the proposal also couched their defense in the recast identity of the state. They asserted that protecting the best interests of children fell within the domain of the state in its guise as the unselfish guardian of the social and national collectivities. As one author argued in a law thesis published early in 1889:

> [T]he State itself is directly interested in the efficacious protection of children; it is entitled to count on these children, who will one day become soldiers and citizens, for the future; but, it is crucial that the race not degenerate; it is crucial to prevent, insofar as it is possible, vagrancy, crime, pauperism, Society's open wounds, which engender and promote a poor upbringing or the absence of any upbringing at all, and which impose on the country extremely onerous costs of assistance; it is crucial, finally, in a land of universal suffrage, not to entrust sovereign powers to ignorant citizens, that is, [to the] incapable and the dangerous.[27]

The child also had rights, according to this author's formulation of the imperative for state action. Most of all, the child had the right "to be protected and fostered from the triple point of view of body, intellect, and morality; his

---

[25] *JOS*, 11 May 1883, 464.

[26] Ibid., 2 May 1883, 423.

[27] Gabriel Melin, *Droit romain: Essai sur la clientèle. Droit français: De la protection légale des enfants légitimes contre les abus de la puissance paternelle* (Nancy: E. Desté, 1889), 16. Melin's use of the term *right* where children's own interest in protection was concerned was both historically and discursively constrained. At the end of the nineteenth century, the notion that children might exercise rights in a manner analogous to adults was not a thinkable proposition. Children's rights as a coherent discourse would not emerge until well into the twentieth century.

outlook, his health must be preserved; his soul must be shielded from the deadly influence of bad examples and bad advice."[28]

The conflicts over the sense and implications of a law designed to protect children by removing them from the custody of their own parents and stripping those parents of their legal authority over their offspring were thus played out in several different languages and turned on several models of what constituted the true purpose and identity of the family. At the same time, these languages and models intersected, overlapped, and contradicted each other, not only in the course of the same debate but often in the construction of a single argument, be it for or against the proposed law. Arguments along the liberal spectrum privileged the issue of the just distribution of power between state and père de famille and saw the problem at hand as one of territorial division and the exercise of rights. Other arguments focused on the rightful exercise of authority in the paternal domain but added to it the grounding of paternal authority in nature. The last set of arguments centered on the definition of parenthood as social duty and demanded that the law enforce a righteous division of responsibility, both economic and moral, between public resources and private families.

The most innovative and ultimately most effective arguments, particularly those of Roussel, blended the notions of power and obligation in a new tapestry of legislative and social reform. In these accounts, the child's interests, perhaps even more than the child, stood at the center of all reconsiderations of the relation between state and family. As one commentator put it in a law thesis reviewing the implications of recent legislative reforms, "[W]e must not forget that above the father's interest, above the interest of society, there is also and above all the interest of the child."[29] This focus on the child was not, as some scholars would have it, simply a device by which public authority could "infiltrate" or "penetrate" the working-class family, although the consequences of the law were often borne most heavily by the destitute and the laboring poor.[30] Instead, it permitted a complete refiguring of the distribution of social authority between the state and the individual parent. Although the direct object of this reconfiguration was the legal authority of the père de famille, the law's underlying orientation around the child's interests meant that the mother, in her role as "natural" protector of her child's interests, might also be drawn into its jurisdiction.

The connections wrought between protection, the child's interests or rights, and the dangers represented by living under one's own parents' roof

---

[28] Ibid.

[29] V. Radenac, *Du rôle de l'Etat dans la protection des enfants maltraités ou moralement abandonnés: Commentaire de la loi du 24 juillet 1889 (Titre II)* (Paris: Arthur Rousseau, 1901), 34.

[30] See Jacques Donzelot, *The Policing of Families*, trans. Robert Hurley (New York: Pantheon, 1979), and Philippe Meyer, *L'Enfant et la raison d'état* (Paris: Editions du Seuil, 1977).

also resolved the problem of territory. They implied that state action could no longer be restricted to those instances in which parents were literally absent from the sites of endangerment or limited to sites outside the home. In the construction of the child's interests within la maison paternelle and the state's interest in protecting them, the debates preceding the enactment of the law successfully described a vacuum in the proper fulfillment of parental right and obligation. These arguments authorized the state to expand into domestic life by rendering the ideological walls of family privacy permeable to its own parental interests.

The law of 1889 and the new vision of state and family it enunciated were grounded in the hope that moral parenthood lay not in a sealed private domain but at the intersection of the natural and the social. In enacting the new civil law, legislators sought to protect children from the destructive influence of unnatural or denatured parents, whose instincts had been weakened by a more general deterioration of France's moral fabric and who placed the satisfaction of their own interests above the best interests of their progeny and their country.[31] Supporters of the laws likewise defended state intervention in terms of this opposition between natural/moral and unnatural/immoral parenthood. One commentator put it this way in 1889:

> Without a doubt, the father is the head of the family and it could not be a question of weakening that in which his authority consists; this authority is legitimate, founded in natural law and necessary to the maintenance and regular functioning of society. It is certain that most often the father makes moderate and reasonable use of it, and that the feelings that move him are affection and [his devotion to] the interests of his children.

"It is no less true," he continued,

> that the facts all too often give cruel lie to these optimistic presumptions. . . . [W]e cannot really rely sufficiently on parents, who are too frequently blinded by their passions, their prejudices, or their vices. If they abuse their rights, if they make use of them to compromise the health, the morality, or the future of their children, the state's intervention seems to us to be quite natural.[32]

---

[31] Illuminating accounts of the visions of demoralization that gripped France in the late nineteenth century can be found in Robert A. Nye's *Crime, Madness, and Politics in Modern France: The Medical Concept of National Decline* (Princeton: Princeton University Press, 1984); Ruth Harris, *Murders and Madness: Medicine, Law, and Society in the Fin de Siècle* (Oxford: Clarendon Press, 1989); and Susanna Barrows, "After the Commune: Alcoholism, Temperance, and Literature in the Early Third Republic," in *Consciousness and Class Experience in Nineteenth-Century Europe*, ed. John M. Merriman (New York: Holmes and Meier, 1979), and *Distorting Mirrors: Visions of the Crowd in Late Nineteenth-Century France* (New Haven: Yale University Press, 1981).

[32] Melin, *Droit romain*, 14–15.

When the moral order of the bon père de famille broke down, in other words, the unselfish action of a benevolent state appeared to be the best and most natural corrective.

By the end of the 1880s, the relation between state and family had been redefined around children's unprotected interests and the intersecting interests of society at large. The maintenance of social order and the provision of proper moral education together demanded that the legal boundaries between public and private be rendered more fluid. Emile Durkheim put it best when in 1888 he described the structure and composition of the modern family. Along with the married couple and their offspring, Durkheim argued, the state was an intimate member of the modern family. "Finally, there is the state," he wrote, "which also, in certain cases, enmeshes itself in domestic life and becomes with every passing day a more important factor in it."[33]

Perhaps most significant of all, Roussel's paradigm worked to dissociate nature from the essential definition of parenthood. In this radical formulation, based on the free play between metaphorically linked institutions, all parenthood could be assimilated to the notion of guardianship. Although nature did not disappear from the rhetorical framework erected around the moral family, it could no longer be invoked in the defense of private paternal right. In this move, Roussel and others ingeniously closed the gap between the law of 1889 and the Napoleonic Code. In eliding natural parenthood with guardianship in parental form, Roussel returned to a definition of parental function that had been conceived, even in 1804, as entirely social and juridical. In this move as well, women returned to the realm of parenthood as guardians whose fulfillment of obligation was open to regulation.

Where the Napoleonic state had once devoted itself to safeguarding the natural rights of fathers in the articles of its Civil Code, the Third Republic thus saw itself as the guarantor of a social order that included the state in the structure of family relations. Ironically, the law of 1889 mandated a solution that separated parental function from the biology of procreation. Defending the principle of family came to mean both the dismantling of families created by blood ties when they failed to meet official norms of parenthood and the constitution of metaphorical and artificial family ties more natural than those of birth.

In describing it as a necessary measure to counteract denatured parents, the authors of the law of 1889 also articulated a nostalgia for a society in which the private life of the family was clearly and permanently set off from

[33] Emile Durkheim, "Introduction à la sociologie de la famille" (lecture delivered at the Faculté des lettres of Bordeaux in 1888), in *Textes*, ed. Victor Karady, vol. 3 (Paris: Minuit, 1975), 12. Durkheim chose the verb *se mêler* to describe the state's entry into family life, a term that also expresses the notion of unwelcome intrusion, or meddling. I have translated it here as "enmeshed" to convey the complex—and not necessarily welcome—manner in which the state worked its way into a realm it simultaneously celebrated as the private and insular.

the public world of politics. The turn among legislators, jurists, and social critics to a language of absolute territoriality, that is, of discerning precisely where the state's rule ended and the father's rule began, obliterated the more subtle operations of the relationship between family and state described earlier in the nineteenth century. The new discourse subtly effaced the historicity of public and private, and the difference between them, while imposing that difference, in various guises and arenas, as the social incarnation of nature. The difference between state and family, particularly where the just exercise of power was in question, was likewise delineated and blurred, simultaneously, by the interests of politics and by the operation of ideologies.

For legislators and reformers involved in the definition of abandon moral, metaphors of territorial dominion, long a mainstay of political theory, provided a useful frame in which the much desired but elusive distinction between state and family might be given fixed coordinates. The contradictions in the projects of reform and the battles between reformers and traditionalists were to reveal, however, that the boundary between state and family, to borrow a phrase from Samuel Weber, was one of dynamic "ambivalent demarcation"; it shifted with each new articulation of the interests of the state and with each new rendering of the essence of the family.[34] This boundary was both the creation and the object of ceaseless cultural contestation. Because the nineteenth-century understanding of the family was locked into a series of metaphors in which the exercise of power had a natural geography, the project of protecting children against their own (un)natural parents could not be justified by simply redrawing the boundaries between family and state. Instead, ironically enough, it demanded that those boundaries be reposited in all their natural rigidity in order to render them more fluid, that they be cast as naturally impenetrable in order to render them more permeable.

Finally, the 1889 legislation also spawned a new set of questions about the gendered exercise of domestic power. As the law on abandon moral entered French civil jurisprudence, the assault on the unnatural exercise of la puissance paternelle quickly turned to what many magistrates and activists considered the most unnatural paternal authority of all: that exercised by

[34] Explaining the indeterminacy of the boundaries between academic disciplines, Weber writes: "The demarcation is ambivalent because it does not merely demarcate one thing by setting it off from another; it also de-marks, that is, defaces the mark it simultaneously inscribes, by placing it in relation to an indeterminable series of other marks, of which we can never be fully conscious or cognizant." See Samuel Weber, *Institution and Interpretation*, Theory and History of Literature, vol. 31 (Minneapolis: University of Minnesota Press, 1987), 145. See also Lynn Hunt, "The Unstable Boundaries of the French Revolution," in *A History of Private Life* vol. 4, ed. Michelle Perrot, and Donzelot, *The Policing of Families*, for important arguments about the construction and significance of an impenetrable private sphere in the nineteenth century.

mothers whose tie to a male partner had been destroyed by death, divorce, or desertion. To be sure, the courts would not exclude fathers from the arena of application. Single fathers as well as husbands would also be divested of their paternal rights by virtue of the law on abandon moral. Nonetheless, the effort to protect children from unfit parents and unhealthy home environments can be seen as an effort to make la puissance paternelle identical with the presence of proper masculine authority in an intact household. The state's right to act in individual families was thus grounded, in large part, in the desire to lay rightful claim to a masculine power usurped by mothers whose own morality was rendered suspect by the literal and moral absence of a proper père de famille. In denaturalizing the foundations of paternal power, the law of 1889 brought the unnatural mother into view in a new and more juridically potent way.

Although the enactment of the law on abandon moral in 1889 brought parliamentary debate to a close, its capacity to disturb existing truths and orders persisted. The vision of public authority irrevocably enmeshed in the private affairs of French families continued to disturb commentators and officials alike. The enactment of the new legislation also raised a series of epistemological questions that would get played out whenever the family entered the space of the justice system and whenever the justice system entered the space of the family. Lawyers, police, magistrates, parents, and children all struggled to determine the truth of abandon moral in their attempts to reconcile particular instances with the elusive principles expounded in the law. These efforts and the conflicts they engendered would translate the law into a set of juridical practices and normative principles essential to the functioning of a new kind of justice, one cobbled together around the apparently deviant family in the space between the norms of civil law and the logic of criminal justice.

Part II

THE MACHINERY OF JUSTICE:
THE INVESTIGATION AND PROSECUTION
OF ABANDON MORAL

WHEN the proposal for a law "on the protection of mistreated or morally abandoned children" was under debate in 1883, the minister of the interior, René Waldeck-Rousseau, included among his many objections the fear that the law would introduce troubling "new machinery" (*des rouages nouveaux*) into the apparatus of state. Such machinery, he argued, would inevitably generate "a certain confusion, equally troublesome for the administration in general as for the work that the honorable M. Roussel pursues with such dedication."[1]

Although no entirely original administrative or judicial institution was created immediately after the law's enactment in July 1889, Waldeck-Rousseau's prediction had some truth in it. The rouages nouveaux generated by the passage of the law were not cast whole but were pieced together from extant procedures, rationalities, and practices. They emerged where public authorities mapped new circuits of investigation and charted new routes between long-established sites of juridical implementation. Despite its apparently piecemeal character, however, the improvised frame for the legal dispossession of parental rights lasted until 1912, a span of nearly twenty-five years, when the hearings were moved from the general civil court to the newly founded juvenile court. Even after 1912, however, the investigation of alleged cases of moral endangerment and the relevant juridical procedures appear to have remained relatively unchanged until after the Second World War, when criminal and juvenile psychiatry began to play a stronger role in child protection cases. Only then would what some historians refer to as a "medico-psychological" approach to endangered children fully supplant the more strictly juridical-moral interpretations and procedures developed in the late nineteenth century.[2]

---

[1] *JOS*, 11 May 1883, 464.

[2] On the invention of the juvenile court and the "psychologization" of family and juvenile justice, see Jacques Donzelot, *The Policing of Families*, trans. Robert Hurley (New York: Pan-

Waldeck-Rousseau's metaphor of troubling new machinery provides a useful analytical tool for examining the particular way in which both the law of 1889 and the actors involved in its drama were situated within interlocking institutional and ideological frames. In invoking metaphors of mechanisms or machines, I do not mean to suggest that these institutions operated with machinelike precision. On the contrary, the movement of the mechanisms of justice in question here was often slowed or even arrested by the frictions produced where parts—and people—met. Pieced together from older elements, sometimes poorly matched, these mechanisms required constant supervision and adjustment to counteract the effects of a particularly complex form of juridical uncertainty. With the passage of time, they called for renovation so that they could continue to meet the demands placed on them by the appearance—if not always the effect—of rational operation.

To be sure, the individual parts of the rouages nouveaux devoted to the question of abandon moral were already well worn when authorities in the justice system put them together in 1889. Fragments of civil procedure, long ago established by the Napoleonic legal codes, were welded to techniques of criminal investigation developed over the course of the nineteenth century. Prosecutors and judges added cases of abandon moral to the wide variety of civil matters they investigated, presented, and heard in their capacity as all-purpose magistrates of the court.[3] Through such conjoinings of institutions and practices, agents of the state charged with applying the law of 1889 attempted to synchronize the language and aims of the public protection of morally endangered children with the movement of late-nineteenth-century civil and criminal justice.

Through the operation of the rouages nouveaux the law emerged from the chambers of the National Assembly in 1889 and was diffused into the ordinary procedural canon of the civil magistrate, the district attorney, the local justice of the peace, the prefect of police, and the local police captain. At the same time, through the imposition of a standard pattern of procedure, a pattern that gave definition to each element of the new machinery and described the periodicity of the machine's broadest movements, the formal text of the law revealed its plasticity. Once engaged in the structures and procedures that comprised the rouages nouveaux, the law of 1889 was continually reinvented, redefined, and reinterpreted by all who fell within its ambit. Simultaneously, those people implicated by the law were similarly defined and interpreted through the lens of the legal text and the rhythms of application it

---

theon, 1979); Jean-Marie Renouard, *De l'enfant coupable à l'enfant inadapté: Le traitement social et politique de la déviance* (Paris: Centurion, 1990); and Yvonne Knibiehler, ed., *Nous les assistantes sociales: Naissance d'une profession* (Paris: Aubier Montaigne, 1980).

[3] In the terminology of the nineteenth-century French judicial system, "magistrate" referred to both the judges (*la magistrature assise*) and the public prosecutors (*la magistrature debout*). See Benjamin F. Martin, *Crime and Criminal Justice under the Third Republic: The Shame of Marianne* (Baton Rouge: Louisiana State University Press, 1990), 321.

dictated. Thus through this new machinery the law touched the populace and, simultaneously, through it the populace could initiate its own contact with—and interpretation of—the law.

It is by now a commonplace in the social history of law and welfare, as well as in the field of legal anthropology, to point out that power is rarely distributed equally among individuals involved in the workings of legal systems. The disparity is most evident between the agents of the state—judges, lawyers, police, court officials—and those people who become the objects of the state's inquiry, especially individuals or groups normally excluded from the exercise of social or political power.[4] There can be no doubt that along with other late-nineteenth-century protective measures, the law of 1889 advanced the normalization of the working-class family through its mechanisms of intervention and its codification of standards of parental behavior.

The law of 1889 should not, however, be understood exclusively as an orchestrated extension of a class-based hegemonic order.[5] Despite the pronounced tendency of the courts to press cases against poor and laboring parents, there were no distinctions of class written into the text of the law. Because the 1889 law provided the only formal means of severing family ties, moreover, some people who solicited the state's intervention in their family affairs also came from solidly middle class backgrounds. In the workings of the court, distinctions of class—along with the equally critical distinctions of gender—tended to be produced in those social spaces the law left open and unmarked. In this sense, the mechanisms of justice often produced quite different experiences for families of different social origins and parents of different sexes.

Yet the elaboration of particular cases and the importance of particular registers of social and sexual difference in those cases should not be separated from the more general questions written into the practice of implementation. The debates surrounding the enactment of the 1889 had been deeply inflected by an ambivalence about the state's right to reconfigure the family at will. That ambivalence returned with a vengeance in the courtroom. Legally unseating any père de famille, and thereby intentionally destabilizing the family, struck a discordant note in the hearts of the French, even (perhaps especially) among those bourgeois legislators, jurists, and philanthropists who were the most outspoken advocates of the law. The intact family

---

[4] See especially Philippe Meyer, *L'Enfant et la raison d'état* (Paris: Editions du Seuil, 1977), and Donzelot, *The Policing of Families*. The question of law, power, and culture has recently been examined in particularly insightful ways by legal anthropologists, especially where it intersects with issues of gender, race, and class. See in particular the introduction and essays in *Contested States: Law, Hegemony, and Resistance*, ed. Mindie Lazarus Black and Susan F. Hirsch (London: Routledge, 1994).

[5] In this I disagree with the editors of *Contested States*, who invoke a rather strict Gramschian notion of hegemony in explaining the relations of power around and in the law in a variety of cultural and historical contexts. See the introduction to Black et al., *Contested States*, esp. 6–13.

remained the ideological cornerstone of a moral society and a coherent, strong nation. Grounding a coordinated effort to control the laboring classes in an act that inspired such anxiety—even with the incentive of opening that family to the supervision of the state—could hardly have been a solid foundation for the kind of controlling "complex" Jacques Donzelot and others have attempted to unmask.[6] When the law was applied to mothers, who could not exercise the formal rights of la puissance paternelle except in the most oblique manner, another, equally unsettling set of anxieties emerged.

If ambivalence tempered the application of the law, so too did a certain measure of formal juridical contradiction. Here, too, the "troublesome confusion" so feared by Waldeck-Rousseau sprang as much from the text of the law as from the mechanisms of application. Despite the fact that almost all of its precedents came from the Napoleonic penal code and later criminal legislation, the law on abandon moral was proposed and approved as a civil measure. It was conceived, in other words, as part of a more subtle and transitory regulation of family affairs, corrective, even preventive, but not— at least in the abstract—punitive.[7]

What did it mean for public officials and for "suspicious" families that the 1889 law on abandon moral had been entered into the body of civil law? How did the imperatives of civil justice shape the court's approach to this new legal terrain? Since the introduction of the Napoleonic codes in the early nineteenth century, jurists in France have viewed civil law as one of the most intellectually challenging areas of legal practice. Whereas French criminal law focuses in large part on the establishment of a particular fact (that is, whether the crime was actually committed by the accused) and pits the state against the defendant, civil procedure concentrates more on the constitution of a case as a complete account of a relationship and focuses in particular on producing a credible narrative of responsibility within the frame of that relationship.[8] In civil law, moreover, the contest takes place

[6] See Donzelot, *The Policing of Families*, esp. ch. 4, "The Tutelary Complex."

[7] See Claudia Scheck Kselman, "The Modernization of Family Law: The Politics and Ideology of Family Reform in Third Republic France" (Ph.D. diss., University of Michigan, 1980), 186–87. Kselman argues that the shift from penal to civil in the conceptualization of the law of 1889 reveals the "radical innovation" characteristic of the Third Republic's family law reforms. On law and family in the early Third Republic, see also Esther Sue Kanipe, "The Family, Private Property, and the State in France, 1870–1914" (Ph.D. diss., University of Wisconsin, Madison, 1976).

[8] To be sure, the question of moral responsibility played an important part in the formulation of the Napoleonic penal code as well, and it became one of the primary themes in the late-nineteenth-century discourse on criminal reform. On the particularly important intersections between medicine and morals in this context, see Robert A. Nye, *Crime, Madness, and Politics in Modern France: The Medical Concept of National Decline* (Princeton: Princeton University Press, 1984), and Ruth Harris, *Murders and Madness: Medicine, Law, and Society in the Fin de Siècle* (Oxford: Clarendon Press, 1989).

between plaintiff and defendant. And unlike the criminal case, which deals in accusations of crime and the meting out of punishment or correction, the conceptual frame of the civil case comprises questions of harm, responsibility, retribution, and compensation.

As to the construction of a case, observers contend that French civil justice has traditionally been much more dependent on calculated moves of interpretation of documents and texts than criminal justice tends to be. As one legal historian puts it, an argument in civil law "requires often lengthy preliminary research, demands the reading of numerous documents, necessitates the interpretation of proceedings whose juridical foundation is often uncertain and subject to dispute." In general, he concludes, civil law is by definition and in application far more "supple" than penal law, and far more reliant on its reconstruction in jurisprudence.[9] The importance of written text to French civil law should not be undervalued. As another legal scholar notes, civil procedure in a code-based legal tradition such as that established in nineteenth-century France "tends to become primarily a written matter."[10] In the particular instance of abandon moral, where each case was constructed through the compilation of a dossier and reviewed in chambers without the presence of a jury or an audience, these problematic qualities of civil procedure—as discursive, textual, and fraught with epistemological uncertainty—became all the more pronounced.

At the same time, the legislation on abandon moral was far from a classical example of civil law. In conceptual terms, the 1889 law, although formally classified as a civil measure and implemented through the civil court system, straddled the logic of civil and criminal law. In some ways, it operated as a kind of subordinate measure to criminal law; according to the text of the 1889 law, certain criminal convictions, particularly those that involved the "sexual corruption of minors," resulted in the automatic suspension of parental rights. However, in its emphasis on moral conditions rather than criminal acts, it exemplified the tendency of civil legislation to rest on uncertainty, to excite controversy, and to demonstrate elasticity.

The law also introduced standards of judgment beyond those imposed by the penal code. Without the certainty of a criminal conviction, the civil magistracy often faced the far more difficult task of establishing a family's moral state of being, predicting its consequences, and determining a course of action that derived neither from the state's correctional apparatus nor from the fundaments of ordinary civil law. Such a state of being—hidden from view,

---

[9] See Maurice Garçon, *La Fin du régime*, vol. 3 of his *Histoire de la justice sous la IIIe République* (Paris: Arthème Fayard, 1957), 182, 186, and 192. Garçon also points to the innovations in family law introduced under the Third Republic as a powerful example of the importance of jurisprudence in civil law and procedure.

[10] John Henry Merriman, *The Civil Law Tradition: An Introduction to the Legal Systems of Western Europe and Latin America*, 2d ed. (Stanford: Stanford University Press, 1985), 114.

known only by its outward traces—could be determined only by reading the public face of a family's interior life, that is, by engaging in the most tenuous kinds of interpretation and reconstruction. As one authority on state-assisted children and the law put it in 1912, "[A]bandon moral cannot be perceived directly; it must be presumed."[11]

How can the historian examine the application of a law centered on a presumed condition, or as the commentator of 1912 also put it, on "a negative fact"? How can one make sense of the "troublesome confusion" that appears to have saturated both the text of the law and its path through the mechanisms of application? I propose here to examine the law as it circulated through the rouages of its own creation, that is, to trace both the forward route of particular cases of abandon moral, from private home to the public stage of the courtroom, and the backward-looking process by which a narrative born in the offices and dossiers of the prosecutor underlay the constitution of a case and defined the course it would take as its contours developed. In order to focus on the moral and political problems that were central to the notion of abandon moral, I am leaving aside the separate provisions in the law's title 2, addressing "la protection des mineurs placés avec ou sans l'intervention des parents," that is, those children whose parents had voluntarily or de facto ceded their rights to the state.

Examining the juridical treatment of abandon moral raises many questions about how the state gained access to and evaluated the intimate life of a family. How did individuals, families, and public authorities enter the domain of justice? How might their actions have influenced the formalized movement of the machine? How might the law's complex structure of discourses and practices have taught public officials and ordinary individuals to take their places as agents and actors in the social dramas that brought family life under the structured scrutiny of the state? Part 2 asks these questions about each of the distinct phases in the making of a case of abandon moral: the initial engagement of the apparatus of justice, the investigation of allegations and suspicions, and the presentation of a case to the court.

The investigation and prosecution of abandon moral also suggests that the state's access to private life was far from perfect, that the discovery and prosecution of abandon moral was far more contingent than public authorities could admit. How, the historian must ask, did accident, uncertainty, indecipherability, and contradiction—springing both from within the text of the law and from the varieties of interpretation at work in the universe of fin-de-siécle France—militate against efforts to impose a rational, machinelike operation of justice? And finally, how did agents of the court manage to create through their choice of cases and arguments an image of justice that eliminated—as much as possible—the traces of uncertainty and contingency?

[11] Emile Alcindor, *Les Enfants assistés* (Paris: Emile Paul, 1912), 85.

CHAPTER 4

Setting the Wheels in Motion

IN THE FIRST movements of the rouages nouveaux accident, passion, fear, and spite played their largest role in the creation of formal cases of abandon moral. In the early stages of accusation and investigation, individual hopes for justice were the greatest, and terror, brought by the realization that accusation brought investigation and suspicion, first struck those who had approached the machinery of justice without caution. In these early stages the meaning of the law appeared to be at its most elastic and, at the same time, the limits on interpretation began to be set and the lines of authority became apparent.

Every case of abandon moral that received a formal hearing was recorded in the registers of the court. Clerks of court inscribed these accounts as they arose in the court docket, interleaving them in the register among the variety of civil cases examined each day by the tribunal de première instance, or the lower circuit court at the Palais de Justice in Paris. These judgment records followed a standard form, prefacing the court's decision with the *exposé*, or summary of relevant facts, presented by the public prosecutor (*le procureur de la République*). The exposé reconstructed each case of abandon moral as it predated the prosecution's inquest, that is, as it awaited discovery or "exposure" by public authorities.

Thus, for example, the procureur presented his case against one Catherine D. on 18 May 1900.[1] For some time, the summary states, Catherine had shown no interest whatsoever in her child. She had taken to drink and begging and had already been sentenced to two months of prison for mendicancy and for allowing her children to beg as well. With these facts, the prosecutor's exposé presented the symptoms of a long-standing condition of moral failing, which, once disclosed by the objective agents and tools of judicial investigation, could serve as the causal foundation for a judgment of déchéance.

The emphasis on exposure here is not accidental. In the logic of the prosecution, cases were built on the foundation of facts that revealed themselves

---

[1] To protect the privacy of the descendants of the individuals named in these case dossiers, I have deleted references to their surnames in the text and notes. Researchers can identify the dossiers by number and date. The dossiers are classified under the Seine departmental justice series D3 U7, located at the Archives de la Ville de Paris et du Département de la Seine in Paris (ADS).

only to the eyes of public authorities. The judge's decisions, nevertheless, were openly based on the prosecution's presentation of those facts as read against the "raw" materials in the dossier. The text of the decisions generally reiterated the prosecution's highly codified story, rewarding the prosecutor rhetorically—and juridically—for his investigative and narrative mastery.[2] Hence, according to the register of court, the presiding judge divested Catherine D. of her parental rights because she had been convincingly "represented as [représentée comme]" prone to drinking and begging, convincingly "represented as" neglecting her children. In grounding his decisions in the prosecutor's representation of the accused, the judge located the hearing's origin and resolution in the prosecutor's satisfactory construction of the case. Because the end of the exposé was to reveal an enduring moral deficiency, rather than the truth of a single criminal act, the integrity of the procureur's narrative was crucial. If, as Hayden White has argued, historical narrative "has as its latent or manifest purpose the desire to moralize the events of which it treats," then the formal narratives exposing a history of abandon moral carried a double moral burden.[3]

Agreement between prosecution and judge seems to have been a prerequisite for bringing a case before the bench. In none of the more than fifty cases heard by the tribunal de première instance in 1890 was the prosecutor's request for déchéance refused. In 1900 only two cases out of more than seventy brought before the court were rejected, and in 1906, out of nearly sixty cases, not a single request was denied. If the exposés presumed a long-standing degenerate condition awaiting discovery, and if the judgments turned more or less exclusively on the prosecution's representation of that condition, both narrative origins obscured precisely how the process of making a case began. What the summaries do not reveal, in other words, is how the emphasis on both discovery and representation masked the more fundamental event that made both possible: the production of a case fit for presentation to the court.

To understand the full trajectory of cases of abandon moral, therefore, we must turn to the investigation dossiers maintained by the Parquet, or office of the public prosecutor. The forty-odd extant dossiers dating from between approximately 1890 and 1910 do not provide sufficient material for a complete social portrait of the population touched by the law, although the variety of characters who populate even these few folders is already striking.[4]

---

[2] These decisions can be found in the registers of the Première Chambre de Conseil, Parquet de la Seine, Tribunal de Première Instance, ADS, D1 U5.

[3] Hayden White, "The Value of Narrativity in the Representation of Reality," in *On Narrative*, ed. W.J.T. Mitchell (Chicago: University of Chicago Press, 1981), 14 n. 11, as cited in Dennis R. Klinck, *The Word of Law* (Ottawa: Carleton University Press, 1992), 297.

[4] Forty-four dossiers dating from 1897 to 1908 have been preserved at the Paris archives. No record of the total number of dossiers compiled by the procureur's office over the years appears

The actors in these officially compiled tales of accusation, inquest, and exposure include a Polish count, an actress, a wine merchant, a factory worker, a traveling salesman, a salesclerk, a journalist, and several women whose means of support ranged from casual needlework to occasional clandestine prostitution. The breadth of the social spectrum in this sample alone begins to suggest that protection law should not be approached in the manner exemplified by Jacques Donzelot, who implies that the law of 1889 was a weapon in the organized repression of the laboring classes, and particularly the bourgeois repression of the working-class père de famille.[5] The fact that single mothers appear to make up close to half of the implicated parents in the registers of court suggests that paternal authority may not have been the most important target of the law. In three sample years, for example, single mothers—either unmarried, divorced, or widowed—accounted for between 40 and 50 percent of all cases decided by the civil tribunal.[6] Single fathers accounted for roughly 30 percent, and decisions involving both parents made up approximately 20 to 30 percent of the total each year.[7]

The project here, however, is not to situate each case as more or less representative of the norm in the larger field of the law's application but to examine the process by which a suspicion of abandon moral was pursued and consolidated into a case. In this context, every one of the surviving files represents something more than the experiences and opinions of the people who populate them: each one shows the construction of a case over time; each one reveals the path of circulation between the institutions of investigation and judgment; each one testifies to a process by which evidence was recognized, collected, and categorized; each one demonstrates the gradual imposition of standardized form on a set of chaotic and contradictory narratives; and each one bears witness to the power of moral questions in turn-of-the-century French civil justice and in the wider cultural currents in which the law found its meaning.[8]

---

to exist. Nor does the archival record offer any explanation for the survival of these particular files among the many that must have been compiled after 1889.

[5] Donzelot's analysis takes a paranoid and damaging turn where his narrative slips into a tale of a rather diabolically conceived social "castration" of the proletarian father through the methods and agents of philanthropy, public assistance, medicine, psychiatry, psychoanalysis, and, last but certainly not least, the collusion of the working-class (and bourgeois) wife with the aforementioned "experts." See Jacques Donzelot, *The Policing of Families*, trans. Robert Hurley (New York: Pantheon, 1979), esp. 45–46.

[6] On women and the Paris courts in this period more generally, see Anne-Marie Sohn, "Les Rôles féminins dans la vie privée à l'époque de la 3ème République" (thèse d'Etat, Université de Paris I, 1993), and "The Golden Age of Male Adultery: The Third Republic," *Journal of Social History* 28, no. 3 (spring 1995).

[7] In 1900 the court issued definitive decisions in about 80 cases; in 1906 the total neared 60; and in 1913 civil magistrates ruled on 116 cases of alleged abandon moral (ADS, D1 U5).

[8] In her discussion of the criminal dossier, Ruth Harris argues that "the rules of evidence were

Because this set of dossiers also includes cases the prosecutor ultimately deemed too weak to pursue, it defines some portion of the outer limit of the law's potential for application. The materiality of the dossier and the documents they contain as themselves a product of judicial action likewise afford the historian a concrete point of access into the consequences of law's application.[9] The dossier, in other words, provides the more ragged histories that lie behind the polished synopses inscribed in the register of court.

The dossiers are perhaps most eloquent in speaking of the creaks and groans of a judicial apparatus just set in motion. Official suspicion that parents might be guilty of abandon moral was raised by a wide variety of events, actions, and signs. It surfaced, for example, when the interest of public authorities was deflected to the question of parenthood from altogether different matters brought to their attention by the soon-to-be-accused. This was the experience of Mme. Ephième E. in 1897. According to the report by the local police superintendent (*commissaire*), agents were sent to investigate after Ephième filed a complaint at the local police station, or *commissariat*. Ephième had charged that her daughter had been abducted, "by force and violence," by one Count de M., who should therefore be arrested for the kidnapping and corruption of a minor. Ephième's accusations implicitly invoked article 334 of the penal code devoted to the sexual corruption of minors through seduction, coercion, rape, or abduction. It is difficult to judge whether this can be interpreted as evidence of the breadth of popular legal knowledge or of the roots of law in popular mores, or as the contribution of the local commissaire with whom she may have lodged a more general complaint.

Upon questioning by the investigating agent, Ephième admitted that the count had been her daughter's lover for seven months and that she had been aware of the liaison from the start. Since Alice had begun earning her own

---

non-existent," in that hearsay and anonymous denunciation were accepted uncritically as valid sources of information. See Harris, *Murders and Madness: Medicine, Law, and Society in the Fin de Siècle* (Oxford: Clarendon Press, 1989), 127–28. The instance of abandon moral, however, suggests that in fact the rules of evidence were quite well established at this time, and that these suspect sources had an explicit and well-defined place in the collection of evidence in both criminal and civil court.

[9] Michel Foucault has called attention to the important connection between the development of regular police surveillance and its material incarnation in what he calls the documentary system. He argues that the 1810 penal code's requirement that "dangerous individuals" be watched stimulated the Ministry of the Interior to establish its own criminal records office, borrowing many techniques of classification from other fields and developing a centralized card index of convictions. See Foucault's *Discipline and Punish: The Birth of the Prison*, trans. Alan Sheridan (New York: Vintage, 1979), 281. See also Foucault's introductory remarks on the dossier in *I, Pierre Rivière, Having Slaughtered My Mother, My Sister, and My Brother . . .* , ed. Foucault, trans. Frank Jellinek (New York: Random House, 1975; Lincoln: University of Nebraska Press, 1982), esp. x.

living as "a lyric artist" in the theater, Ephième explained, she had considered her fifteen-year-old daughter "free to do as she pleased." After interviewing Alice and the count separately, the agent concluded that the violence reported by Ephième had been generated by an ordinary domestic squabble and that the charge of "seduction of a minor"(*détournement de mineure*) should be dropped.

Ephième's moral character, however, was another matter. The accounts given by Alice and the count suggested that not only had Ephième been aware of her daughter's relationship with the count but that she had actively encouraged Alice's theatrical career as a means of attracting a rich lover and had actively supported Alice's rendezvous. "I am of the opinion," the commissaire concluded in his report,

> that there has been no assault, no abduction or seduction of a minor, but that there is, in this matter, an unfit mother, who facilitates one of her daughter's debaucheries, and readies herself to facilitate those of her second, [a mother] whom we must at the very least divest of her *puissance paternelle*.[10]

Thus the tables turned in the course of the inquiry, shifting suspicion to the complainant herself. The police agent's inquiry into Ephième's household led soon after to a new and extensive investigation of Ephième's status as a parent and moral guide.

Children picked up by the police for vagrancy or petty crimes also provoked the turn of official interest from child to parent. In the case of M. et Mme. C., the investigation of a possible case of abandon moral began after their children had been taken into police custody several times running for begging and vagrancy. After the children's fifth arrest between June and October 1908, the prefecture's Service de Sûreté, the criminal investigation bureau, launched a preliminary inquiry into the children's background. Two weeks later, the head of the prefecture's division devoted to the protection of infants addressed a letter to the procureur: "[H]aving been arrested several times for begging or sent to my prefecture as homeless children, these children attracted my attention, and, consequently, I felt I had to order an investigation of the manner in which they were being raised and cared for by their parents."[11] Here, too, public authorities transformed the original disturbance into the symptom of a more serious hidden family pathology. Further investigations of M. et Mme. C. ensued.

The prescription to take a child's actions or condition as possible evidence of parental misconduct had, by this time, been codified into the canon of police investigation and the discourse of child protection. It seems clear that belief in an inevitable connection between child delinquency and hidden

[10] ADS, D3 U7, Dossier 849 (1897).
[11] ADS, D3 U7, Dossier 3363 (1908).

parental deficiency had penetrated far beyond the police station by the late nineteenth century. Othenin d'Haussonville, in a lengthy article on childhood in Paris published in the mid-1870s, informed his readers that child criminals were more often than not the offspring of convicts, "beggars, vagabonds, missing parents, or prostitutes."[12] Loys Brueyre, a longtime administrator in the Bureau of Public Assistance's Enfants Assistés division and active in many private charitable organizations, also claimed that young criminals were in large part produced by the moral degeneracy of their parents. Arguing against the return of the juvenile offender to his family, Loys Brueyre warned that

> [t]he paternal household, where he most often found only the spectacle of demoralization, vices, the effects of alcoholism and debauchery, did not change during the child's pretrial detention. The same causes must inevitably produce the same effects, all the while aggravating them. It is the recidivist who lies in wait for the child.[13]

Where philanthropic and reformist discourse fell short of breath, science and art took over. Theories of both hereditary and environmentally caused moral degeneration abounded in the literature of psychiatry, criminal anthropology, and moral philosophy during the last decades of the century.[14] On the literary front, Emile Zola, greatly influenced by these scientific understandings of morality, continually reminded his readers that the demoralized family was certain to produce even more corrupt—and corrupting—children. Nana is doubtless Zola's finest and, for the reformers of the Third Republic, most terrifying image of this moral economy shared by parent and child. She literally incarnates her parents' bent for dissolution from the moment of her birth, and her life describes a course of further demoralization made inevitable by the exposure to the excesses of vice inherent in her environment, in her parents, and in her own desires.[15] As Nana is the inherently and environmentally corrupted product of her parents, so too does she further her parents' own moral degeneration; Nana's mother, Gervaise, is destroyed by her daughter's "fall."[16]

In Zola's work, as in the theories of science, criminology, and philanthropy that moved public authorities to seek out and sever the parental root

---

[12] Othenin d'Haussonville, "L'Enfance à Paris," *Revue des deux mondes* 17 (1876), 484–85.

[13] Loys Brueyre, "Comité de défense des enfants traduits en justice," *Revue philanthropique* 1 (1897): 389–90.

[14] See Robert A. Nye, *Crime, Madness, and Politics in Modern France: The Medical Concept of National Decline* (Princeton: Princeton University Press, 1984), esp. chap. 4: "Heredity or Milieu: The Born-Criminal Debate and the Foundation of Criminology."

[15] Emile Zola, *L'Assommoir*, trans. Leonard Tancock (Harmondsworth, England: Penguin Books, 1970), esp. 354.

[16] Ibid., 358.

of juvenile deviance, environment stimulated hereditary predispositions.[17] Where earlier in the century delinquent or vagrant children were considered independent subjects by police and social observers, by the 1880s and 1890s they were read almost exclusively as the expression of their parents' moral disorder. It is small wonder, then, that the movement of police investigative procedure followed suit.

The police station was far from the only site where investigations were set in motion, however. Following the law of 1889, which prescribed the automatic loss of la puissance paternelle upon the parent's conviction for certain felonies, magistrates in the criminal courts also began to direct their attention to the parental status of the people they sentenced. These crimes included the prostitution of one's own children, the violent assault or complicity in the assault of one's children, or the prostitution of other minors. Félix B., for example, condemned to fifteen months of imprisonment by the tribunal correctionel de la Seine for the prostitution of minors (*l'excitation habituelle des mineurs à la débauche*), became the subject of a new inquest. "We must know," the procureur wrote in his request to the Service de Sûreté for further investigation, "his ordinary conduct vis-à-vis his own children in order to request the divestiture of his paternal authority."[18]

Even in the absence of any of the criminal convictions listed in the articles of the law of 1889, other crimes and multiple convictions were taken as warning signs of the disruption in the code of moral responsibility that defined parenthood, at least in the courtroom, in the late nineteenth century. Criminal conviction of any sort could thus be invoked as a sign of dangerous moral deviance, and hence as grounds for the dispossession of parental rights. That a single procureur managed all public prosecution in both the criminal and civil chambers of the tribunal de première instance in Paris clearly facilitated the juridical translation of such "evidence" from the criminal to the civil context.[19]

When a child appeared before the criminal court, the increasingly powerful notion that the family was the "cradle of vice" underscored the imperative for background investigation. Armandine G., for example, was arrested and convicted for vagrancy and solicitation. As a consequence of her arrest,

---

[17] On Zola and his interest in nineteenth-century theories of heredity, see Jean Borie, *Mythologies de l'hérédité au XIXe siècle* (Paris: Editions Galilée, 1981).

[18] ADS, D3 U7, Dossier 743 (1897).

[19] Although only one procureur de la République was appointed at a time, he directed a large staff of assistant prosecutors, who also presented cases to the court. According to Benjamin F. Martin, there were twenty-six such *substituts* working in the Paris court in 1880, and more than thirty by 1910. See Benjamin F. Martin, *Crime and Criminal Justice under the Third Republic: The Shame of Marianne* (Baton Rouge: Louisiana State University Press, 1990), 171. The fact that all prosecution was organized under the supervision of the procureur, however, suggests that the circulation of suspicion and evidence did not depend on his personal participation in each case.

the investigating judge (*juge d'instruction*) attached to the criminal court ordered the police superintendent of the Gare quarter to pursue a separate inquest on the girl's family. The request, printed on a mass-produced form, read as follows: "We must look for the cause of these children's misconduct; if it results from their poor upbringing [*mauvaise éducation*], from their parents' indifference or lack of supervision, or from the bad influence of the children's cohorts . . ." In addition, the superintendent was to determine "if they could be returned to their parents with no ill consequence, or if the latter seem unfit to exercise parental authority."[20] Less than two months later, the procureur wrote up his request that Armandine's mother be stripped of her parental rights.

A third avenue to a judgment of déchéance de la puissance paternelle was opened by the profound transformation in the meaning of the paternal *droit de correction* by the last decades of the nineteenth century. Originally designed as the legal means by which families and the state could collaborate in the maintenance of social order, the droit de correction allowed fathers to request that the court incarcerate their "unmanageable" children for a limited period of time. In principle, only the family father could exercise this right, although in his absence, mothers, guardians, and other relatives might also seek such a court order.

During the first half of the century, requests for correction were honored with relatively little complication, particularly when the children were under the age of sixteen.[21] Changing attitudes toward children and the turn from punishment to reeducation or rehabilitation in the treatment of delinquent or unruly children brought the practice of correction paternelle under severe scrutiny and led ultimately to its obsolescence by the 1930s.[22] At the same time, suspicions grew that social and familial disruptions apparently caused by the actions of a disobedient child might in fact be the symptom of deeper parental inadequacies. Public authorities may also have become increasingly

---

[20] ADS, D3 U7, Dossier 1702 (1901). The use of a single form for a variety of family structures accounts for the use of the plural—"ces enfants"—in this particular case. The text of the request left blanks only for the investigating judge to fill in his own name, the name of the child in question and his or her crime, and the quartier of the commissaire to whom the request was addressed. A handwritten note at the bottom of the form provided the commissaire with the current whereabouts of the child and her mother.

[21] *CN*, bk. 1, title 9, art. 376, reads: "If the child is less than sixteen years of age, the father may have him detained for a period not to exceed one month; and, to that end, the presiding judge of the arrondissement tribunal must, on the father's request, deliver the warrant of arrest." For children over sixteen, the next article adds, the judge must confer with the public prosecutor before granting or refusing the paternal request.

[22] See Bernard Schnapper, "La Correction paternelle et le mouvement des idées au dix-neuvième siècle (1789–1935)," *Revue historique* 263 (1980). See also Arlette Farge and Michel Foucault's concluding commentary in *Le Désordre des familles: Lettres de cachet des Archives de la Bastille au XVIIIe siècle*, ed. Farge and Foucault (Paris: Gallimard, 1982).

uncomfortable as the invocation of the droit de correction became more prevalent among the laboring classes. The tendency to investigate a request's origins, according to this thesis, and the uncertainty about granting it thus increased in step with the rising number of requests from the more marginal elements of the social body.[23] By the 1890s, then, the desire to have one's own child imprisoned began to signify not the responsible exercise of parental discipline but parental disinterest or even deliberate and malicious mistreatment.

The law of 1889 codified this mounting suspicion regarding requests for corrective incarceration: article 2 specified that every *mise en correction* might be possible grounds for the divestiture of parental rights. Thus, to borrow the words of sociologist Philippe Meyer, "[E]very father requesting correction could, in the wake of an investigation of his family, see the use of his right of correction turned back against him."[24]

This was certainly the experience of one Etienne M., a ragpicker who had requested the mise en correction of his oldest daughter sometime in the early autumn of 1897.[25] The chief justice, in accordance with common procedure, ordered the superintendent of Etienne's quartier to investigate. In his report, a preprinted form used for background checks on requests for correction, the commissaire wrote out his impressions, as the form asked, of "the behavior and morality of parents and child, the attitude of the former toward the latter, the objectionable influences which might be working upon them." Etienne, the commissaire reported,

> his wife, and his daughter are all of the same moral status. M., who was incarcerated at Ville Evrard as an alcoholic, has in no way profited from the experience. He drinks like [,] brutalizes his wife and daughter. The latter, scarcely fourteen, is completely [   ]. She constantly spends the night away from home, and it is well known in the neighborhood that she has a lover. The mother supports the daughters. As for the father, he does not [   ] to reprimand except when he is drunk.

The report concluded, "It is not a mise en correction but rather the divestiture of paternal right that should be instigated."[26] From these observations, made in the service of an entirely different judicial procedure and initiated

---

[23] See Philippe Meyer, *L'Enfant et la raison d'état* (Paris: Editions du Seuil, 1977), 59. According to Schnapper, the fees involved in requesting correction paternelle were prohibitive for most working-class families until the late 1880s, when they were systematically waived where indigence could be proven (Schnapper, "La Correction," 336).

[24] Meyer, *L'Enfant*, 65.

[25] ADS, D3 U7, Dossier 825 (1897).

[26] In what might be construed as a kind of resistance to the formal standardization represented by the preprinted form, the police agent left the entire form blank, confining his remarks to his own written statement. The letter, written in a poorly schooled hand, contained several illegible words, indicated here by the blanks in the quotation.

by Etienne himself, the "innocent" supplicant became the suspect; the investigation shifted from child to parent.

The indirect push or backfiring impulse was not the only gesture that could move the cogs of judicial investigation. More intentional solicitation, marked by the amateur exposition of cases, also engaged the procureur's attention; almost half of the surviving dossiers were opened upon the receipt of a letter of denunciation. These letters were generally addressed directly to the procureur and were written by spouses, family members, neighbors, and, in some cases, children. The quality of the paper, the neatness of the hand, and the literacy of the author vary as much as the internal structure of the letters does not.[27] If the letter of denunciation qualifies as a particular genre of popular writing, then it was apparently well known throughout the many layers of class and generation that defined the population of fin-de-siècle Paris.[28]

These letters should not be taken as transparent communications of the dramas and conflicts of domestic life, even if we discount the role of what some might see as individual bias or motive; nor were they accepted at face value by the officers of the court to whom they were addressed. As evidence of the way in which the judicial apparatus found the raw materials for the cases it constructed, however, the letters of denunciation can be unpacked in other, ultimately more revealing ways. Each text, for example, takes as its rhetorical point of departure the collapse of individual or community tolerance for witnessing—or experiencing—what its author considered dangerous abuse. Each describes a particular vision of the "unfit" parent. Each fuses the "evidence" of abuse provided by specific occurrences to the insider's "knowledge" of the parent's moral profile. In short, the letters provide an opening into popular understandings of the operation of justice and the way in which the law was redeployed for the brief moments it seemed to be at their disposal. It illuminates the important role the ordinary social actor played in the law's interpretation and application.

---

[27] These letters, written between about 1898 and 1906, suggest the success of the Ferry Laws of the early 1880s, which called for universal primary education. The letters written by children tend to show fewer grammatical errors and misspellings than those written by the generation of their grandparents and even those written by adults in their twenties and thirties. According to Carlo Cipolla's reading of French census data, by 1901 only 3 percent of Parisians (men and women) over the age of ten were counted as illiterate, whereas the rate for all of France was 17 percent. See Carlo M. Cipolla, *Literacy and Development in the West* (Baltimore: Penguin Books, 1969). For a comprehensive discussion of literacy and primary education in France, see also François Furet and Jacques Ozouf, *Lire et écrire: L'alphabétisation des Français de Calvin à Jules Ferry*, 2 vols. (Paris: Editions de Minuit, 1977). See also James Smith Allen, *In the Public Eye: A History of Reading in Modern France, 1800–1940* (Princeton: Princeton University Press, 1991).

[28] On popular letter-writing practices in the nineteenth century, see Roger Chartier, ed., *La Correspondance: Usages de la lettre au XIXe siècle* (Paris: Fayard, 1991).

Above all, the letters must be read as supremely self-conscious and "interested" narratives. They are fictions, in the sense articulated by Natalie Davis in her book on sixteenth-century letters of supplication, in that they are highly crafted accounts designed to move and persuade a powerful addressee. Their "truths" cannot be disentangled from the authors' highly circumscribed choice of "language, detail, and order."[29] In the letter of denunciation, form and force of persuasion derived not only from the admixture of personal interest and empathy but also from the careful mimicking of legalistic language and logic, and from the attempt to render popular mores compatible with a particular—and not always complete or useful—understanding of the norms of the law and its jurisprudence.[30] Finally, the letters were suffused with—and shaped by—fin-de-siècle obsessions with journalistic and fictional scandals, with the effects of truth produced through recourse to rational, empirically grounded modes of representation, and with the revelation of unexpected causal connections.

Through the invocation of conventional structures of legal discourse and reportage, the letters "made cases." They presented the facts, examples, and observations on which, the authors argued, the danger to the child or children in question could be established. "I have the honor," wrote one young girl addressing the procureur on her own behalf, "to submit to your esteemed consideration the following facts." "I have the honor," a grandmother began her letter, "to set forth [*exposer*] the following facts for you."[31] "It is a matter of a little girl," began another appeal to the procureur.[32]

The parallels between these openings and the language and form of the prosecutor's formal exposition to the court cannot be accidental. Here, as in the prosecution's account of a case against an unfit parent, the emphasis lay on the exposition of relevant facts and on the concurrent exposure of the accused's essential moral character. The facts introduced into the letters of denunciation, like those foregrounded in the prosecution's constructions,

---

[29] See Natalie Zemon Davis, *Fiction in the Archives: Pardon Tales and Their Tellers in Sixteenth-Century France* (Stanford: Stanford University Press, 1987), 3. On style, narrative, and the complexities of justice in the eighteenth century, see Sarah Maza, *Private Lives and Public Affairs: The Causes Célèbres of Prerevolutionary France* (Berkeley: University of California Press, 1993). Ruth Harris treats the question of stylization and the production of juridical truth in nineteenth-century criminal courts in *Murders and Madness*, esp. 213–28.

[30] An exemplary approach to this general problem can be found in Michael Sonenscher's work on labor and law in the eighteenth century, *The Hatters of Eighteenth-Century France* (Berkeley: University of California Press, 1987), and *Work and Wages: Natural Law, Politics, and the Eighteenth-Century French Trades* (Cambridge: Cambridge University Press, 1989). For a comparative approach to popular knowledge and the law, see Mindie Lazarus Black and Susan F. Hirsch, eds., *Contested States: Law, Hegemony, and Resistance* (London: Routledge, 1994).

[31] ADS, D3 U7, Dossier 2711 (1906).

[32] Ibid., Dossier 1318 (1900).

tended to combine accounts of particular events with assertions about the true and enduring features of an individual's moral nature. *Facts*, in other words, signified both carefully narrated events and essential interpretations.

Thus, for example, a neighbor denounced one Mme. Valerie S. with the exposition of the following facts: Mme. S., the author asserted, was "without resources, almost mad, and alcoholic," and "incapable of rearing her child." One time, she added, "the mother, drunk, took the child to a painter . . . to have her pose entirely nude." Another time, she "had to intervene to prevent the mother from strangling the little one." The child finally had been forced to flee from a domestic life made intolerable by her mother's "cohabitation with [a] man who disgusts her and whose relationship with her mother she cannot comprehend." In the opinion of the author, these incidents revealed Valerie's deeply ingrained and dangerous proclivity to vice.

The neighbor offered confirmation of her interpretation as well, arguing against the common misrepresentation of Mme. S. as one of the most respectable members of the community. Thus, the letter concluded, the procureur should also take note of the facts that Mme. S. had been fired from her job as a nurse by the head doctor, who "identified her as alcoholic and mentally deficient." The local priest, the child's godfather, likewise had described Mme. S. as "deficient and incapable of rearing the child." No doubt the moral authority gained in naming these particularly authoritative witnesses was lost neither on the letter's author nor on the procureur. Ironically, the case of Mme. S. is one of the few among the dossiers in which the local priest appears to have been invoked as an expert on the moral life of a particular family. On one hand, this may testify to a thorough secularization of the Paris justice bureaucracy by the 1880s. On the other hand, it may be the expression of the decline in popular religiosity by the end of the nineteenth century, as historian Pierre Sorlin has argued.[33]

The denunciation in the case of Mme. S. and others like it also followed the narrative model provided on a daily basis in the *faits divers* columns—a hybrid of what we might call the metropolitan news roundup and the most sensational yellow journalism devoted to "miracles" and acts of inhuman violence—in the popular press. At least one investigation, moreover, was directly affected by the existence of the faits divers. On 22 August 1906 a newspaper item entitled "A Bad Father" appeared in the faits divers of the *Petit Parisien*.[34] "A revolting scene took place last night at number 29 rue de la Pointe d'Ivry, in the quarter of la Gare," the column began. The article, like the letters, combined the description of habits and reputations with the

---

[33] ADS, D3 U7, Dossier 3172 (1908). Pierre Sorlin, *La Société française*, vol. 1, *1840–1914* (Paris: Arthaud, 1969), 211–17. Gérard Cholvy and Yves-Marie Hilaire argue for a more complex understanding of the variations in nineteenth-century religious practice in *Histoire religieuse de la France contemporaine, 1800/1880* (Paris: Bibliothèque historique Privat, 1990).

[34] The clipping from *Le Petit Parisien* was included in Dossier 2735 (1906).

narration of a clear sequence of events. Monsieur C., it reported, "was given to drink. In order to gratify his vice, he did not work." Mme. C., an invalid, had recently passed away. The care and support of the family had been left to the eldest daughter. "This sad event," the article added in comment, "in no way modified the father's behavior." The latter regularly threatened his daughter, "whose conduct, meanwhile, was admired throughout the neighborhood." The tale then turned to the particular. The previous evening, the father had come home drunk and struck his daughter, who then had fled, taking her two brothers with her. All three children had been taken in by "kindly" neighbors. The article concluded with the note that "[a] complaint was lodged at the office of M. Rocher, commissaire of the quarter, and a request for the divestiture of paternal authority was entered."

The circulation of popular papers such as *Le Petit Parisien* expanded dramatically in the very years the civil court began to take on the question of abandon moral.[35] Thus the faits divers column provided a growing Parisian reading public with a veritable primer, instructing it not only in the art of moral diagnosis but in how to tie the narration of events and the interpretation of behavior to an appeal directed at public authorities. It also taught narrative strategies designed to make apparent order out of unfixed signs, the same strategies that provided the court with the foundation for legal action.[36] Other publications, such as the *Gazette des Tribunaux*, also made the structure and language of legal proceedings available for popular consumption. The appetite for crime fiction, with its own logic of exposition, disclosure, and decoding, appeared toward the end of the century to be insatiable.[37]

---

[35] Between 1889 and 1900 the number of issues of *Le Petit Parisien* printed per day rose from three hundred thousand to more than one million, whereas other papers in the same genre, such as *Le Petit Journal*, had already reached a daily printing of more than nine hundred thousand in the 1890s. Rising literacy as a result of the Ferry laws on primary education, according to one historian, again played an important role in this readership explosion. See Micheline Dupuy, *Le Petit Parisien: İLe plus fort tirage des journaux du monde entier*M (Paris: Plon, 1989), esp. 56, 60, 67. On newspapers and popular reading practices in Paris around the turn of the twentieth century, see A.-M. Thiesse, "Mutations et permanences de la culture populaire: La lecture à la Belle Epoque," *Annales: Economies, Société, Civilisations* 39, no. 1 (1984), esp. 73–74.

[36] On the structure of the faits divers, and in particular on the "literary" construction of the relationship between effect and cause in the fait divers, see Roland Barthes, "Structure du fait divers," in his collected *Essais critiques* (Paris: Editions du Seuil, 1964). For a more thematic analysis, see Alain Monestier, ed., *Le Fait divers*, catalog, Musée national des arts et traditions populaires (Paris: Editions de la Réunion des musées nationaux, 1982). On the sensational reporting of crime in the popular press, see Nye, *Crime, Madness, and Politics*, esp. 203–14. Foucault is also useful here for his stress on the importance of the fait divers as a frame for popular images of delinquency in the nineteenth century and for making crime into material for mass consumption (Foucault, *Discipline and Punish*, 286–88).

[37] The popularity of Eugène-François Vidocq's memoirs remains an excellent index of the reading public's interest in crime stories. First published in 1828, Vidocq's memoirs appeared in multiple revised editions, abridgments, and extracts across the century (Vidocq, *Mémoires de*

Given the growth of the Parisian police force, the importance of law in the regulation of society, and the increasingly litigious nature of the French during the Third Republic, moreover, it is likely that many people could claim at least one personal encounter with the judicial system.

If the structure of the letters speaks to a familiarity with the general rules of juridical prose and the language of criminological explication, the selection of incidents they included, as well as the choice of modifiers used to describe the moral condition of a parent, resonated with a language particular to the law of 1889. One author, writing to denounce his wife, explained that his mother-in-law had been "scandalized by his daughter's conduct," where paragraph 6 of the second article of the law noted that "notorious and scandalous misconduct" could serve as definite grounds for a decision of déchéance. Other letters emphasized drunkenness (*ivrognerie*) and the frequency of abuse (*mauvais traitements*), which were also addressed in paragraph 6, the catalog of parental misconduct most open to interpretation in the entire text of the law.[38]

Two letters do suggest that some authors might have had far more than a passing familiarity with the specific tenets of the law on abandon moral. One, written anonymously by a member of a child protection society, included in his litany of accusations frequent references to "debauchery," "misconduct," and "drunkenness," again, all formal terms of the law.[39] No doubt the protection societies, like the author's own Société de sauvetage de l'enfance, provided their members with abundant information about the law and its provisions, and they may well have encouraged vigilant members to

---

Vidocq, chef de la police de Sûreté, jusqu'en 1827 [Paris: Tenon, 1828–29]). Eugène Sue's *Les Mystères de Paris* realized similar success from its first publication in serialized form in the early 1840s. See Pierre Orecchioni, "Eugène Sue: Mesure d'un succès," *Europe* (1982): 643–44. See also Louis Chevalier's classic but problematic discussion of nineteenth-century literature centered on crime in *Laboring Classes and Dangerous Classes in Paris during the First Half of the Nineteenth Century*, trans. Frank Jellinek (Princeton: Princeton University Press, 1973). On the intersection of literacy and social concerns in the crime fiction of the nineteenth century, see D. A. Miller, *The Novel and the Police* (Berkeley: University of California Press, 1988).

[38] ADS, D3 U7, Dossier 2699 (1906). Whereas other paragraphs in articles 1 and 2 list specific acts or criminal convictions for which parents can be deprived of their rights, paragraph 6 describes the less tangible aspects of parents' moral status. It states that legal authority can be taken from parents who, "by their habitual drunkenness, their notorious and scandalous misconduct, or by mistreatment, compromise the health, the safety, [or] the morality of their children." *Mauvais traitments*, it should be added, did not necessarily refer to physical abuse, which was not treated explicitly in protective legislation until "la loi sur la répression des violences, voies de fait, actes de cruauté et attentats commis envers les enfants" (law on the suppression of violence, assault, acts of cruelty and attacks committed against children) was passed in 1898. The different status of physical abuse is also reflected in the penalties dictated by the 1898 law, a criminal measure.

[39] ADS, D3 U7, Dossier 2702 (1906).

present their own charges of parental misconduct in a form as close to the state's text as possible.[40]

The second letter, addressed to the prosecutor by the family of a disbarred lawyer earning his living as a journalist in Algeria, contended that the child's father "abandoned her morally," one of the surprisingly few uses of the law's official title in these letters. It also included the direct citation of articles 2 and 3 of the law of 1889, by virtue of which, the authors argued, the unfit father should be divested of his rights.[41]

The vocabulary shared by accusers and the text of the law of 1889 does not necessarily imply that these letters were written with a copy of the law on the author's desk, although at times this may perhaps have been the case. Instead, the widespread use of a particular moral language suggests that the law owed as much to the popular understanding of abuse and immoral conduct as the letters owed to the codified provisions of the law. Unless they were the sheer instruments of malice, the letters had to carry weight not only with the office of the prosecutor but also in the experience of the accuser. The act of bearing witness, in other words, was powerfully shaped by the same cultural medium in which the legal text itself had come to life.

While the letters resounded with the language of law and official legal procedure, they also incorporated certain formal and stylistic elements that contradicted the tenets of that language when used in its official milieu. In particular, the authors tended to emphasize their own relationship to the people and events they described, and their personal stake—at least as they presented it—in the state's intervention. The power of their accounts thus relied not on the disinterested and detached reproduction of a true story, as it did in the prosecution's exposition, but in the situated and interested nature of their testimony.

This strategy is manifest in a letter accusing one Mme. G. of exposing her daughter to moral danger. The accuser, the Widow D., explained her own interest in bringing the facts of a case of parental misconduct to his attention. Eight days ago, she wrote in her letter to the procureur, she had found and taken in from the street a naked and "repulsively dirty" five-year-old girl (a condition "betraying in an irrefutable fashion," she added parenthetically, "the immorality of the environment in which she lives"). The widow went on to provide details about the abuses the child had suffered at home, which, she explained, she personally had been able to extract "from the mouth of

---

[40] Domenique Dessertine has written a comprehensive study of the Société de sauvetage in Lyons, after Paris, France's second center of activism around the enfant moralement abandonné (Dessertine, *La Société lyonnaise pour le sauvetage de l'enfance, (1890–1960): Face à l'enfance en danger, un siècle d'expérience de l'internat et du placement familial* [Toulouse: Erès, 1990]).

[41] ADS, D3 U7, Dossier 1713 (1901).

the little victim herself." As she closed her request for action, the Widow D. stressed her own charity and empathy.

> I have sheltered this little girl, terrorized by abuse [*mauvais traitements*], for the past ten days. I cannot keep her any longer. . . . I hope, Monsieur le Procureur, that your generous intervention will provide this unhappy child with a happier future.

Ten witnesses added their names to that of Mme. D., she explained, as evidence of their support for her accusations and, implicitly, as an endorsement of the author's character.[42]

Even the anonymous letters of denunciation played on the authors' relation to the family, their interest in its moral essence and in the fate of the children, and their means of access to the intimate life of the family. Because reputation in the community and information provided from within the family were privileged evidence in the process of establishing the truth of the charge, this specificity could not have been mere narrative convention. It suggests that the moral foundation of a family's domestic life was not taken to be a private matter in the nineteenth century but was constituted through the play of rumor and reputation that was, in the ongoing, collective, and public process of judgment, a sum of appearances. What actually went on behind closed doors could not then and cannot now be recovered with certainty. These narratives suggest, however, that a family's private life was in essence very much a public matter. The structure of these letters also reveals the existence of a strong popular interest in delimiting the private and the familial as spaces within an apparently totalizing regime of public order.[43]

Surprisingly, children sometimes wrote directly to the procureur themselves. Their letters appear to have adhered to a structure similar to that of the letters sent by adults. They too tended to open by announcing the intention to "lay out the following facts" and then presenting a melange of characterological analysis, descriptions of habits and long-standing domestic conditions, and the detailed narration of particularly revealing incidents. They too stressed the author's privileged position in the exposure of private domestic ills.

The child's narrative position, however, was unique. The denouncing au-

---

[42] Ibid., Dossier 2714 (1906).

[43] On the experience of interpenetrating neighborhood and family life among the Parisian working classes, see Arlette Farge, *La Vie fragile: Violences, pouvoirs, et solidarités à Paris au XVIIIe siècle* (Paris: Hachette, 1986), recently translated by Carol Shelton as *Fragile Lives: Violence, Power, and Solidarity in Eighteenth-Century Paris* (Cambridge: Harvard University Press, 1993). See also David Garrioch, *Neighborhood and Community in Paris, 1740–1790* (Cambridge: Cambridge University Press, 1986), and Georg'Ann Cattelona, "Control and Collaboration: The Role of Women in Regulating Female Sexual Behavior in Early Modern Marseille," *French Historical Studies* 18, no. 1 (spring 1993): 13–33.

thor was also the victim, the direct object of both the parents' abuses and the procureur's interest. Apparently uncomfortable with the betrayal of their own parents, they often stressed the severity of their suffering and the extent of their virtuous forbearance. Marthe F., for example, described how her mother had physically abused her and repeatedly attempted to force her into prostitution, "[a] veritable persecution," she explained, "of which I was the victim." "Monsieur le procureur de la Republique," the appeal closed, "I am a respectable girl and I want to earn my living honorably."[44] Another letter came from a boy of fifteen, who alleged that his mother took many lovers "who beat me and force me to call them father." He also claimed that his mother had once forced him to act as courier in her traffic in stolen wine, had accused him of stealing from her in the course of that illicit transaction, and then had attacked him with an iron. "Monsieur," young Léon J. entreated the prosecutor at the end of his account, "I want very much to remain a good boy rather than becoming a *vicieux*—and who knows, later a criminal—from witnessing the kind of business I mentioned above."[45]

The position of the author as victim allowed these children both to appeal for specific judicial action (although in this small sample of letters few did) and, more commonly, to plead for the prosecutor to extend protection and mercy to them. "I come to put myself under your benevolent protection and very humbly beg you to tell me where my duty lies," wrote one fifteen-year-old girl who desperately sought safe refuge from her father and his new companion. Another girl, almost twenty at the time she wrote to the procureur, ended her description of the "ten years of suffering in my parents' house" with the plea only that the prosecutor "protect me from their attacks." A third girl, also aged fifteen, described the neglect that she and her sister had suffered since their father had remarried. "[W]e place our trust in you, monsieur le Procureur, that you might make our father remember that he has daughters."[46] Only Marthe F., in her second letter to the procureur, announced that she was seeking a judgment of déchéance and that she had already filed a request for déchéance maternelle against her mother.

The fact that several of these juvenile authors acknowledged that their letters, and the decision to send them, were the product of a consultation with the local commissaire also suggests that many of these denunciations had been profoundly shaped by the contribution of police agents. Such were the circumstances, for example, behind the production of Marthe F.'s complaint against her mother and her decision to leave home. "I only resolved to do this today and only after having consulted *Mr. le Commissaire de Police de Lilas*, to whom I explained my situation. It was he who . . . advised me to

[44] ADS, D3 U7, Dossier 1490 (1901).
[45] Ibid., Dossier 1687 (1901).
[46] Ibid., Dossiers 2711 (1906), 2753 (1906), and 854 (1898).

write to you," she explained to the procureur in her first letter.[47] The coherence of these accusations and their authors' apparent familiarity with the language and terms of the law may perhaps be explained by ad hoc procedural and lexical tutorials provided by the local officials. Consultation with the local commissaires in fact appears to have been common practice in the effort to resolve domestic struggles. One father, whose request to have his son placed in correction later returned to haunt him, noted in his letter to the presiding judge that he was entering his plea for the temporary incarceration of his son after describing his son's "terrible conduct" to Monsieur le Commissaire de Police.[48] What may have begun as undirected or inchoate grievances, in other words, may well have been tailored to the norms of the law in passing through these first layers of judicial filtering provided by the local precinct station.

The children's admission that the commissaire had guided their actions may also begin to explain the process by which knowledge about the law, its requirements, and its moral vocabulary was diffused throughout the urban population at large. It suggests that at the local level representatives of the state willingly put the law into the array of tools with which ordinary people could settle their affairs, informing them of their right to use it if they seemed unaware of its existence or utility. This picture is a far cry, then, from the more common assumption in the history of social welfare that unwelcome agents of public order indiscriminately exploited the law as a passkey to the most intimate spaces of family life.

At the same time, however, in these letters we get a clear if fleeting glimpse of what Foucault has described as power's "capillary form of existence." As much as the law appeared to invest ordinary people with the capacity for autonomous action, and as much as they seemed to have initiated and directed the movement of the law's application, their agency, indeed the very possibility of their agency, was immediately and indelibly inscribed within the terms of the law and the juridical apparatus built around it. And in many instances, an apparently free act of will eventually brought the deprivation of a significant part of the civil identity on which that act had been predicated. As the course of the investigations provoked by these initial suspicions and complaints reveals, the position of these independent actors ultimately became as circumscribed by the mechanisms of justice as that of the people they accused.[49]

---

[47] Ibid., Dossier 1490 (1901).

[48] Ibid., Dossier 2739 (1906). The full extent of the commissaire's particular role in local and private affairs awaits further research.

[49] Foucault, "Prison Talk," in *Power/Knowledge: Selected Interviews and Other Writings, 1972–1977*, ed. and trans. Colin Gordon et al. (New York: Pantheon, 1980), 39.

CHAPTER 5

Investigation

ACCIDENT, deflection, and direct solicitation all underlay the initiatory gestures that first set the wheels of justice in motion. In each of those first movements, the law of 1889 began to be invoked, interpreted, and contested well before the cases were ever presented to a judge or entered the annals of French jurisprudence. Individuals with various kinds of knowledge of the law claimed that the stories they presented to the public authorities fell clearly within the law's reach. Similarly, public authorities attempted to demonstrate that the facts they discovered lined themselves up under the sign of the law that they, as its representatives and guardians, knew from a superior vantage point. In these first turns of the machinery of justice, the room for creative application of the law to one's own domestic struggles was clearly delineated by the way in which the judicial apparatus invited or allowed that application. Quite soon, however, the gears meshed, other parts of the machine were engaged, and an increasingly regularized movement of justice gained momentum.

As that movement widened and quickened, however, it was accompanied by an increase in friction between the state and the objects of its examination and, at times, between some of the more ill-fitting gears of the state apparatus. The problems of evidence and the narrative representation of moral status also grew more complex as police and magistracy attempted to divine the presence of a viable case. A veil of epistemological uncertainty darkened the cases of abandon moral that were produced through the inquiries that followed the first stirrings of official suspicion. In the best-made cases, uncertainty could be banished as various oblique representations of a particular private domestic condition harmonized and reinforced each other's claims. At worst, authorities were left with a snarl of conflicting and unstable testimony that made it impossible to establish "the negative fact" of moral abandonment with any confidence.[1]

To be sure, these processes of "truth making" remain common to most efforts of juridical inquiry. In instantiating the law on abandon moral, however, these investigations and the truths they produced had effects far beyond the evolution of a particular case. The investigations, and particularly the efforts to reconcile narratives of good and bad parenthood produced in both official and popular sites, resulted in a new form of practical moral codifica-

---

[1] Emile Alcindor, *Les Enfants assistés* (Paris: Emile Paul, 1912), 85.

tion. Making cases of abandon moral, in short, also contributed to the making of morality in modern France.

Making moral order through the application and interpretation of law happened locally, case by case. How, then, did the courts transform raw suspicions and allegations into "confirmed" cases of abandon moral? The procureur usually opened an investigation as soon as he received the first request to do so, be it from police, judge, neighbor, relative, or child.[2] He delegated the actual work of the inquiry, however, to three other sets of officials working in the Parisian institutions of justice: the local commissaire de police; agents of the Service de Sûreté at the central Prefecture de Police; and the justice of the peace (*juge de paix*) presiding in the quarter of Paris in which the accused parents were officially domiciled.[3] Each branch would conduct its investigation separately and send the results directly to the procureur, who would then present the case to the judge presiding over the Seine's tribunal de première instance. These three sites of inquiry appeared to have been the essential minimum in each case documented in the surviving files, although in some cases, as we shall see, other officials and designated experts were also engaged in the process of the investigation.

Take, for example, the case of Léon and Pauline H. A dossier was opened by the Parquet, or procureur's office, after the prefecture of police completed a report on Léon and his family dated 2 December 1905.[4] That report, provoked by the daughter's arrest for solicitation on 13 November, summarized the history of Léon's employment as an administrator and police captain in Algeria until his forced retirement and his return to Paris in 1901. Although

---

[2] Whereas in criminal proceedings the supervision of this sort of investigation was left to a special magistrate, *le juge d'instruction*, in civil affairs the entire investigation was orchestrated by the procureur's office in the court of first instance. On the history and organization of French criminal justice, see Benjamin F. Martin, *Crime and Criminal Justice under the Third Republic: The Shame of Marianne* (Baton Rouge: Louisiana State University Press, 1990), esp. chaps. 4–5.

[3] Each arrondissement in Third Republic Paris was divided into four quarters, each of which had a precinct station. The central station, or *commissariat*, for the arrondissement was located in one of those quarters and was generally open between 8 A.M. and 10 P.M. The Sûreté was a separate branch of the central police administration in Paris and conducted all criminal investigations, as well as background checks, surveillance operations, and the taking of testimony. In 1881 the vice squad, or Service de Moeurs, was merged into the Service de Sûreté. All branches of the police in France were, like the administration of the Bureau of Public Assistance, ultimately under the authority of the Ministry of the Interior. The juge de paix, however, was appointed with lifetime tenure and served as all-purpose arbitrator in his community. He also presided over some civil proceedings and could be consulted in criminal cases under consideration elsewhere in the judiciary system. In the case of abandon moral, the juge de paix also served in this advisory capacity (Martin, *Crime and Criminal Justice*, 42–53, 166). See also Jill Harsin, *Policing Prostitution in Nineteenth-Century Paris* (Princeton: Princeton University Press, 1985), esp. 136, 337–38.

[4] ADS, D3 U7, Dossier 2541 (1905).

Léon had taken a degree in law, he had not been able to find employment, and despite his government pension, the family had been reduced to selling its possessions, taking furnished rooms, and turning to charity. Given Léon's income, the report's author found this degree of economic distress "abnormal" and "difficult to explain." The report also addressed the state of the family's dwelling, where, the author remarked, "filth reigns." Of the four-teen-year-old girl, the agent noted rather laconically that she was "*vicieuse* and prostitutes herself." The mother, who sold "knickknacks"—"bouquets, paper, etc."—in the street with her daughter, had once tried to kill herself by jumping from the window. The report concluded, as was typical of many official inquiries on the civil, economic, and moral status of a family, with the agent's assessment of what he had observed: "Under these conditions, we can only conclude that it is necessary to remove the young Marthe H . . . from her milieu." One week after this report was completed, the head of the first division wrote a note to the procureur advising him that Marthe appeared to be "in moral danger" and that the procureur should begin his own investigation of her case immediately.

On 26 December the justice of the peace of the fourth arrondissement, after receiving the procureur's request for his official opinion on whether a request for déchéance should be submitted to the court, completed his own report. Far less detailed than the initial police inquiry, the judge noted merely that the family H. appeared to live exclusively off Léon's pension. The justice described the mother as "neurotic" and observed that when he had confronted her with the possibility of losing her child, she had "protested energetically." It was possible, the judge remarked, that the parents were exploiting their daughter, but in the end he could not endorse the legal divestiture of their rights.

One month later, the commissaire of the quarter of Saint Gervais in the fourth arrondissement began his own two-day-long investigation, taking statements from the mother, Pauline H., and from several other residents of the neighborhood. In her interview of 24 January 1906, according to the summary of the inquiry, Pauline had provided "precise information" but had protested against the allegations brought against her family. She claimed that her daughter was not vicious, that she did not walk the streets, and that she had never had a single lover. Pauline provided the police with a list of witnesses who would support her claims.

The neighbors and colodgers interviewed that day varied in the amount of information they could or were willing to provide. According to the police report on the interviews, the coal merchant from whom the family bought their fuel stated only that he "knew nothing about the family." A former landlord, however, was far more forthcoming. He claimed that the family H. depended exclusively on charity and noted that Léon H. spent all his time in bed. When strangers arrived, he remarked, "[T]he [aforementioned] H . . .

would leave his bed and lie down on the floor. It was in that position that he received his visitors." He also accused the husband and wife of morphine addiction and charged that the daughter "hung around with the neighborhood thugs" and "seemed to have nothing more to learn about sex."

Two days later the inquiry continued. The commissaire took statements from the family's current landlady, who contended that they never paid their rent. Whenever she threatened Léon H. with eviction, she added, "[H]e gets in bed and won't budge from it." She too accused Léon and Pauline of a morphine habit, which, in her opinion, must cost the family at least three francs a day, a significant sum for the family, since the Prefecture put Léon H.'s pension at 1,250 francs per year. Finally, she claimed that their room, in which there was but one bed, remained in a state of "repulsive filth."[5]

As their last witness, the police interviewed the porter at the lodging house. He claimed that Léon and his wife both spent all their time in bed and that they were often visited at home by various emissaries from the Bureau of Public Assistance and other charities. He had observed, he added, that the daughter "goes out at night and hangs around with thugs." He had also refused to rent temporary rooms to her and her "friends," he added, "because the girl had the demeanor of a prostitute."

Two other documents completed the dossier: the Sûreté's rather brief report, dated 29 May 1906, and an undated internal memo from roughly the same time and addressed to an assistant prosecutor (*substitut*). The note, apparently from the procureur himself, summarized the important elements of the case as it had been established thus far. After remarking on the parents' denial that their daughter was a prostitute and the fact that the justice of the peace had advised against a judgment of déchéance, the procureur suggested in the note that the case could be pursued only if supplementary investigations were conducted. The case, opened on 11 December 1905, was shelved on 9 June of the following year.

The investigation of Léon and Pauline H. exemplifies the long and circuitous route of the procureur's investigation. From criminal court to precinct station, from justice of the peace to concierge, representations of Léon and Pauline were tested against the elusive demands of the law and the court. Throughout the investigation, officials wrestled with the flexibility of the "immoral conduct" clause. How far could the images of the couple's behavior and habits be taken in the establishment of "notorious and scandalous misconduct"? In the ongoing interpretive improvisation that marked these inquiries, representations of this family's "abnormal" economic cir-

---

[5] On the importance of domestic hygiene in reading the morality of the poor, see Ann-Louise Shapiro, *Housing the Poor of Paris, 1850–1902* (Madison: University of Wisconsin Press, 1985).

cumstances, its fall into addiction, sloth, and filth, and the daughter's appearance of sexual availability were aligned to give particular substance to the law's empty category. Culturally and historically potent norms of "proper" family life, of individual conduct, and of reputation, in other words, were put to work filling in the law's mostly unspoken requirements. And conversely, the process of producing a case articulated and reinforced these codes of family morality. The investigation of Léon and Pauline also demonstrates the relative value of the various representations and interpretations the police collected. Not surprisingly, an informed nay from the justice of the peace or the suspicion asserted by the local commissaire usually drowned out the voices of ordinary individuals, whose authority carried less weight with the prosecutor and his staff.

The investigation of Léon and Pauline H. took roughly six months to complete. Although a reliable average length of time between the opening and closing of a case cannot be established from this sample of dossiers, the cycles of investigation represented here ranged between one month and two years, including several files that were reopened. A brief period of inquiry did not necessarily mean that the case had been dropped any more than a long period meant the irrefutable establishment of juridical truths. The court divested one Widow G. of her parental rights in 1902 after an investigation lasting only one month.[6] By contrast, the procureur pursued the case of Jean Baptiste B. for well over a year, until it was eventually shelved in early 1907.[7]

Although the case of Léon and Pauline passed only into the hands of the procureur, the agents of the Sûreté, the commissaire, and the juge de paix, additional official characters were called in for other investigations, and other types of formal documents appeared in the files. The procureur, for example, might send requests for information to commissaires and justices in other towns and even other departments when a parent had moved from Paris, had recently moved to Paris from another region, or could not be located at all. Particularly in cases originating in conviction, arrest, or the mere allegation of criminal activity, a request often went out for a copy of the accused's criminal record. Official extracts from the municipal civil registries were common to all but the most slender dossiers, especially the registration of marriages, births, deaths, and divorces, documents confirming the civil status of the family members under investigation.

Although they were not solicited by the prosecutor, certificates of medical examination also appear in some of the dossiers. In general, fin-de-siècle France saw a great explosion in the role the medical expert would play in the

[6] ADS, D3 U7, Dossier 1702 (1901)
[7] Ibid., Dossier 2681 (1905).

exercise of justice, where doctors testified with increasing frequency in criminal trials.[8] As they had not been central figures in the drafting of the law of 1889, however, physicians did not yet have a fixed place in the prosecution of cases of abandon moral, even those based in an allegation of a parent's physical or sexual assaults on his or her children. The medical certificates preserved in these dossiers had in fact been produced on the initiative of family members eager to provide further evidence of either guilt or innocence. Thus, for example, in a case opened in 1906, Mme. Jeanne C. had taken her children to a doctor for physical examination to strengthen her charge that her husband was abusing them sexually. Despite the fact that it did not provide the confirmation she sought, the doctor's statement was included in the prosecution's dossier. The manner in which Jeanne C. provided the procureur with evidence that ultimately did nothing to support her claims suggests that the transfer of information between doctor and magistrate, like the movements of the rouages as a whole, could not be controlled once it had been initiated. The conduits of official documentation had, by the turn of the century, clearly developed an order of their own.[9]

Despite the magistracy's obvious interest in expert opinion, making a case against a parent suspected of abandon moral was equally if not more dependent on the testimony of the amateur. Neighbors, friends, boarders, and landlords provided the best and in many ways the only means by which the court and the police could probe the secret recesses of family life. These witnesses appear not to have suffered from reticence in presenting their own impressions of the events and characters in question. They were, moreover, often as deft in making moral judgments, and as quick to make them, as the investigating officials. The French proverb A good reputation is worth more than a belt of gold (*Bonne renommé valait mieux que ceinture dorée*) must surely have based its aphoristic truth in the historical and cultural power of community opinion in the most ordinary of social relations.

Neighbors certainly played an important part in the investigation of young

---

[8] See Ruth Harris, *Murders and Madness: Medicine, Law, and Society in the Fin de Siècle* (Oxford: Clarendon Press, 1989), esp. 138–54, and Robert A. Nye, *Crime, Madness, and Politics in Modern France: The Medical Concept of National Decline* (Princeton: Princeton University Press, 1984), esp. chap. 7, "The Boundaries of Responsibility: Asylum Law and Legal Medicine in an Era of Social Defense."

[9] ADS, D3 U7, Dossier 3000 (1907). The medical statement is included in an attached dossier from 1906, which documents Jeanne C.'s first attempt to have her husband's parental rights withdrawn by the courts. Consulting doctors, however, even in cases where the physical abuse of a child was the central element of the case against an "unfit" parent, was by no means a common practice at this time. Jacques Donzelot argues that despite the increasingly important role of the social worker and the child psychiatrist, the investigation of cases of "endangered children" remained primarily in the hands of the police into the 1940s and 1950s. See Donzelot, *The Policing of Families*, trans. Robert Hurley (New York: Pantheon, 1979), 118.

Fanny L.'s charges against her father.[10] In the course of his investigation, the commissaire of the quarter of Folie-Méricourt took the statements of seven witnesses over two days in March and April 1898. These signed statements included one from a seamstress, who claimed she had a clear view from her window of what went on in the neighboring apartment, one from Fanny's employer, also a seamstress, who stated that Fanny "complains often of being mistreated by her parents," and one from Mme. de B., yet another seamstress, who testified that from her apartment on the same floor as that of Monsieur L. she heard "the sound of continual disputes and the cries of the two young girls who are being mistreated and whose parents batter them with coarse language." Other witnesses included the concierge at a former dwelling, who proclaimed that the conduct of Monsieur L. and his second wife had been "a daily scandal." Two other residents at Monsieur L.'s current address also claimed to have heard the noises of frequent dispute and mistreatment. The concierge of that building also testified that on the whole the family constituted "a bad household."[11]

Historians have often argued that the urban fabric of France has long been riddled with structures of mutual surveillance. Michelle Perrot, for example, contends that in working-class quarters in the nineteenth century "[t]he disapproval, tolerance, or indulgence of one's neighbors determined the law by which one lived."[12] Ironically, such conventions and social relations also determined the substance of "private life," particularly the private life that mattered most to investigating authorities. The moral aspect of intimate family relations was thus ultimately located not behind the closed doors of the individual dwelling but in the more permeable interpenetrating spaces of the building and the neighborhood. In this series of official statements, as in many others contained in the prosecutor's files, witnesses stressed their par-

---

[10] ADS, D3 U7, Dossier 854 (1898).

[11] For an illuminating and personal account of the life of a concierge, see Bonnie G. Smith, *Confessions of a Concierge: Madame Lucie's History of Twentieth-Century France* (New Haven: Yale University Press, 1985).

[12] Michelle Perrot, "Roles and Characters," in *From the Fires of Revolution to the Great War*, ed. Michelle Perrot, trans. Arthur Goldhammer, vol. 4 of *A History of Private Life*, ed. Philippe Ariès and Georges Duby (Cambridge: Belknap Press of Harvard University Press, 1990), 177. On urban life in the ancien régime, see Arlette Farge, *Fragile Lives: Violence, Power, and Solidarity in Eighteenth-Century Paris*, trans. Carol Shelton (Cambridge: Harvard University Press, 1993), and Farge, ed., *Vivons dans la rue à Paris au XVIIIe siècle* (Paris: Gallimard/Julliard, 1979). For an exemplary consideration of neighborhood relations, particularly on informal networks of cooperation among working-class women, see Christine Stansell's book on nineteenth-century New York, *City of Women: Sex and Class in New York, 1789–1860* (New York: Alfred A. Knopf, 1986), esp. 55–62. See also Susan Dwyer Amussen's suggestive exploration of the construction and use of reputation in the early modern English village, *An Ordered Society: Gender and Class in Early Modern England* (Oxford: Basil Blackwell, 1988), 95–133.

ticular point of access to the private affairs of their neighbors: the open window, the thin wall, the stairwell, the doorway. The credibility of their testimony derived from a confidence, shared in part by the procureur, that their information was privileged by the superior vantage of close and continuous physical proximity.

Neighbors also proved themselves quick to offer a definitive interpretation of the evidence they presented, and quick in particular to tie it into a master narrative they assumed to be at the heart of the inquiry. In these amateur interpretations, the aural experience of one's neighbors' domestic quarrels signified the truth of the implied charge of mistreatment, and the keeping of a tidy room proved that the charge of parental neglect must be unfounded. Thus, for example, one Widow D. wrote in her 1906 letter to the procureur that she had found five-year-old Marcelle G. in the street one day, "completely naked" and "repulsively filthy." Marcelle's situation, Widow D. explained in a parenthetical remark, "indisputably reveal[ed] the immorality of the milieu in which she lived."[13] These sorts of accusations and interpretations provide an important window onto the site where popular understandings of the orderly and moral family intersected with the signs of moral danger as conceptualized by the agents of the law. They suggest once again the unacknowledged complicities produced at the intersections of official and popular norms and representations.

Establishing with certainty the essence of individual motive lies far beyond the scope of the historian's own prying eyes. Coercion and complicity, not always easily distinguishable, played a strong part in animating the law in its social context.[14] No doubt many people looked on these official requests for information as opportunities to settle old accounts. Others probably spoke to police with an eye toward establishing their own virtue, fearful that public authority might turn its sights on them. Still others, whose statements contradicted the accusations under investigation, may have acted out of personal or community loyalty.[15] It is no less likely, moreover, that some

---

[13] ADS, D3 U7, Dossier 2714 (1906). Widow D.'s letter is undated, but its place in the dossier suggests a date of composition somewhere around November 1906.

[14] On eighteenth-century roots of the complex relationship between police agents and the denizens of Paris, see Farge, *Fragile Lives*, esp. 131–68; Alan Williams, "Patterns of Conflict in Eighteenth-Century Parisian Families," *Journal of Family History 18*, no. 1 (1993), esp. 39–52; and Erica-Marie Benabou, *La Prostitution et la police des moeurs au XVIIIe siècle* (Paris: Librairie Académique Perrin, 1987). On the police in nineteenth-century Paris, see, among others, Harsin, *Policing Prostitution*, esp. 133–65, and Clive Emsley, "Policing the Streets of Early Nineteenth-Century Paris," *French History 1*, no. 2 (1987): 257–82. Several of the essays collected in Philippe Vigier et al., eds., *Maintien de l'ordre en France et en Europe au XIXe siècle* (Paris: Créaphis, 1987), also address the question of policing nineteenth-century Paris, placing particular emphasis on the role of the police in times of revolutionary disorder and the development of militant labor politics.

[15] In her book on prostitution in nineteenth-century Britain, Judith Walkowitz has also sug-

came to the support of their suspected neighbors out of solidarity against the prying eyes of the police. Some letters of denunciation explicitly justified the willingness to speak against a neighbor with assertions of genuine concern for the well-being of the children the authors believed to be endangered. "I am very concerned about the child," one woman wrote to the procureur in 1908. "If there is a way, I would like very much to adopt this child and take her from her mother's, where she is very unhappy and is provided only with a bad example."[16] Another letter, written anonymously in 1906, referred to the "child martyr" who could be observed from "an empty apartment" on the same floor as her parents', "alone in the kitchen at mealtime, gnawing on bones or licking empty or nearly empty plates." "Save this child," the letter concludes, "who, in everyone's opinion will be better off anywhere than with her parents."[17] Genuine concern for children such as these may well have been one of many factors that moved people who might otherwise despise and avoid the police.

The fact that the neighbors' statements lie embedded in official police reports also suggests, however, that coercion may have played an equally important a role as "intention" or humanitarian concern in the shaping of testimony, although it leaves fewer visible traces in the documents. A "request" from the police for an official statement might easily have caused the majority of Parisians to tremble, if not from guilt, then from fear of the less than gentle methods for which the police force was notorious. Waldeck-Rousseau, whose Ministry of the Interior supervised both the domestic police force and the Bureau of Public Assistance, expressed strong reservations about the use of police in the protection of endangered children, arguing that "the prefecture of police represents surveillance, force, and even repression, and that a project of assistance must on one side be all voluntary trust, and on the other, all benevolence."[18]

Waldeck-Rousseau's fear of police excesses was not unreasonable. Although relations with the local commissaire may have been somewhat smoothed by the lubricant of familiarity, the agents of the Sûreté—the central police investigation bureau—who also interviewed neighbors and collected statements, were well preceded by their reputation: the Sûreté was renowned throughout the nineteenth century for its brutal interrogations, for the extraction of confessions from suspects in the criminal cases they inves-

---

gested that neighborhood tolerance quickly gave way when public authorities began to exert pressure, particularly among the poor, although she gives more credence to the fear of economic penalty than she does to other kinds of forces that might shape relations between prostitutes, their neighbors, and agents of public order. See Judith R. Walkowitz, *Prostitution and Victorian Society: Women, Class, and the State* (Cambridge: Cambridge University Press, 1980), 201–8.

[16] ADS, D3 U7, Dossier 3172 (1908).

[17] Ibid., Dossier 2734 (1906).

[18] *JOS*, 11 May 1883, 465.

tigated, and even for the blatant manufacture and destruction of evidence. Although cases of suspected abandon moral were not criminal matters, and although the majority of the people interviewed were neither suspects nor the usual vulnerable informants typically employed by the agents of the Sûreté, any interaction with these officers was surely touched by the knowledge of both their methods and the minimal checks on their powers.[19] Even in these civil affairs, the structures and techniques of criminal investigation, as well as the instability of the testimony they produced, were thus incorporated into the regular procedural machinery devoted to the collection of evidence.

Investigation did not, however, stop with the interrogation of witnesses. Procedure also demanded that the police and the magistracy interview the parents and children who were the objects of the court's investigations. Their statements stand alongside and in dialogue with those of their acquaintances and neighbors that were entered into the official record. Not surprisingly, accused parents generally attempted to shut down the investigation by asserting their innocence and, at times, by turning on the people who had testified against them. Fanny L.'s father, for example, denied the charge that he beat and neglected his daughters, explaining to the police that his daughter's complaint was yet another instance of her general "insolence" and her hostility toward her new stepmother. Fanny's stepmother also attempted to undermine the credibility of both Fanny's complaint and the testimony of neighbors who claimed to have heard the sounds of mistreatment coming from their apartment. "If the neighbors heard them screaming," she protested in her statement, "it's because every time I wanted to chastise them, they went to the window to bring the neighbors. They have always wanted to get me in trouble with their father."[20] Although her charge of staged misrepresentation was an unusually creative way of casting doubt on both the testimony of the children and the neighbors' observations, it also revealed once more the degree to which evidence was understood to turn on the question of credible representation. Her explanation likewise underscored the endemic possibility of deception in both the construction and the apprehension of "facts" related to the juridical treatment of a family's moral life.

Statements made to police by accused parents also suggest that parents were routinely apprised not only of the imminent charge of abandon moral but also of the details of the information that had been provided by other witnesses. Denying the truth of the court's information in 1897, for example, one Monsieur Etienne M. systematically disputed the facts that supposedly revealed his moral deficiencies as a parent.[21] The record of Mme. Louise L.'s

---

[19] On the coercive aspect of interrogation in a criminal investigation and the centrality of the informant, see Martin, *Crime and Criminal Justice*, 44, 78–81.

[20] ADS, D3 U7, Dossier 854 (1898).

[21] Ibid., Dossier 825 (1897).

interrogation at the commissariat of Charenton in 1909 explains that the interview began with a formal reading of the charges of "debauchery" that had been leveled against her.[22]

Accident and lack of knowledge or foresight, so vivid in the origins of the cases, also played a role in the collection of evidence. In their efforts to justify or explain away the testimony of the neighborhood, parents often backed deeper into the charges they were attempting to elude. In 1898, for example, Ephième E. spoke with surprisingly consistent nonchalance of her daughter's sexual affairs and her own concern that the daughter's current lover's resources would not be adequate to support her daughter in the style to which he had initially accustomed her, thus unwittingly providing the best "evidence" of her own parental inadequacies.[23] Making a statement or responding to charges clearly had as dangerous consequences for the family caught in the machinery of justice as did the lodging of a complaint.

Children also had their opportunity to make statements to the authorities. Eugénie C., whose bad reputation and record of arrest had brought her parents under suspicion in 1897, denied that her parents were responsible for her actions. "If I steal," the statement she gave to the Sûreté reads, "it is because the individuals I frequent pushed me to do it, and they beat me."[24] Like their parents, the children questioned by the police appear to have been well aware of the informal accusations and the official suspicions that had inspired their interpellation. Some of the children revealed a fairly specific awareness of the law when they were questioned more closely. Eglantine C., for example, claimed to the commissaire that since her mother died, her father had been making sexual advances toward her. At the end of her statement, taken down in the first person in 1906, the eighteen-year-old declared: "I ask that an inquiry be carried out, that my father be dispossessed of his rights, and that a guardian be appointed for me."[25] Although it is quite likely that Eglantine received coaching from somewhere, perhaps from the police themselves, her statement suggests once more the degree to which the law was made available to the populace, and the degree to which ordinary people's invocation of it had significance in the complex operation of justice. In Eglantine's case, the court did in fact strip her father of his authority, this time in spite of the justice of the peace, who had advised against such a decision.

What becomes apparent in all of these documented investigations is the degree to which the effective operation of the machinery of justice depended on the piecemeal collection and interpretation of unstable subjective accounts. Each representation of the scene and characters under investigation

[22] Ibid., Dossier 3399 (1908).
[23] Ibid., Dossier 849 (1897).
[24] Ibid., Dossier 826 (1897).
[25] Ibid., Dossier 2735 (1906).

was inflected by the tones of individual interest, each one shaped by the witness's particular point of contact with the family, each one weighted by the relative status and credibility of the author, and each one compromised by its production through an encounter with agents who, as Waldeck-Rousseau had put it, represented "surveillance, force, and even repression."

The logic of investigative procedure did not ignore the difficulties inherent in making a case from these aggregates of highly charged and unevenly situated narratives. The official reports were not pure transcriptions of the individual statements but mediated narratives, efforts to subordinate the statements—or, in some reports, summaries of them—to an overarching linear narrative of police investigative procedure. Even statements apparently recorded verbatim were laden with the evidence of their collection. Quotation marks, summaries, prefatory remarks, and concluding interpretations all reveal the manner in which these statements were the product of a most peculiar sort of authorial collaboration. Unlike Davis's collaborative letters of remission, these statements, even those most sympathetic to the investigation, speak of the violence with which "evidence" was captured and presented in the framework of official inquiry.

As they collected the statements as partial elements of a larger picture, police agents and magistrates also read them as incomplete renderings of a larger whole. They weighed the credibility of contradictory reports and attempted to reconstruct from them not an absolute truth but a truthful and viable representation of the moral universe of the families under investigation. No doubt the opinion of the justice of the peace or the commissaire de police carried more weight than that of the neighboring seamstress, but even these more "professional" assessments were based on the same norms of popular knowledge and opinion against which they were considered. The juge de paix of Charenton, for example, noted in his opinion on the family of one Louise L. that "[n]eighbors and residents of the quarter judge them harshly."[26]

Taken together, the dossiers suggest that authorities built their investigations around the intersections of several sets of signs representing serious domestic disorder. Of greatest concern, it seems, were allegations of sexual misconduct, drunkenness, familial violence, neglect, and economic instability. Thus reports compiled by local police, justices of the peace, and agents of the Sûreté consistently presented mothers who appeared to have more than one lover, mothers and daughters who seemed to be prostitutes, and parents of both sexes who were alleged to lead their amorous lives before the eyes of their children. Evidence of parental drunkenness and alcoholism also regularly signified danger to investigating authorities, as did reports of parents who beat their children in ways that seemed to exceed the

---

[26] Ibid., Dossier 3399 (1908).

limits of "proper" chastisement or reports of regular violent conflict between parents themselves. Neglect similarly was known through a range of signs, encompassing both the material—failure to provide proper food, clothing, and shelter—and the moral—failure to provide a proper moral education, good examples of behavior, or evidence of affection. Among the signs of dangerous economic disorder were parents who seemed to have no regular employment, parents who failed to pay the rent and thus were often forced to relocate the family, and parents who appeared to live solely off their children's legitimate or illegitimate gain.

A host of other clearly codified signs of moral danger also emerge from the court dossiers, including the use of insulting or obscene language, accusations of sexual abuse, the coming and going of too many visitors or strangers, a child's truancy, evidence of a parent's or child's criminal activity, overcrowding, and the sights and smells of extreme poverty and "inadequate" domestic hygiene. The persistent presence of these issues in officially generated reports suggests that apart from collecting detailed information about particular cases, investigative practice served to create a foundational set of symptoms that gave narrative substance to the law's definition of abandon moral. The consistent manner in which witnesses addressed the matters of moral conduct, employment history, patterns of family conflict, and the abuse of alcohol in their statements to the authorities suggests further that questions derived from these issues shaped the frame within which investigators drew on the ordinary residents of Paris in constructing both particular cases and the practical meaning of the law.

The dossiers also suggest that no single sign of disorder worked alone. Abandon moral emerged most consistently at the intersection of several different types of familial disorder, where drunkenness seemed to coincide with indecent displays of sexual activity, as in the case of Jules B., for example, or where allegations of physical abuse accompanied "evidence" of prostitution, as in the case of Mme. G.[27] At the same time, these intersecting signs of moral danger gained their authority only where they also intersected with the narratives and codes of moral disorder offered by—or extracted from—the ordinary people caught in the mechanism of official investigation.

That the articulation of these codes took place within a frame of institutional and procedural regularity could not wholly undo the fact that investigation was as subject to accident, contradiction, and indeterminacy as the gestures that had first raised official suspicions. Nevertheless, by the time a viable case reached the courtroom, the procureur had done his best to ensure that the traces of uncertainty had been effaced by his efforts to fit the contours of each case to both the dynamic processes of justice and the ambigious categories of the law.

[27] Ibid., Dossiers 2739 (1906) and 2685 (1906–7).

CHAPTER 6

Judgment

UNTIL NOW, the chapters in part 2 have followed the forward movement of these cases, from initial contact with the justice system through the various twists and turns of the investigational structures, from one site of inquiry to the next, from one set of official hands to the next. At each point on the chronological and institutional trajectory that defined a case, both the authorities and the individuals they confronted attempted to build a solid foundation of truth for the assertion or denial of abandon moral. They positioned themselves and each other in the web of relations that defined the life of the family in question and in the social and material fabric of the quarter. Most characters in these dramas of denunciation, exposure, and investigation implicitly emphasized their own authority to "expose the facts," whether it was the local justice of the peace or the seamstress living downstairs.

At the same time, however, their testimony spoke to the power of a tacit but shared belief that a completely transparent knowledge of one's neighbors' intimate life was a logical and representational impossibility. Ironically, "inside" testimony, that is, the statements from family members, was subject to the greatest suspicion: parents, driven by their own "interests," would consistently deny the allegations of abuse through the intentional misrepresentation of themselves and their domestic lives, and children might exploit a charge of abuse to amplify their own inevitable gripes against their parents. Only when their testimony slipped into the unintended revelation, or when it had been corroborated by "outside" representations, did the family's testimony gain currency in the prosecution's final construction—or rejection—of a case. A veracious likeness of the moral character of family relations could therefore be compiled only from the overlay of a series of partial renderings, themselves the unstable products of culturally encoded inferences, assumptions, and interpretations.

It is precisely this process of weighing, comparing, and superimposing that the procureur followed in constructing his cases. Many allegations, judged too weak or inconclusive to be pursued, were rejected before they ever reached the eyes of the presiding magistrate. Unfortunately, the lack of any reliable documentary trail obstructs efforts to estimate the number of cases opened and subsequently dropped by the procureur, although the variety and eccentricity of many of the accusations in the surviving dossiers suggest that the number of files well exceeded the number of cases actually brought before the civil tribunal.

For those cases that appeared suitable for a court hearing, however, the procureur and his staff wove a "definitive" account of the family's moral condition from their collection of already-semiworked pieces that had been filed in the dossier. Shards of contradictory evidence were discarded. Series of mutually reinforcing narratives were welded into more universal generalizations. In the hands of the procureur and his staff, in other words, the rough edges of a representational uncertainty were smoothed to the standards of the law and the demands of jurisprudence.

This is not to suggest that the prosecutor fabricated his cases in the sense that he built them from nothing, nor that his suppression of contradiction produced a falsehood. Representational reworking was an essential element in the final preparation of a case prosecuted by the state. In the particular order of late-nineteenth-century French jurisprudence, where the judge's task was to evaluate the prosecutor's construction of guilt, and not, as in the Anglo-American tradition, the more open (at least in principle) consideration of a case actually argued before him, finishing and sealing a case in advance were critical to the ordinary functioning of justice. The epistemological uncertainty generally inherent in civil procedure—and most especially in the juridical establishment of abandon moral—made such apparently solid reconstructions all the more crucial if the law was to function at all. In short, if facts were to be exposed, the cultural work of their construction had to be suppressed for the machinery of justice to give the appearance of rational, effective operation.

The art of the procureur, then, was to reread, reconstruct, and re-present his evidence and his charges against the textual and jurisprudential backdrop of the law. Concerned most of all with the strength of his cases, the procureur polished the final renderings by sorting his facts into the legitimate categories of the text of the law. The linear process of investigation so well documented by the order and contents of the dossier here broke down under the procureur's search for an irrefutable image. In his hands, the most apparently stable facts were extracted from their documentary context and re-presented as the raw materials of the case. Crystallized, buttressed, and confirmed, they became the foundation of the procureur's decision to enter a formal request to the court for the divestiture of parental rights.

The high number of decisions for déchéance recorded in the registers of court points to the procureur's entrenched reluctance to pursue cases that were not, in his judgment, absolutely airtight. The dossiers, many of whose documentary trails end without explanation or with only the briefest of penciled notes, similarly attest to the procureur's tendency to drop weak cases without seeking a judgment. Again, the registers of the civil court support this impression of the magistracy's conservatism. Both the relatively low number of cases heard annually by the Parisian courts and the low percentage of decisions against the procureur suggest that he screened his cases as

much for conventional legitimacy as for the "truth"—even a well-founded
and confirmed "truth"—of the moral abuse of children.

In the formal request for déchéance, the procureur tied his carefully
worked representation of the family's moral essence to the aims and provisions of the law. In the case of Ephième E. and her rights over her daughter
Alice, for example, the procureur "exposed" the following "facts" in the
statement he submitted to the judge on 28 February 1898:

> That from the marriage of B . . . Louis Elie, and E . . . Marie Ephime [*sic*], were
> born Alice Julie Désirée[,] 17 years of age[,] Eva Marie Félicité Georgette, 15
> years of age, Georges Fernand Edouard, 14 years of age, that Monsieur B . . .
> abandoned his wife and his children, that he has been convicted numerous times,
> that the wife B . . . does not work and lives only off the product of her oldest
> daughter's prostitution, that she pushes the youngest daughter to follow the ex-
> ample of her elder sister.[1]

The "facts" of a case that had originated in competing charges of kidnapping, violence, greed, and moral corruption were thus flattened into a family
portrait of occupational "irregularity" and persistent moral failings. The "expert" opinion of the local justice also lost its specific contours; only a brief
note recording whether or not the justice had approved the request for déchéance was entered into the register. In the last instance, his status and his
assigned place in the rouages of the justice system, rather than the relationship between the information he had gathered on the family and the conclusions he had drawn from it, affirmed the authority of the court's decision.

The conventions structuring the prosecution's exposé turned representation into proven and enduring moral deficiency. This fitted well, and indeed
was prescribed by, the logic of paragraph 6 of the law's second article,
whereby the revelation of persistent "notorious and scandalous misconduct"
might provide sufficient grounds for a judgment of déchéance. The case of
Ephième and her absent husband is again exemplary; the prosecutor's exposé of facts compressed the tangled collection of interpretive narratives
hidden in his files into a simple set of truths configured according to the
abstract determinants of the law and packaged for the consumption of the
court.

In fact, packaging was by no means irrelevant to the conduct of these
hearings. In the constitution of a formal request for déchéance, as elsewhere
in the rouages of justice, the printed form stood as the emblem of systematic
formal standardization.[2] Only a few blanks in the lengthy request form sub-

---

[1] ADS, D3 U7, Dossier 849 (1897).

[2] Ironically, a printing school for boys in the ranks of the Seine's Service des Enfants Moralement Abandonnés quickly became a major site for the production of government forms and
documents, particularly those necessary for the everyday operation of the Bureau of Public
Assistance. Although it is not clear whether these children, some of whom no doubt had been

mitted by the procureur allowed for specificity: a paragraph-size space was left for the exposé of facts, and short blanks permitted the prosecution to enter the name of the accused and the date and to specify whether the accused was parent to one or more children. In all other respects, the petition applied an identical juridical metanarrative to every case: the procureur, after "exposing" the facts of the case—facts by now almost incidental to the movement of the machine—was requesting that the tribunal, "in accordance with the law of 24 July 1889, article 2, paragraph 6, declare [the parent(s) in question] dispossessed with regard to their child[ren], of paternal authority and all the rights it confers." Radically diverse narratives, pulverized and reconstituted in the mills of situated representation and "definitive" interpretation, were thus ultimately bracketed at the empty center of the mass-produced case, embodied in the universally applicable mass-produced forms of bureaucratic red tape. This material incarnation was the final step in the prosecution's effort to make cases resonate with the law.

In our own fascination with the courtroom, late-twentieth-century observers often expect that the intrigue of a crime will be matched by the drama of the trial. A battle between titans of rhetorical brilliance—or at least of limitless amoral maneuvers—and the startling revelation of detail and motive define even our most banal legal melodramas. Fin-de-siècle France also had an apparently insatiable appetite for the scandal and drama of criminal trials.[3] Then, as now, however, much of the work of the court was far more mundane. Hearings, silent bureaucratic procedures, and pro forma decisions occupied a far greater part of the juridical apparatus than did the cause célèbre.

If cases of abandon moral were constructed using the personnel and techniques of criminal investigation, they partly recovered their civil status when they reached the civil tribunal at the Palais de Justice. At the same time, the exceptional nature of these cases, negotiated between the judge and the procureur, foreshadowed the imminent development of administrative justice.

---

removed from their parents' custody by the terms of the law of 1889, produced these particular forms, it is not to be ruled out as a possibility. On the Ecole d'Alembert and its print shop, see the survey of its history published by the Administration Général de l'Assistance publique à Paris, *Les Ecoles professionnelles du service des enfants assistés de la Seine: L'école d'Alembert (1882–1909) à Montévrain* (Paris: Berger-Levrault, 1909).

[3] On the sensational criminal trial in the late nineteenth century, see Ruth Harris, *Murders and Madness: Medicine, Law, and Society in the Fin de Siècle* (Oxford: Clarendon Press, 1989), as well as Joëlle Guillais-Maury, *La Chair de l'autre: Le crime passionnel au XIXe siècle* (Paris: Olivier Orban, 1986); Mary S. Hartmann, *Victorian Murderesses: A True History of Thirteen Respectable French and English Women Accused of Unspeakable Crimes* (New York: Schocken Books, 1977); and Edward Berenson, *The Trial of Madame Caillaux* (Berkeley: University of California Press, 1992). Ann-Louise Shapiro provides a lucid and penetrating account of the gendering of criminality in this period in *Breaking the Codes: Female Criminality in Fin-de-Siècle Paris* (Stanford: Stanford University Press, 1996).

Most significant in this oddly configured juridical drama was the procureur himself, who represented both the child's interests and those of the state. Although they are somewhat cryptic on this question, both the dossiers and the registers of court suggest that parents had no legal representation in the hearings on abandon moral, and quite often they did not even attend the proceedings. The drama of the "discovery" and investigation, moreover, ended somewhat anticlimactically in these closed hearings. Although it was in the final hearings that the lethal blow to individual parental authority would fall, both uncertainty and suspense—at least in most instances—had long before been stifled. In many ways the formalized moment of the hearing represented the phase of the machine's movement least affected by the friction of interpretative reordering.

Once the procureur had submitted his request, the accused parents were summoned to the chambre de conseil of the tribunal de première instance for the formal hearing. Here, according to the standardized summons they received, they would be questioned one last time and would be given the opportunity to respond to the allegations of parental inadequacy. In many cases, particularly those in which the children had long before been abandoned into the care of another individual, the Bureau of Public Assistance, or a private charitable institution, it seems that the parents neither responded to this notification nor appeared on the assigned date. If the court was satisfied that all reasonable steps had been taken to find and inform them, the judgment proceeded without them.

No jury sat on these hearings. Instead, the cases were presented directly to the judge. Although the judge had a certain degree of latitude in whether to rule for divestiture, the law brooked no modification in the application of the penalty. Until reforms introduced in the interwar period, there was no possibility of softening the treatment of negligent or "morally dangerous" parents through sentences of mandatory supervision, reeducation, or partial loss of rights.[4] The law of 1889 in its original form called for judgments of all or nothing, an aspect that particularly enraged some of its severest critics.[5] Al-

---

[4] The law of 1889 stood untouched until 15 November 1921, when the concept of partial divestiture was introduced. The standard of notorious and scandalous misconduct in the determination of morally unfit parents was also amended to an even more open-ended notion of lack of necessary moral guidance. According to one commentator, this measure implied that judges would consider "bad examples set for the child," as well as the earlier signpost of "provoked scandal." In 1935 a decree-law continued this trend from dispossession to surveillance; parents deemed incompetent in the rearing of their children would be placed under state observation but would not necessarily lose their rights or the physical custody of their offspring. See Denise Bouchet, *Le Rôle de l'Assistance publique dans l'application de la loi du 24 juillet 1889 "sur la protection des enfants maltraités ou moralement abandonnés"* (Lyons: Imprimerie Grosjean-Fourgerat, 1938), 16, 32–33.

[5] In a note prefacing *La Fille Bazentin*, a didactic play criticizing the insensitivity of the Bureau of Public Assistance published in 1908, the author wrote: "Wouldn't it be preferable, in

though an appeal could be filed within six days of the original decision, parents could not petition the court to restore their rights and their children to them until three years had elapsed from the date of judgment, if that decision survived appeal. In a culture obsessed with the ties of blood, maintaining the stability of the family, and preservating paternal authority as a central cultural and social touchstone, the decision to dissolve the legal relationship between parent and child could hardly be taken lightly.

The registers of court, as formally standardized as they are, do suggest certain patterns of ruling in cases where the court agreed to break the legal and custodial ties between parents and children. Single parents, male and female, were much more likely to bear the brunt of the law. Among the most common reasons single fathers—usually widowers—lost their children in 1900, for example, were the apparent lack of any material support of their children, physical or sexual assault on them, imprisonment or criminal conviction, as well as the ubiquitous charges of habitual inebriation and scandalous misconduct. The court ruled against the single mother—usually widowed or unmarried—where evidence of prostitution, neglect, drunkenness, and scandalous misconduct had been presented by the prosecutor. Living in common-law relationships with partners other than the children's biological parent also brought suspicions on both men and women but was not in itself sufficient grounds for a decision of déchéance. Single mothers and fathers also appear to have accounted for the majority of dispossessions voluntarily solicited by the parents themselves, usually on grounds of indigence.

Ironically, the widowed or unwed mother appears to have been the most common object of this law designed to break the Napoleonic consecration of paternal authority. Decisions against these women often accounted for up to half of the cases heard in an average year. Suspicions of female-headed households and women workers immediately made the single mother the paradigmatic deviant parent.[6] The strategies that single working-class mothers adopted in the face of their extreme vulnerability further tarnished their moral credibility. Thus mothers who abandoned infants to the care of the state when they could not afford to raise them appeared to prosecutor and judge to have lost their maternal instincts.[7] Similarly, those women for whom

place of pronouncing the brutal separation of beings joined by ties of blood, to leave the children with their parents, while charging the Administration [of Public Assistance] with exercising constant surveillance over those conferred to it[;] morality and justice would thus both be served." See Edouard David, *La Fille Bazentin: Pièce social en quatre actes sur l'Assistance publique* (Amien: Imprimerie du Progrès de la Somme, 1908), x.

[6] On the chain of pejorative associations embedded in dominant visions of women workers, see Joan Wallach Scott's essay on sexual difference in nineteenth-century political economy, "'L'ouvrière! Mot impie, sordide . . .': Women Workers in the Discourse of French Political Economy," in *Gender and the Politics of History* (New York: Columbia University Press, 1988).

[7] See Rachel G. Fuchs, "Preserving the Future of France: Aid to the Poor and Pregnant in Nineteenth-Century Paris," in *The Uses of Charity: The Poor on Relief in the Nineteenth-*

survival depended on cohabiting with a man, whose time spent earning wages precluded keeping a home up to the standards of "decency," or who turned to casual prostitution as a means of support were read as degenerate and as violating the natural sanctity of the maternal role. It was in the case of single mothers, in other words, that the points of moral reference for bourgeois adjudicators clashed with the economic necessities and the sometimes distinct moral order of the urban poor. Thus if the text of the law appeared to threaten the integrity and dignity of the père de famille, the implementation of the law threatened the independence of single mothers. If the original intention had been to preserve children from the abusive exercise of paternal power, in the courtroom the law was used to preserve children from "inadequate" and denatured maternal sentiment.

After the judgment had been rendered, the second order of business was the designation of a legal guardian. Here, as in other cases where the loss of parents entailed the search for an appropriate substitute, the court, and the law itself, preferred that a *conseil de famille* be constituted, and that a guardian from within the family be selected (*tutelle de droit commun*). The first rulings on the exercise of tutelle and the custody of children were thus provisional. Once the court was certain that no appeal would be filed, once the conseil de famille had met, and once the prospective guardian's moral and material profile had been examined more closely, attributions of legal guardianship and custody would follow in a second ruling.

Although family members were preferred in the selection of a legal guardian, the provisions of the civil code did not exclude the exercise of tutelle by unrelated individuals. The search for guardians documented in the prosecution's files also suggests that material resources were as significant a consideration as moral stature. Several dossiers contain letters from potential tuteurs who claimed they were too poor to take on the care of another child. This must have been particularly common when children were still at an age when school attendance was mandatory and the parents involved were too poor to provide any sort of child support. If a child could not contribute to the income of an already economically vulnerable family, he or she could hardly have been a welcome addition to the household.

In many cases, a suitable and willing individual guardian could not be found. Under the sway of theories of moral degeneration that stressed envi-

---

Century Metropolis, ed. Peter Mandler (Philadelphia: University of Pennsylvania Press, 1990); *Abandoned Children: Foundlings and Child Welfare in Nineteenth-Century France* (Albany: SUNY Press, 1984); and *Poor and Pregnant in Paris: Strategies for Survival in the Nineteenth Century* (New Brunswick: Rutgers University Press, 1992), for persuasive arguments against this theory of stunted maternal instinct. On the other side of the debate, see Edward Shorter, *The Making of the Modern Family* (New York: Basic Books, 1977), for a prime example of how historians have reproduced the conclusions of nineteenth-century bourgeois observers in taking abandonment as a sign of the "modern" degeneration of maternal morals.

ronment and heredity simultaneously, turn-of-the-century magistrates were particularly wary of families in which the moral corruption in one branch appeared to compromise the moral status of the entire clan. In cases where a father lost his rights, the courts often hesitated to place the children under the legal authority of their mother, even if she was legally separated or divorced from her spouse. One commentator described the problems inherent in leaving children with their natural mothers this way:

> This solution, which would in theory be an excellent one, could have, in the majority of cases, the most serious and substantial drawbacks, for the mother who has been subordinated to marital authority, obliged to live under the same roof as her husband, would be unceasingly dominated by the unfit father and, consequently, unable to exercise her own authority freely.

Citing Senator Roussel's report from 1882, the author added:

> One must note, as M. Roussel put it so well, that even when the mother is not personally rendered unfit to exercise parental authority by participating in the actions which led to her husband's dispossession, the mere fact of their life in common—of contact with the father and the experience of his influence—is of such importance that if the mother were invested with rights over the child, the effect of the decision against the father would be canceled out.[8]

Even when wives were granted the right to exercise paternal authority, moreover, the law required that if they remarried the conseil de famille meet to approve her continued investment with parental rights. Without that meeting, a mother would automatically lose her rights of guardianship upon remarriage.[9]

Once more, then, a mother's claim to parental authority was cast as contingent, her solitary exercise of it considered an exception to the rule. In the case of a ruling of déchéance, moreover, she was further compromised by the combination of her daily exposure to her husband and by the weakness of moral fiber that came, according to fin-de-siècle medical and moral experts, with being a woman. Although the registers of judgment are often vague on the status of married couples in question, it seems that a woman was far more likely to gain legal guardianship if a definitive separation could be shown. In general, the husbands of those few women who did retain parental rights over their children had abandoned their families altogether and could not be found, were imprisoned with long sentences, or had been incarcerated or hospitalized indefinitely.

If no suitable guardian could be found among family members, the law stipulated that legal guardianship be exercised by the Bureau of Public As-

---

[8] Gabriel Melin, *Droit Romain: Essai sur la clientèle. Droit français: De la protection légale des enfants légitimes contre les abus de la puissance paternelle* (Nancy: E. Desté, 1889), 164.

[9] Ibid., 74.

sistance. Even then, the child might stay in the custody of an individual or a private charitable organization, rather than entering the ranks of children in state care. That guardianship would take the form designed for the legal tutelle of infants or foundlings abandoned into the care of the Service des Enfants Assistés.[10] In 1890 sixty children were put under the legal guardianship of the Bureau of Public Assistance, and almost three hundred more were put in the care of a guardian found in their extended families. The following year, the bureau exercised legal tutelle over close to one hundred children and was caring for another eighty-eight whose status as moralement abandonné was still unconfirmed by a legal decision. According to the director of the Bureau of Public Assistance, by 1899 the total number of children in the care of the state as moralement abandonné throughout France had risen to more than twenty thousand.[11]

Although the judges appear to have regularly granted the procureur's requests for déchéance, they did at times also rule in favor of the accused parents. In the July 1901 hearing of a case against Pierre and Laure B., for example, the procureur framed his argument as a textbook example of every one of the provisions of article 2, paragraph 6. Drawing out the themes of habitual drunkenness, scandalous behavior, and physical and moral endangerment, he informed the judge that "Monsieur and Madame B . . . drink, that Madame B . . . especially is a chronic alcoholic; . . . she brutalizes her children, whom she leaves untended and sometimes without food." Completing the full spectrum of family dysfunction, he ended his charges with the additional claim that "Monsieur and Madame B . . . make scandalous scenes and come to blows before their children."[12]

Despite the procureur's meticulous exploitation of the form and language of the law, and despite the certainty in which he bathed his allegations, the judge chose in this case to produce his own picture. In his account, the recent revelation of "new facts" undid the procureur's portrait of chronic immorality. Since January 1901, the judge countered, "[T]he conduct of Monsieur and Madame B. . . seems to have improved noticeably. . . . [T]hey seem to be taking care of their children, showing them a great deal of affection and making them attend school regularly." In addition, Pierre had found work, and Laure, no longer drinking, "was taking care of her children as

---

[10] See chap. 2, art. 11 of the 1889 law on abandon moral: "If tutelle has not been constituted in conformity with the preceding article [on family guardianship], it is to be exercised by the Bureau of Public Assistance, according to the laws of 15 *pluviôse*, year XIII, and 10 January 1849, as well as article 24 of this law" (*JO*, 25 July 1889, 3654).

[11] Seine, Conseil Général [CGS], no. 93, *Rapport sur le service des enfants moralement abandonnés présenté par Henri Rousselle* (1891), 5; CGS, no. 32, *Rapport sur le service des enfants moralement abandonnés présenté par Henri Rousselle* (1892), 10; and Henri Monod, *L'Assistance publique en France en 1900* (Paris: Imprimerie nationale, n.d.), 38.

[12] ADS, D3 U7, Dossier 1474 (1900).

well as her home." In this case, then, the procureur's careful screening and meticulous construction did not produce a decision of déchéance.

In the majority of cases, nonetheless, the judge did accept the procureur's charges. The documentary record of these hearings took a fuguelike form in which the structure and tone of the procureur's exposé were, two beats later and in a slightly different register, re-created in the judge's decision. In the summary of the decision against Widow A. in March 1900, for instance, the procureur's argument stressed the facts that she lived out of wedlock with her lover, that she "frequently got drunk," and that she "mistreated her children and did not give them the care they required." The judge's explanation of the grounds for his ruling mirrored this account: Widow A., according to "reliable" information, "was given to habitual drunkenness"; she "had been found in the street in an obvious state of drunkenness"; and she "never took care of her children."[13] The judge supported his representation of the case with the additional "fact" that the widow's neighbors had declared her "unfit to maintain custody of her child [*sic*]."[14] Quite often the judge's restatement of the case included many more detailed facts than did the procureur's formal presentation, suggesting that his knowledge of the cases derived as much from his own review of the prosecution's dossiers as it did from the prosecution's testimony. The actual encounter between procureur and judge on the day of the hearing, then, offered even less room for accident or improvisation than a first glance might reveal. The machinery of justice seems to have operated with the greatest efficiency in the chambers of court.

In both the decisions that stripped parents of their rights and those that denied the procureur's request for déchéance, the judges tended to recall the place of representation in the collection of evidence and the construction of a case. In the hearing on the parental status of Monsieur and Madame B., the judge opposed the procureur's argument to a series of apparently more reliable representations: the couple's behavior "appeared" to be improved, their attitude toward their children "appeared" to have changed, and they "manifested" the signs of parental affection more clearly. Likewise, in the case of Widow A., the text of the judgment stressed both the credibility of the prosecution's representation and that of moral rendering provided by neighborhood opinion.

Even when all apparent resistance had been eliminated from the "rational" functioning of justice, the repressed construction of the case returned in the judge's use of this language and logic of appearance. The final move-

[13] Public drunkenness had been outlawed in 1873 through legislation sponsored, among others, by Senators Théophile Roussel and René Bérenger. See Susanna Barrows, "After the Commune: Alcoholism, Temperance, and Literature in the Early Third Republic," in *Consciousness and Class Experience in Nineteenth-Century Europe*, ed. John Merriman (New York: Holmes and Meier, 1979), 211–12.

[14] ADS, D1 U5 (23 March 1900).

ments of the machinery of justice were thus shaped by the regularization of paradox where the exposed "objective facts" were prefaced in the judge's rendering with the qualifiers of representation. The accused no longer *was*, but was "represented as," "known to be," and "considered." The enduring tension, therefore, was that despite their status as persistent traces of the epistemological uncertainty and representational disorder that were themselves amplified by the negative definition of abandon moral, these representations of moral character came to serve as definitive evidence in the rendering of legal decisions about the family. Although this kind of uncertainty was intrinsic to the operation of civil justice in the nineteenth century, its depth and its persistence were especially apparent in the case of abandon moral.

The state's regular judicial regulation of the ideologically sacrosanct private life of the family could be tolerated only through a particularly strong reliance on the paradoxes of procedure. The more the courts' actions became a fixed part of the judicial and social landscape, the more firmly they were based in the representation of an oblique view of a family's domestic experience as capturing the central truths of individual moral nature and of the moral essence of family relations.

The ease with which this judicial machinery functioned in the final stages of constructing and judging a case should not lead the historian to think that silence reigned supreme once a judgment was rendered and the apparatus shut down. The decision itself was not always the final product of the investigation and hearing; nor was it necessarily the last document to be entered in the prosecution dossier. Friction was in fact never entirely eliminated from the juridical procedures that structured cases of abandon moral. Incensed protests, from both indirect and direct participants, commingled with the pronouncements of individual ruling, and inefficiency, overefficiency, inhumanity, and judicial conservatism were only some of the charges leveled against the manner in which the law of 1889 was used in the decades that followed its promulgation.

From within the world of public and private child protection, critics railed against the magistracy's apparent reluctance to use the law with the vigor it seemed to require. As early as 1891, for example, cries of bureaucratic distress resounded in the chambers of the Seine's General Council. Although the law was new and, as one council member put it, "still in its trial run," the council's subcommission on public assistance charged the magistracy with betraying the sense and aims of the new law. According to the commission's report, officers of the court appeared unwilling to relinquish a notion of la puissance paternelle that defined it as sacred, natural, and, for the most part, inviolable. Overall, the report claimed, "[T]he justice system is hesitant and fumbling." The commission demanded "less timidity" from civil magistrates, particularly in the application of article 2, covering instances of parental abuse and moral degeneracy.[15] Although the Service admitted a bit more satisfaction with the magistracy's use of the law in 1894, the call for more aggressive application was nevertheless renewed that year. At the same time, the Paris Municipal Council was raising its own objections to the reluctance of magistrates in the criminal courts to call for the divestiture of parental authority in the application of the 1874 law on the employment of children in "the itinerant trades."[16]

Many critics ascribed the resistance of the civil justices to their particular devotion to Roman law and, by extension, to its more absolute vision of paternal authority where patria potestas was unassailable. Councillor Henri Rousselle also accused the courts of ignoring the new law out of an unshakable loyalty to an archaic legal philosophy. "[L]a puissance paternelle must be sacred only for those parents who are worthy of exercising it," he railed in 1894.[17] Similar complaints marked departmental reports on the Service des Enfants Moralement Abandonnés throughout the 1890s, and the general protest against judicial inertia continued well into the interwar era.[18]

Even when decisions of déchéance had been reached, neither law nor court provided the means of certain enforcement. Four weeks after the decision of déchéance de la puissance paternelle had been handed down in the case of Monsieur and Mme. C., for example, the procureur received a terse note from the director of the Bureau of Public Assistance in Paris. According to the court's ruling, tutelle was to be exercised by the Bureau of Public Assistance. The weak mechanisms of enforcement, however, forced the director to send a memorandum asking where the children might be found.[19]

For his part, Paul Strauss, a member of the General Council who was later elected senator and then named minister of hygiene after World War I, was incensed by the apparent contamination of the Bureau of Public Assistance's public identity when it was driven to enforce the law. "It is unacceptable," he wrote in his 1896 report on the Service, "that a benevolent administration

[15] CGS, no. 93 (1891), 5 and 14.

[16] Paris, Conseil Municipal [CMP], *Rapport présenté par M. Georges Berry au nom de la commission de la mendicité professionnelle sur l'exploitation de l'enfance* (7 March 1892), 18–20. For more on the 1874 law on the employment of children in *les professions ambulantes*, see chap. 2.

[17] CGS, no. 1, *Rapport sur le service des enfants moralement abandonnés présenté par M. Henri Rousselle* (1894), 21.

[18] "Judges often recoil from declaring even a partial divestiture," Denise Bouchet wrote in her law thesis of 1938. "[M]any magistrates continue to consider *la puissance paternelle* more of an unassailable right, taking the place of *patria potestas*, rather than a right which only rests on whether its bearer fulfills all the attached obligations" (Bouchet, *Le Rôle de l'Assistance publique*, 38).

[19] ADS, D3 U7, Dossier 3363 (1908).

presents itself to the public in the guise of a *gendarme* or police constable. . . . [T]his use of force does not facilitate the Bureau of Public Assistance's moralizing task."[20]

The ambivalence about intervention that had left its marks on the creation and application of the law on abandon moral thus struck again and struck hard. It affected even the most adamant proponents of protection, those who consistently denied any residual attachment to a "sacred paternal power" when it came time to actually use the law against parents. The work of preserving the safety and best interests of the child appeared once again to compromise the assertion of the state's higher moral aims as well as its benign paternal identity. That the sanctity of la puissance paternelle had not been entirely undone by the enactment—or even the formal application—of the law of 1889 thus emerged in the general reluctance to do the dirty work and in the fear that the violence ineluctably bound into the law would sully the image of protective public authority. Given this reluctance to destabilize paternal authority, the large proportion of single mothers among the ranks of the juridically dispossessed seems even less surprising.

Meanwhile, some parents and family members whose lives had been suddenly and permanently transformed by their encounter with the rouages of justice continued their battle, unwilling to be silenced by the authority of the court's ruling. Decisions were appealed and in some cases overturned.[21] Other rulings were the object of furious and desperate letters to the procureur after the case had, in one way or another, been put to rest. Some people protested against the state's unwillingness to pursue a hearing when they had borne such convincing testimony against the parent in question. Jeanne C., for example, wrote to the procureur twelve times in 1906 and 1907, entreating him in each letter to protect her children from their "dangerous" father, who maltreated them and subjected them to "obscene acts." When the case was shelved without a hearing in April 1907, she continued her campaign and forced the prosecutor to open a new dossier with her letter of May 1908. The second file ends with a poignantly terse note from the Sûreté dated 29 May 1908, remarking only that Jeanne C. had "already addressed many identical complaints to the Parquet."[22]

Others still, like the brother of Elie M., who had lost his parental rights in 1907, argued that the judgment had been hasty and that the wrong parent had been punished. In his letter to the procureur, Elie's brother, a member of the municipal council of Vanves, contended that despite the fact that Elie had

[20] CGS, no. 12, *Rapport général au nom de la 3ᵉ commission sur le service des enfants secourus, des enfants assistés et des enfants moralement abandonnés présenté par M. P. Strauss* (1896), 118.

[21] See, for example, ADS, D3 U7, Dossier 3090 (1907), in which Madame R., deprived of her rights by a decision of December 1905, had them legally restored more than two years later.

[22] Ibid., Dossier 3000 (1907).

been condemned to prison for a murder attempt on his wife, he was nonetheless a fit parent. Evidence of Elie's moral standing included his faithful service in the colonial army in Anam and his brother's certainty that the accusations leveled by Elie's now ex-wife were the product of calculated deceit. His daughter's testimony that Elie had raped her, moreover, was discounted in this letter by the fact that she had been coached by her mother and was herself "vicieuse" by temperament. The entire case, according to Elie's brother, was thus the fabrication of a vengeful ex-wife. Curiously, the dossier on Elie M. shows no evidence of a response to this letter, despite the unusually elevated status of its author.[23]

Some of these letters appear to have yielded results, either in the overturning of a decision or in the reopening of a case—however briefly. For the most part, however, they appear to have had little impact at the Palais de Justice, particularly once the procureur had shelved a case or a final judgment had been rendered. When the machinery of justice ground to a halt, in other words, these individual protests appear to have been little more than the last echoes of its crashings, grindings, and hums, echoes silenced by the covers of the dossiers as they were literally and procedurally closed.

Protest nevertheless continued to be an essential element in the unfolding of the individual case, as well as a fundamental attitude in the critical literature of the next century. Other changes in the legal infrastructure between the turn of the century and the outbreak of war in 1914 ensured that the problem of misused parental authority would be thoroughly subsumed in the problem of protecting vulnerable children. The year 1898 saw the passage of a law on the corporal abuse of children (*la loi sur la répression des violences, voies de fait, actes de cruauté et attentats commis envers les enfants*). This legislation introduced a more modified form of limiting parental right by denying abusive parents the custody of their own children, *le droit de garde*, while leaving their rights—la puissance paternelle—intact. The *loi organique* of 1904, reorganizing the integration and care of children under the Bureau of Public Assistance, assimilated the enfants moralement abandonnés into its more general category of wards, or *pupilles assistés*. Decisions of déchéance thus were placed side by side with the exposure or formal abandonment of infants as causes of abandonment and the justification for the state's paternal protection. Taking children from their biological parents, in other words, became a natural part of both abandonment and protection.

In 1912 hearings on abandon moral were shifted from the first chamber of the inferior court to the newly established juvenile court. This institutional reorientation, like the Bureau of Public Assistance's revision of its administrative categories, signaled the fact that déchéance de la puissance paternelle

---

[23] Ibid., Dossier 2789 (1906).

was being moved out of the realm of general civil law and civil right, where the status of the father as a citizen was at stake in the privation of his parental rights as père de famille and where the legal status of the single mother was already compromised. The new location of parental rights in a frame of administrative law devoted, at least in principle, to dangerous and endangered children's best interests can perhaps best be read as the consequence of the previous decades' efforts to resolve the conflict of interest between children and their parents that had first been raised by the law of 1889. The transfer of these hearings from the tribunal de première instance to the juvenile court was thus the institutional embodiment of the ultimate subordination of parental right to the interest of the child, as defined and protected by the state, a formula that had first been suggested by the logic of the 1889 law, if not by its early application.

Some forty years after the law was enacted, however, even after the institutional frame around it had been transformed, and even while the project of protecting children from their own parents in the twentieth century would turn increasingly from moral to psychological investigations into (and explanations of) the dysfunctional family, the ambiguities brought by the elusive nature and definition of abandon moral continued to plague those charged with the application of the law. As one legal commentator observed in 1938, abandon moral remained locked in the epistemological difficulties that had marked the law's initial appearance in the civil court. On the eve of the Second World War the juridical essence of abandon moral remained elusive. Abandon moral, this author contended, could still be understood only as

> a complex and imprecise situation which is characterized by a series of parental negligences in the rearing of children; it is a negative case defined by a lack of care, it is a phenomenon which is therefore reconstituted from its consequences. . . . And, increasingly, as the legislator seeks out these cases of abandon moral, he is confronted with the widest variety of situations, even where the notion is most applicable.[24]

Despite the inability of the French justice system to overcome the indeterminacy embedded in the notion of abandon moral, the efforts to identify and interpret it within the mechanisms of justice had important consequences. Bringing abandon moral into the court provided a new site for the conflict and alignment of diverse moral discourses. It permitted a new degree of state participation in the moral normalization of the family.

The juridical treatment of abandon moral also contributed toward the larger remaking of civil justice in the late nineteenth and early twentieth centuries.[25] The difficulty of appropriating concepts and practices simul-

---

[24] Bouchet, *Le Rôle de l'Assistance publique*, 9.

[25] On the transformation of law at the end of the nineteenth century, see François Ewald, *L'Etat providence* (Paris: Grasset, 1986).

taneously from both civil and criminal justice fostered the development of a third terrain of law wherein protective regulation of the family would prove far more possible.

The introduction of abandon moral into the machinery of civil justice also provided a new legal status and often a new life experience for children made visible through the lens of abandon moral. Like the law of 1889 and its jurisprudence, the category of the enfant moralement abandonné would also be marked by ambivalence and indeterminacy. It is to that category and its trajectory in the logic and practices of state guardianship under the Third Republic that I turn next.

Part III

PETITS PARISIENS INTO PEASANTS: THE GUARDIAN STATE AND THE CHILD IN MORAL DANGER

ALTHOUGH the law of 1889 signaled a critical moment in the codification and regulation of abandon moral, the terrain defined by the new social problem was not limited to morally dangerous parents; nor was it defined in exclusively juridical terms. Under the early Third Republic, the problem of abandon moral was worked out simultaneously in the interlocking fields of legislation, jurisprudence, and administration. Each of these arenas of governance, however, embraced different themes in the development of particular ideologies and practices. Where the text of the law and the commentary surrounding it focused primarily on parental character and the regulation of parental rights in the name of moral protection, and where the civil magistrates examined the moral quality of the relationship between parent and child, administrative efforts to articulate and act on the problem of abandon moral focused almost exclusively on the child and his or her relationship to the guardian-state.

The morally endangered child was thus as central to the developing discourse on abandon moral and to the institutionalization of public responses to this new social problem as were deficient or delinquent parents. As the court dossiers suggest, the trajectory of governmental concern about morally dangerous families began as often with the inquiry into the background of a child arrested for vagrancy or petty crime as it did with the fear that immoral parents threatened the moral well-being of their offspring. While the question of the demoralizing parent monopolized much of the debate on regulating the family under the early Third Republic, the plight of street children and minors arrested for petty offenses fueled some of the rising interest in drafting a law on abandon moral and the divestiture of parental authority in the late 1870s and 1880s.

The problem represented by children whom public authorities considered moralement abandonnés was at once conceptual and practical. What kind of children would fall within the category of moralement abandonné? What children would be excluded from it? If, as republican ideology insisted, a proper family environment was essential to the formation of a virtuous citizen, a moral parent, and a productive worker, how could the ostensibly intrinsic formative properties of life with one's birth parents be reproduced for children bereft of that naturally moralizing and socializing experience? How could the degrading effects of life in a denatured and morally dangerous family best be counteracted? How, in short, could the republican state instantiate the metaphorical parental identity so crucial in its wider reforging of relations between government and the governed? How, as one Parisian official put it, could public authority act "en bon père de famille"?[1]

The department of the Seine and the Paris Bureau of Public Assistance attempted to address these questions almost a decade before the National Assembly gave abandon moral its formal juridical definition in July 1889. That year, celebrating the passage of the new law, departmental councillor Henri Rousselle congratulated his colleagues on their prescient activism in founding a special service for the public protection of the moralement abandonnés at the beginning of the decade.

> Nowhere have you innovated with more daring and success. Nothing stopped you, neither the timidities born of routine, nor financial difficulties, nor juridical obstacles, and, cheered on by public opinion, you pursued your task and brought with you the Administration [of Public Assistance] and parliament itself.

The law of 1889, Rousselle added, could be traced directly to the department's philanthropic activity in this area. "That legislative reform was inspired by you, gentlemen," he declared, "and it is because of you that it succeeded."[2] Although Rousselle's triumphant hyperbole effaces the more complex history of the 1889 legislation, it also suggests that the relationship between formal codification and everyday practice was more complex than the common narrative structure of enactment and implementation tends to suggest.[3]

To be sure, concern over the moral constitution of the urban working class or poor child in the late nineteenth century was by no means the exclusive domain of departmental officials. Private philanthropy also embraced and developed the notion of the enfant moralement abandonné in this period,

---

[1] Seine, Conseil Général [CGS], no. 18, *Rapport présenté par M. Curé au nom de la 3e commission sur le budget du service des enfants moralement abandonnés pour l'année 1888* (1888), 3.

[2] CGS, no. 15, *Rapport présenté par M. Rousselle au nom de la 3e commission sur le service des enfants moralement abandonnés* (1889), 2.

[3] Many works on child protection imply a linear relationship between legislative action and practical implementation. Although this is not always an incorrect assumption, the story of the practices surrounding morally abandoned children suggests the importance of reexamining this position. For an example of this linear approach, see Lee Shai Weissbach, *Child Labor Reform in Nineteenth-Century France: Assuring the Future Harvest* (Baton Rouge: Louisiana State University Press, 1989).

particularly in large cities such as Paris and Lyons, and created its own institutions for the care and rearing of these children.[4] Although historians have only recently begun to research the role private charities played in the production of state policy, it is clear that philanthropists in the late nineteenth century were extremely active in the area of moral protection and may well have been instrumental in amplifying the note of urgency public authorities injected into their own deliberations and projects. In addition, it was not unusual for public officials to involve themselves in private philanthropic activities. The Parisian magistrate Georges Bonjean, for example, ran a private organization for the care and rearing of abandoned children while also presiding over cases of alleged abandon moral in the civil court.[5] The production of these new categories and strategies often took place at this kind of intersection of public and private child protection, intersections populated by individuals such as Bonjean who straddled the identities of public servant and private philanthropist.[6]

Despite the apparently blurred boundaries between public and private action in this field, however, by the early 1880s the protection of morally endangered children had been explicitly identified as a matter of state interest. Among public bodies concerned with abandon moral and its consequences, the department of the Seine's Service des Enfants Moralement Abandonnés would prove to be particularly influential in the early decades of the republic. The creation of a new service marked one of the first stages in the process of formalizing abandon moral and the enfant moralement abandonné as social problems of central concern to public officials on both a local and a national level. It provided the first imprimatur of legitimacy for a new institutional infrastructure designed to protect endangered and potentially dangerous children. The experience of the Service des Enfants Morale-

---

[4] See, for example, Domenique Dessertine's history of one charitable organization in Lyons, *La Société lyonnaise pour le sauvetage de l'enfance (1890–1960): Face à l'enfance en danger, un siècle d'expérience de l'internat et du placement familial* (Toulouse: Erès, 1990). See also Lee Shai Weissbach, "*Oeuvre Industrielle, Oeuvre Morale*: The *Sociétés de Patronage* of Nineteenth-Century France," *French Historical Studies* 15, no. 1 (spring 1987). For a survey of the more general role of private charity in child protection before the Third Republic, see Danielle Laplaige, *Sans famille à Paris: Orphelins et enfants abandonnés de la Seine au XIXe siècle* (Paris: Centurion, 1989).

[5] Ironically, Bonjean was the object of public scandal when the newspaper *La Lanterne* accused his private organization, La Société générale de protection pour l'enfance abandonnée ou coupable, of illicitly extracting subsidies from the Paris Bureau of Public Assistance. The scandal also emerged in reports and letters published in *Le Temps* and *Le Petit Journal* between June and December 1881. See the clippings preserved at the APP, series DB:75, *Enfants abandonnés*.

[6] The international congresses on children in moral danger included representatives from both public and private organizations. See, for example, Belgium, Ministère de la Justice, *Congrès international pour l'étude des questions relatives au patronage des détenus et à la protection des enfants moralement abandonnés. Anvers, 1890* (Brussels: E. Guyot, 1891). The first such congress was held in 1889.

ment Abandonnés over the course of the 1880s seemed to reinforce the ideas of parliamentary reformers such as Senator Théophile Roussel: only the legal empowerment of the state to protect children from their own parents could provide an adequate guarantee that the state-directed education of the moralement abandonnés would not be undone by the abuse of parental rights.

The history of the Service des Enfants Moralement Abandonnés also reveals important aspects of the mechanisms by which the Third Republic and its public servants gave practical and institutional substance to the state's identity as surrogate or metaparent to those children it deemed endangered. It suggests as well the ways in which evolving conceptions structured administrative practice and, conversely, the ways in which the demands of everyday administration destabilized and recast governing categories, ideologies, and rationalities.[7]

Introducing the category of the morally abandoned child into the discourse and practices of state child protection was an especially volatile experiment. It threatened the foundations of the extant institutional apparatus for the assistance of foundlings and poor orphans, which dated from the first decades of the nineteenth century. It pushed public authorities to redefine the limits of the state's relationship to individual children, to their parents, and to literal and metaphorical family forms. Without a clear sense of the explosive potential of their work, the Seine officials who founded the Service des Enfants Moralement Abandonnés contributed directly to the Third Republic's larger assault on the logic of the Napoleonic Code, an assault that produced, among other effects, the 1889 law on abandon moral.

The entwined histories of the Service des Enfants Moralement Abandonnés and the category of the enfant moralement abandonné yield an important window onto the process of administrative rationalization under the early Third Republic. The department's struggle to find appropriate means of rearing and supervising the morally endangered children in its care enfolded a critical second order of struggle: to eliminate contradiction, to find a regime of care that would domesticate the dangerous and bring order to the disorderly. Here, as in the discussion of legislation and justice, attention to the historical specificity of Third Republic France is critical. Although some

---

[7] In this endeavor, Foucault's account of the relationship between rationalities and practices is especially useful. Studying the operation of any regime of government, Foucault contends, is a matter of "examining how forms of rationality inscribe themselves in practices or systems of practices, and what role they play within them, because it's true that 'practices' don't exist without a certain regime of rationality" (Michel Foucault, "Question of Method," trans. Colin Gordon, in *The Foucault Effect: Studies in Governmentality*, ed. Graham Burchell, Colin Gordon, and Peter Miller [Chicago: University of Chicago Press, 1991], 79). The interview with Foucault first appeared in *L'impossible Prison: Recherches sur le système pénitentiaire au XIXe siècle*, ed. Michelle Perrot (Paris: Editions du Seuil, 1980).

social theorists, most notably Max Weber, have ascribed the desire for ratio-nality to modern bureaucratic functioning in abstracted form, the process of rationalization cannot in fact be extracted from historical contingencies, from the web of dominant ideologies, or from historically bound elaborations of particular and localized knowledges, practices, and techniques of administra-tion.[8]

The story at the center of part 3 is thus the story of a category—the enfant moralement abandonné—consumed by its internal ambiguities and contra-dictions as representatives of the state struggled to elaborate a rational ad-ministrative form tailored precisely to its contours. By the turn of the twen-tieth century, the collision between the desire for rational administration, the available techniques and institutions used to provide state guardianship for children dislocated from their families of birth, and the instabilities embed-ded in the category of enfant moralement abandonné ultimately resulted in the dissolution of the Service and the conceptual evisceration of the cate-gory. Through this history, then, we can begin to illuminate the fine texture of government in late-nineteenth-century France. Most of all, the history of the Service des Enfants Moralement Abandonnés and the category of the enfant moralement abandonné discloses the ways in which ambiguity and contradiction structured the Third Republic's effort to reshape the most fun-damental relationships between government and the governed at the intersec-tions of legislation and administration and, at that intersection, through its attempts to give effective institutional form to the parental identity it em-braced.[9]

---

[8] For Weber's account of rationality and administration, see the translated extract from *Wirt-schaft und Gesellschaft* entitled "Power and Bureaucracy," in *Max Weber*, ed. S. M. Miller (New York: Thomas Y. Crowell, 1963), esp. 64–75. Foucault offers the historian this line of inquiry by distinguishing Weber's "ideal type" of administrative rationality from his own con-cern with the history of the *dispositif*, or apparatus of administrative order (Foucault, "Questions of Method," 80–81).

[9] On the particular distinctiveness of the modern French state as producing and unifying the social, particularly since the Revolution of 1789, see Pierre Rosanvallon, *L'Etat en France de 1789 à nos jours* (Paris: Editions du Seuil, 1990), 96 and 125–26.

CHAPTER 7

Defining a Population, Defining an Administration

THE DEBATE ON how public authorities should protect and rear morally endangered children began in the late 1870s with the same breath that animated the attempt to define exactly who they were. The search for appropriate institutions and regimes of care was an essential part of the process by which the fluid category of enfant moralement abandonné was given more concrete form, a process that included but was not limited to the drafting of the 1889 legislation. At the same time, every attempt to fix the category of the enfant moralement abandonné raised the question of how the state might fix and enact its own identity as a guardian figure fulfilling its moral—and moralizing—obligations. The search for a fixed category, the effort to match it with a specific regime of state care, and the constitution of the state's identity as substitute parent through institutional and administrative practices were necessarily and ineluctably entwined.

These processes were also joined by a common underlying logic of comparison and differentiation. From the beginning, public authorities conceptualized the category of enfant moralement abandonné in relation to extant categories, institutions, and policies designed for other types of children placed in the state's care. How, they asked, were the moralement abandonnés different from other categories of state wards? What particular kind of state-supervised regime of care would those differences require? How, finally, could the state best substitute itself, through policy and administrative practice, for the delinquent parents who had, in the eyes of reformers, so blithely exposed their children to moral danger?

Beginning in the late 1870s, officials in the department of the Seine, the administrative region encompassing Paris, moved to the forefront of French administrative innovation. These officials, particularly the members of the Seine's departmental council, were the first to begin to sketch the conceptual portrait of the moralement abandonnés. With the founding of the Service des Enfants Moralement Abandonnés in 1880, they were also the first public authorities in France to begin to devise practical schemes intended both to protect these children and to defuse the potential social danger they appeared to embody. "There was a perilous lacuna in that area of assistance to children," departmental councillor Henri Rousselle observed in his 1889 review of the Seine's efforts to care for morally abandoned children. "It became necessary to take in and rear [*éduquer*] these unfortunates: wisdom advised it, humanity demanded it, it was at once an act of reparation and of social safeguarding."[1]

If the imperative for action was clear to public officials such as Rousselle, at least in retrospect, departmental records suggest that the course to be taken was not as immediately apparent. First, the law that would eventually formalize the juridical meaning of *abandon moral* existed only in draft form for most of the 1880s. Even when it was finally enacted in 1889, however, the text of the law defined the morally endangered child only through the actions of his or her parents. Further, although the 1889 law stipulated that the children removed from their parents' custody would be placed with approved guardians or in the care of the Bureau of Public Assistance, it neither defined nor required any particular structure of care. Department officials such as Rousselle thus recognized that if a new administrative structure were to be erected, it would have to be without the foundation of legally defined categories or formalized national guidelines.

How, then, did the Seine authorities begin to piece together their strategies in the late 1870s and early 1880s? How did they establish their institutional and practical frames of reference for defining the category of the moralement abandonnés and creating the appropriate structure of care for them? Most often, officials sought to define the problem of the moralement abandonnés against existing categories, institutions, and practices. Because the problem of the morally endangered child first was cast as a gap in the institutions of public assistance devoted to children, departmental authorities and administrators in the Bureau of Public Assistance looked to the administration designed for the rearing of infants and poor orphans abandoned into the care of the state, the Service des Enfants Assistés. Dr. Thulié, member of the Seine's General Council and *rapporteur* for its subcommittee on assistance, suggested in 1879 that the department simply borrow the practices established for foundlings and orphans: "[W]e could . . . send these children [the moralement abandonnés] to farmers and industrialists, and create placement districts for them comparable to those for our *enfants assistés*."[2]

Even in 1879, however, the particularity embedded in the category of the enfant moralement abandonné militated strongly against Thulié's suggestion. Tempting though it was, Seine officials found that the Service des Enfants Assistés could not provide an easily translatable model. In fact, despite the department's apparent reflexive turn to this well-established administration as prototype, the effort to define this new category of child and its proper

---

[1] Seine, Conseil Général [CGS], no. 15, *Rapport présenté par M. Rousselle au nom de la 3e commission sur le service des enfants moralement abandonnés* (1889), 3.

[2] CGS, no. 26, *Rapport sur le service des enfants assistés présenté au nom du 3e commission par Dr. Thulié* (1879), 29.

administrative form threw the conceptual and practical limits of the Service des Enfants Assistés into stark relief.

Seine officials centered their concern on two interrelated issues, both of which appeared to obstruct any simple assimilation of the moralement abandonnés into the conventions governing assistance to abandoned infants. First, early attempts to define the moralement abandonnés identified them as precisely those children formally excluded from the department's Service des Enfants Assistés. Most important, the Enfants Assistés strictly limited admission by age: in the 1880s no child over the age of twelve could be taken in as a ward of the state.[3] The earliest working definitions of the moralement abandonnés, however, generally placed them between the ages of twelve and sixteen. Councillor Rousselle, for example, used this age range to contrast the wider aims of the new Service to those of the Enfants Assistés. Because the Service's primary role was "to provide a vocation to its wards," he explained, the new Service should primarily take in older children, who "could be immediately placed in apprenticeship." At the same time, he cautioned, the children should not be too far into their teens "because the legal age of apprenticeship would be past and because their nature is more refractory to the effects of education."[4]

Despite Rousselle's emphasis on the practical demands of vocational education, the determinants of the upper age limit in particular intersected with other powerful concerns about the relationship between a child's age and the course of his or her moral formation. In the pedagogy and psychology of the late nineteenth century, age signified both the degree of a child's moral corruption and the potential for reform.[5] As one Doctor Vingtrinier had written in an influential 1840 treatise on prison reform, "If children, according to the

[3] The 1811 decree founding the Service des Enfants Assistés in France limited admission to poor orphans and abandoned children born out of wedlock or to unknown or untraceable parents. Another ministerial decree, dated 8 February 1823, further limited admission to children under the age of twelve. The 1811 decree had had no such limits. For a general account of the changing criteria for accepting children into the Service des Enfants Assistés in the nineteenth century, see Albert Dupoux, *Sur les pas de Monsieur Vincent: Trois cent ans d'histoire parisienne de l'enfance abandonnée* (Paris: Revue de l'Assistance publique à Paris, 1958), esp. chap. 9, "L'Assistance aux enfants trouvés et abandonnés au XIXe siècle." For the complete text of the 1811 decree, see *Sur les pas*, 184.

[4] CGS, no. 15 (1889), 9.

[5] Kathleen Alaimo has extensively examined new definitions of adolescence and its dangers in the late nineteenth century in her doctoral dissertation, "Adolescence in the Popular Milieu in France during the Early Third Republic: Efforts to Define and Shape a Stage of Life" (Ph.D. diss., University of Wisconsin, Madison, 1988). See also Alaimo, "Shaping Adolescence in the Popular Milieu: Social Policy, Reformers, and French Youth, 1870–1920," *Journal of Family History* 17, no. 4 (1992): 419–38. Michelle Perrot also addresses the question of youth, adolescence, and social anxiety in "Sur la ségrégation de l'enfance au XIXe siècle," *La Psychiatrie de l'enfant* 25, fasc. 1 (1982), and "Quand la société prend peur de sa jeunesse en France, au 19e siècle," in *Les Jeunes et les autres*, ed. Michelle Perrot, vol. 1 (Paris: CRIV, 1986).

Horatian expression, take like wax the impression of vice, *cerus in vitrium flecti*, they also take the impression of virtue."[6] Age, in other words, was not only a measure of the child's relationship to the social world of labor, law, and institutional incorporation, it also signified the status of the child's intellect, morals, and character. Age stood for both the relative potential for change—that is, the child's position on the scale of educability—and the degree to which time had permitted the accumulation of unhealthy experiences and moral scars.

The parameters of age also drew on the conceptual and institutional conventions of criminal justice. The upper limit of the range, age sixteen, coincided exactly with the legal definition of penal majority, the age at which delinquent youths were treated as adults in the criminal justice system.[7] These parameters of age and potential criminal status were critical to all further articulations of the essence of the enfant moralement abandonné. Even before this category of children was named, it was defined in the entwined terms of age and potential or actual delinquency: "[C]hild vagabonds from twelve to sixteen years old."[8] On the whole, the defining age range of the morally abandoned child rested on a logic of exclusion. The moralement abandonnés were those too old for existing regimes of child protection and too young for the existing regime of correction. The tendency to identify the category of the enfant moralement abandonné through a process of exclusion would have important conceptual and practical consequences. Most of all, it would ensure both the internal instability and the liminality of the new category in ways that ultimately rendered it impossible to institutionalize as a distinct and permanent category of state-protected child.

The threat of deviance, although an important consideration in setting the boundaries of age, also constituted an independent point of reference in the wider consideration of what differentiated the moralement abandonnés from the enfants assistés. In contemporary commentary, as in the language of administration, the new category of abandoned child appeared to emerge far more from conceptions of the dangerous vagabond than from images of the comparatively innocent abandoned infant.[9] Othenin d'Haussonville, for ex-

---

[6] Dr. [Arthus-Barthélemy] Vingtrinier, *Des prisons et des prisonniers* (Versailles: Klefer, 1840), 133.

[7] The original, 1810 version of article 66 put the age of responsibility at sixteen. Revisions enacted in 1906 raised the age of penal majority to eighteen. On late-nineteenth-century understandings of juvenile delinquency, adolescence, and the age of penal majority, see Alaimo, "Shaping Adolescence," 431–32.

[8] CGS, no. 26 (1879), 28.

[9] In fact, as Rachel Fuchs demonstrates, it was far from the case that state-assisted foundlings—*les enfants assistés*—were deemed purely innocent victims. The *petit parisiens* were generally assumed to be illegitimate; administrators and the populace at large saw in them both the signs of parental immorality and the vehicle for transmitting the sins of the parents to future generations. Fuchs also notes, however, that this attitude underwent considerable revision to-

ample, who frequently wrote on social and moral conditions in Paris in the 1870s, described the city's population of "young vagabonds" as one of the "blights" of modern civilization. These children, he wrote, were

> little nomads who wander, without a fixed home, parentless, without protection . . . the majority of whom, after having crowded the holding room at the Prefecture de Police, faced the solitude of the cells at the Petite Roquette, and tasted the charms of prison camaraderie at Poissy or Melun, end by making the one-way voyage for the beaches of New Caledonia.[10]

As the categorical reembodiment of Haussonville's vagabonds, the enfants moralement abandonnés were also defined in terms of a linear trajectory of experience and time, both essential elements in the nineteenth-century logic of reform.[11] Well past infancy, these children were nearing an age at which they would no longer be educable, and at which the demoralizing habits and tastes they had acquired might harden into permanent characterological attributes. Old enough for legitimate apprenticeship, they offered little proof that they had been sufficiently indoctrinated with an acceptable ideology of work and its moral benefits. Neglected by their parents, they were likely to have wrought for themselves a dangerously different kind of education, learning the arts of petty crime in the street instead of the standards of moral conduct they should have received in the home. In this light, then, even the most apparently innocent enfant moralement abandonné contained the germ of dangerous criminality. For the Parisian officials charged with inventing a regime of care for the enfant moralement abandonné in the 1880s, this view would resonate strongly within their growing concern about the blurred lines between innocence and criminality, educability and impressionability.[12]

If the trajectory of precocious and prolonged exposure to the demoralizing forces of modern urban life pointed toward a criminal future, it did not determine a criminal status for them in the present. In these first articulations of the new category, the enfants moralement abandonnés were in fact defined in opposition to the juvenile offender. Along with their experience of demoralizing family life and their exclusion from the structures of state child pro-

---

ward the end of the century as opinions on childhood changed and the importance of renewing an ailing and diminishing population overshadowed earlier concerns. See Rachel G. Fuchs, *Abandoned Children: Foundlings and Child Welfare in Nineteenth-Century France* (Albany: SUNY Press, 1984), esp. chap. 2, "Attitudes and Public Policy toward the Family."

[10] Othenin d'Haussonville, "L'Enfance à Paris," *Revue des deux mondes* 17 (1876): 482.

[11] On the importance of linear time as the frame for "evolution" in nineteenth-century theories of reform, see Michel Foucault, *Discipline and Punish: The Birth of the Prison*, trans. Alan Sheridan (New York: Vintage Books, 1979), esp. 160–61.

[12] On the increasing concern about youthful impressionablity and immorality, see Annie Stora-Lamarre, *L'Enfer de la Troisième République: Censeurs et pornographes (1881–1914)* (Paris: Editions Imago, 1990), esp. chap. 3, "La Marée pornographique." See also Perrot, "Quand la société prend peur de sa jeunesse," 20–22.

tection, the morally abandoned were also fundamentally defined in the early 1880s by what appeared to be a dangerous and unjust inclusion in the categories of criminal justice. According to Senator Roussel, the term *enfant moralement abandonné* was in fact first used in the 12 June 1879 report of the Société générale des prisons, a private reform organization of which Roussel was a prominent member. "This expression," Roussel noted in 1882, "was soon welcomed with favor by the press, at the same time as the noble creation of the new service to which the Administration of Public Assistance in Paris gave this same name." A central element of the campaign for the new legislation, Roussel added, was the need to give the term a "more precise legal definition."[13]

In the widening debate about the need to develop more refined distinctions between types of criminal offenders, authorities found a concrete foundation for differentiation between the enfant moralement abandonné and the young delinquent. Most important in these discussions was the category created by the law of 5 August 1850 on youth and criminal responsibility: minors acquitted for having committed their crimes "without discernment" according to article 66 of the penal code but still deemed to be in need of institutional correction.[14] In 1879 the Seine's General Council openly deplored the ways in which abandoned or endangered adolescents fell under the 1850 law by default. According to the annual report of the Service des Enfants Assistés from that year, the only "protective" action available to authorities was for the police to arrest these older children in the name of "preventing vagrancy." If their parents did not claim them from police custody, the children would be taken to court. There, the magistrate would generally acquit them for having acted "without discernment." Exempted from criminal conviction but still thought to be culpable and in need of state supervision, the children would be sent to an agricultural colony or other correctional establishment for "reeducation."[15]

In the late 1870s, the policing practices subtended by the 1850 law lay behind much of the official impetus to develop more precise boundaries for this ambiguous category of children. According to the council's subcommission on assistance, these older children's only crime was having been abandoned. Instead of helping them, members argued, arresting them and placing them in penal institutions were the equivalent of inducting them directly into

---

[13] France, Assemblée nationale, Sénat, *Rapport fait au nom de la commission chargée d'examiner: 1° La Proposition de loi ayant pour objet la protection des enfants abandonnés, délaissés ou maltraités, présenté par MM. Théophile Roussel, Bérenger, Dufaure, l'amiral Fourichon, Schoelcher et Jules Simon. 2° Le Projet de loi sur la protection de l'enfance présenté par M. Cazot, Garde de Sceaux, Ministre de Justice*, no. 451, Sénat session 1882, annexe au procès-verbal de la séance du 25 juillet 1882 (Paris: Imprimerie du Sénat, 1882), 27.

[14] On the law of 5 August 1850, see Jean-Marie Renouard, *De l'enfant coupable à l'enfant inadapté: Le traitement social et politique de la déviance* (Paris: Centurion, 1990), 38–41.

[15] CGS, no. 26 (1879), 28.

a "school of vice."[16] Looking back on the years before the founding of the Service des Enfants Moralement Abandonnés, Councillor Rousselle stressed the problem of the state's culpability in promoting the further demoralization of the morally endangered child through the operation of this correctional mechanism. Through the limits imposed by article 66 of the penal code and the law on juvenile correction of 1850, Rousselle argued, "[Society] had no other haven for him than the house of correction, that is to say, an unhealthy milieu where the young innocent could not enter without being tarnished and whence he could rarely leave uncorrupted." The demoralizing experience of the prison, Rousselle added, ensured that the once-innocent abandoned child would become, "through a kind of social determinism, a soldier in the army of crime." Like the members of the Société générale des prisons a decade earlier, Rousselle claimed that the only solution was to provide this category of children with "another refuge." This refuge, embodied for Rousselle in the Seine's new Service des Enfants Moralement Abandonnés, would permit authorities to differentiate between the morally endangered child and the truly delinquent one. No less important, it would prevent the slippage between the categories of the morally abandoned and the delinquent that officials such as Rousselle saw as the inevitable result of treating these children as juvenile offenders.[17]

One other critical aspect of the conceptualization of the new category lay buried within these assumptions about age and delinquency. Social and criminological commentary almost universally identified vagrancy and juvenile crime as a male phenomenon.[18] The criminal "deviance" attributed to girls found wandering the city streets, in contrast, was given an explicitly sexual cast; for police, urban authorities, and philanthropists, adolescent girls in public spaces could be read only as juvenile prostitutes.[19] Ironically, the gendered distinctions between vagrancy and prostitution collapsed in Paris in 1893, when the court of appeals ruled that girls under sixteen could no longer be treated as prostitutes when arrested for solicitation but would be assimilated into the more generic category of vagabonds.[20] It is unlikely,

---

[16] Ibid.

[17] CGS, no. 15 (1889), 3.

[18] See Lenard R. Berlanstein, "Vagrants, Beggars, and Thieves: Delinquent Boys in Mid-Nineteenth Century Paris," *Journal of Social History* 12, no. 4 (summer 1979). See also Philippe Meyer, *L'Enfant et la raison d'état* (Paris: Editions du Seuil, 1977), esp. chap. 2, "Le Territoire de l'aveu."

[19] See, for example, Haussonville, "L'Enfance à Paris," 505. On prostitution in Paris, see Jill Harsin, *Policing Prostitution in Nineteenth-Century Paris* (Princeton: Princeton University Press, 1985). For the campaign against child prostitution and "white slavery" led by Senator René Bérenger at the turn of the twentieth century, see Alain Corbin, *Women for Hire: Prostitution and Sexuality in France after 1850*, trans. Alan Sheridan (Cambridge: Harvard University Press, 1990), 289–98.

[20] Henri Monod, *Les Enfants assistés de France* (Melun: Imprimerie administrative, 1898), cxxviii–cxxix.

however, that the sexual—and sexed—nature of their presumed delinquency was masked by these administrative gestures.

Defined from the first in terms of the potentially criminal vagabond, the category of the enfant moralement abandonné was implicitly gendered as male. Again, this rather abstract conceptual element would have significant institutional and practical consequences. To be sure, it was not that girls would be lacking from the rolls of the moralement abandonnés in departmental care. Over the life of the Service as an independent administration, girls comprised on average one-third of the moralement abandonnés. Between 1881 and 1888, girls made up an average of 31 percent of the new admissions to the Service des Enfants Moralement Abandonnés. In 1882, for example, the Service took in some 290 girls and roughly 650 boys.[21] Despite these figures, however, the abstract—and ideologically loaded—determinants of the category tended to efface the female population both in the wider discussions of the problems posed by the enfants moralement abandonnés and in the efforts to determine appropriate regimes of care for them. Only when administrators shifted from the abstract and universal to particular and practical questions about vocational training and sexual restraint would the question of sexual difference arise.

The masculine essence of the category of the enfant moralement abandonné—as opposed to the mixed-gender population taken into state care under this rubric—was most commonly elaborated in the administration's rhetoric of prescription and prognostication. In the introduction to his 1894 report on the Service des Enfants Moralement Abandonnés, Councillor Rousselle proclaimed the main goals of protecting the morally endangered child: "To make the child into an honest man, a productive worker, and a brave soldier concerns both the wealth and the strength of the fatherland [*la patrie*]."[22] Rousselle's language exemplifies the common understanding in late-nineteenth-century France that the endangered child of greatest interest to la patrie was the male child.[23] Beneath the apparently neutral discussion of relations between the French state and endangered French children lay an intricate and highly gendered vision of public ties between the "fatherland" and future generations of male social, economic, and political actors. In this double articulation of the enfant moralement abandonné as both neutral ob-

---

[21] CGS, no. 15 (1889), 10.

[22] CGS, no. 1, *Rapport général présenté par M. Rousselle au nom de la 3e commission sur le service des enfants moralement abandonnés* (1894), 2.

[23] Lee Shai Weissbach has also noted this ideological investment in children as the literal embodiment of the future—again, especially as workers, soldiers, and citizens—in his study of child labor legislation in the nineteenth century (*Child Labor Reform in Nineteenth-Century France: Assuring the Future Harvest* [Baton Rouge: Louisiana State University Press, 1989]). See also Colin Heywood, who notes the importance of military recruitment statistics in the campaign for child labor legislation (Heywood, *Childhood in Nineteenth-Century France: Work, Health, and Education among the "classes populaires"* [Cambridge: Cambridge University Press, 1988], 147–56).

ject of state protection and, implicitly, as the male subject of the future, Rousselle was not alone.[24]

A French philosopher has recently argued that *man* has served as a gendered but universal signifier in modern language. In a parallel fashion, albeit perhaps more subtly articulated, *child* (*l'enfant*) served as a universal signifier in the nineteenth-century discourse on the morally endangered child.[25] Within the bureaucratic enclave of the Bureau of Public Assistance, the discussions of how the moralement abandonnés were to be protected from their past and molded for the future embraced a similar slippage. Official discourse vacillated between male-gendered terms that carried an apparently neutral charge and male-gendered terms fully engaged in the hierarchies of social roles and cultural values that differentiated men from women from the moment of birth. The female enfant moralement abandonné was, conceptually, a contradiction. Only where administrators addressed the more concrete questions of particular institutions and practices, such as vocational training or apprenticeship, was the gender specificity of girls categorized as moralement abandonné(e)s materialized.[26]

The contradictions of gender, the threat of criminality, and the uncertainties of age and educability all ensured that the moral status of the enfant moralement abandonné would remain indeterminant. This moral ambiguity continually disrupted the Seine's efforts to stabilize both an effective definition of the population in question and the regime of care that population required. Most of all, it was unclear to administrators whether the enfant moralement abandonné should be considered primarily the victim of immoral parents or a potential agent of demoralization. Councillor Rousselle summed up this enduring conundrum. Morally abandoned children, he stated decisively, "menace society, which must be protected." Yet, Rousselle asked, "[W]hat made them so, if not that same society of which they are the victims?"[27] The uncertainty about the moral status of the enfant moralement abandonné turned departmental officials in two directions at once; while Parisian authorities proclaimed with great confidence that children in moral dan-

[24] See, for example, Jules Simon, *L'Ouvrier de huit ans* (Paris: A. Lacroix, Verboeckhoven et Cie, 1867).

[25] This philosopher, Luce Irigaray, also writes: "[T]he subject is always inscribed as masculine, even when it would pose itself as universal or neuter: *man*. Yet man—at least in French—is not neuter, but sexed" Unlike English, the French language assigns gender to all nouns. See Irigaray, *Ethique de la différence sexuelle* (Paris: Editions de Minuit, 1984), 14 (emphasis hers).

[26] On sexual difference and the logic of child assistance, see also my article "When the Child Is the Father of the Man: Work, Sexual Difference, and the Guardian-State in Third Republic France," *History and Theory* (1992) *beiheft* 31: History and Feminist Theory, 98–115, reprinted in *Feminists Revision History*, ed. Ann-Louise Shapiro (New Brunswick: Rutgers University Press, 1994).

[27] CGS, no. 1 (1894), 3.

ger needed state protection, they could not say with equal conviction to what degree that protection should be prophylactic and to what degree corrective.

The consequences of this fluid conceptualization were deeply troubling, and not only on a discursive level. The new category radically challenged the polarities that had previously organized the state's treatment of the young. In need of more rigorous supervision and education than the enfants assistés, but not so delinquent that they belonged in the institutions of the penal administration, these children fell between the cracks of the existing regimes of public child rearing, education, and correction. They illuminated the rigidity of existing institutions and conceptual models through which the state protected the abandoned child or corrected the delinquent one. In locating the category in the shadowy interstices between innocence and corruption, and between impressionable youth and hardened adult, Parisian officials were forced to look for solutions in a new and similarly interstitial region: the space between the institutional strategies of protection and those of correction.

The core of the Seine's new Service des Enfants Moralement Abandonnés was shaped by administrators' continuing efforts to develop a theory of placement tailored to the specific problem of children in moral danger. These attempts to articulate general principles took place on several conceptual levels and made use of a variety of languages. First, for most public officials the ideal program for the moralement abandonnés would necessarily involve physical relocation: authorities would extricate children from the unhealthy environments that threatened their moral well-being and place them in surroundings deemed morally salubrious. Administrators and commentators frequently employed the language of agriculture to explain their aims. Arguing in 1892 against the use of distinctive uniforms for those moralement abandonnés in the care of provincial foster families, for example, Councillor Rousselle claimed that such visible distinctions prevented the children from "taking root in the soil where they had been transplanted."[28] Similarly, in 1909 a report issued by the Bureau of Public Assistance argued that to transform "little vagabonds" into good workers and citizens, "first it is necessary to 'transplant' these children, to have them live in an absolutely new environment."[29]

The moral geography of placement was not the only important frame of reference for developing a regime of care tailored specifically for this category of children in state care. Officials also addressed the problem of characterizing the forms of supervision and training best suited for the moralement

[28] CGS, no. 38, *Rapport général présenté par M. Rousselle au nom de la 3e commission sur le service des enfants moralement abandonnés* (1892), 9.

[29] AGAPP, *Les Ecoles professionnelles du service des enfants assistés de la Seine: L'école d'Alembert (1882–1909) à Montévrain* (Paris: Berger-Levrault, 1909), 1–2.

abandonnés. Here, too, the language of agriculture provided the basic tropes that would serve as the standard of measure in the development of concrete plans for rearing this category of children. One member of the Seine's General Council exemplified the department's developing ideal through this construction: "With the gentlest binding a tree can be made to take the form one wants (nature is mastered)."[30]

At the heart of the department's concern about placement and the metaphorical and institutional relationships it instantiated lay the fundamental question of the state's role in forming moral character and regulating habit. Here, Parisian officials grounded the question of placement and its moralizing effects in contemporary efforts to reconstruct the state as metaphorical guardian or parent. In protecting a child from dangerous influences, and in creating a moralizing structure of everyday life through the development of effective administrative practices and policies, officials simultaneously confirmed and enacted the new regime's parental identity.

The vision of character shaping through the constitution of moralizing "familial" identities and relations, along with the emphasis laid on the inculcation of work skills and the discipline of labor, came together in administrators' identification of appropriate placements with the essential task of *éducation*. The term *éducation*, used to describe the simultaneous formation of the moral and the social self, carried strong connotations, which were in turn well embedded in the history of pedagogic thought in France. These historically and politically situated understandings of education, particularly those developed during the Enlightenment and the French Revolution, would in fact serve as a blueprint for the self-conscious reformers of the early Third Republic.[31] In the 1870s Emile Littré, enthusiastic republican, disciple of Auguste Comte, and lexicographer, reinscribed the eighteenth-century notion of education in the vocabulary of the later nineteenth century. "Education," he argued, "pertains simultaneously to the heart and the mind, and comprises knowledge given to us and the moral guidance of our sentiments."[32]

To be sure, all was not static in the century between the Revolution and the establishment of the republican Third Republic. By the end of the nineteenth century, prevailing notions of education also took on important social

[30] CGS, no. 18, *Rapport présenté par M. Curé au nom de la 3e commission sur le budget du service des enfants moralement abandonnés pour l'année 1888* (1887), 7. On agricultural metaphors in the discourse of industrial labor reform, see Weissbach, *Child Labor Reform*, esp. xii. The influence of Jean-Jacques Rousseau's *Emile* on nineteenth-century educational philosophy is quite evident in this councillor's choice of language. See Rousseau, *Emile, ou de l'éducation*, ed. Marcel Launay (Paris: Flammarion, 1966), esp. bk. 1.

[31] On revolutionary visions of education, see Marie-Françoise Lévy, ed., *L'Enfant, la famille et la Révolution française* (Paris: Olivier Orban, 1990). See also Yves Roumajon, *Enfants perdus, enfants punis. Historique de la jeunesse délinquante en France: Huit siècles de controverses* (Paris: Editions Robert Laffont, 1989), esp. "Les débuts de l'éducation."

[32] Emile Littré, as cited in Roumajon, *Enfants perdus*, 121.

inflections. In the context of the growing body of thought on the moral and economic status of the laboring classes, education thus also came to describe the particular structure of vocational training, the inculcation of the skills and habits of labor. In late-nineteenth-century usage, particularly where poor or laboring-class children were concerned, *education* described a total apprenticeship of manners, morals, and métier.[33]

Where the state's care of the moralement abandonnés was concerned, education also implied the project of civilizing the untamed. In the first annual report on the new agency, written in 1881, Dr. Thulié described for his colleagues an archetypal first encounter between an enfant moralement abandonné and the disciplinary order of the Service.

> When the child comes to our Service . . . he is like a wild animal caught in a snare and caged. For him everything is subject to suspicion, he seeks a crack through which to escape, but the regularity of existence and above all the rest that comes without fail at a fixed time, gradually calms him. He is quite astonished no longer to know hunger and not to have to risk pursuit and arrest in order to provide for his basic needs. It is then that counsel intervenes; it is when he physically enjoys this regular state of well-being that he can be made to understand that through work, this well-being could last forever, and the satisfaction of the stomach is, for this savage, evidence more convincing than the world's best treatises.[34]

Thulié's words encapsulated many of the Service's most fundamental concerns about rearing and educating the moralement abandonnés. Whereas the first order of business in the Service des Enfants Assistés was to ensure that the infants in its care survived through the first tenuous months of life, the primary issue for the Service des Enfants Moralement Abandonnés was to tame the "savage" child. This domesticating education, moreover, would act first through the body, with the strictly routinized satisfaction of basic physical need.[35] Only later, in appeals to the child's intellect, could the route to civilized humanity be represented as a causal chain between the satisfaction

---

[33] The literature on the relationship between education and the discipline of the poor in the nineteenth century covers a wide range of topics. See, among other works, Robert J. Bezucha, "The Moralization of Society: The Enemies of Popular Culture in the Nineteenth Century," in *The Wolf and the Lamb: Popular Culture in France from the Old Regime to the Twentieth Century*, ed. Jacques Beauroy, Marc Bertrand, and Edward T. Gargan (Saratoga: ANMA Libri, 1976); Lee Shai Weissbach, "*Oeuvre Industrielle, Oeuvre Morale:* The Sociétés de Patronage of Nineteenth-Century France," *French Historical Studies* 15, no. 1 (spring 1987); and Isaac Joseph, Philippe Fritsch, and Alain Battegay, "Disciplines à domicile: L'édification de la famille," *Recherches* 28 (28 November 1977).

[34] CGS, no. 18, *Rapport sur le service des enfants moralement abandonnés présenté au nom du 3e commission par M. Thulié* (1881), 2.

[35] On the relationship between the discipline of the body and the larger project of normative reform, see Foucault's *Discipline and Punish*, esp. pt. 3, chap. 1, "Docile Bodies."

of appetite, the performance of respectable labor, and a restored moral sensibility.

The comparison of the urban vagabond to a wild animal resonated widely in the late nineteenth century. One of the most powerful fantasies about modern life was the notion that while some sectors of society advanced the cultural, technical, and intellectual achievements of humankind, other representatives of the species were undergoing a literal devolution in the streets of the modern world's great capitals. By the last quarter of the century, social science and criminology had cast the savage as anything but noble.[36]

Deficient moral and familial education was thus a particularly dreadful specter for public officials charged with protecting and rearing morally endangered children. Arresting the "civilizing process," negligent parents in effect marooned their offspring in the urban wilderness, where they would be forced to lead the most degraded type of existence. Against the backdrop of hysteria generated by France's demographic crisis, the idea of losing able-bodied children to the moral plagues of parental failure and urban experience seemed almost as dangerous to collective survival as the nation's high rate of infant mortality and comparatively low fertility.

With their emphasis on combating the combined dangerous influence of modern life and negligent or ignorant parents, the debates on the proper placement and education of the enfants moralement abandonnés brought Seine officials face-to-face with the more general educational projects and institutions of the new republican regime. The advent of the liberal Third Republic in the 1880s brought a new moral weight to all questions pertaining to the formation of future citizens and mothers of citizens. As in the Revolution of 1789, the moral health of the nation was attached to education in its broadest sense. From the household to the classroom, all educational situations became a matter of overwhelming public and political concern.

For committed republicans, childhood thus represented nothing less than the window of opportunity for ensuring the reproduction of a moral population. For many activists, the stabilization of republican France in the late 1870s and 1880s turned on this vision of education, for the liberal Third Republic staked its future as much on the molding of the young as on the reform of political institutions, if not more so. In this view, mandatory secular primary instruction promised that universal manhood suffrage would not be exercised under the sway of ignorance or "superstition," the republicans' euphemism for the "archaic" religiosity and clerical influence they abhorred. State-run primary schooling for children between the ages of six and thir-

---

[36] Susanna Barrows notes the importance of the paradigm of pathological atavism in nineteenth-century social science and criminal anthropology, especially in the work of the influential Cesare Lombroso. See Barrows's *Distorting Mirrors: Visions of the Crowd in Late Nineteeth-Century France* (New Haven: Yale University Press, 1981), 125–26.

teen, established by the Ferry Laws of the early 1880s, would thus provide the means for instilling secular civic virtues in children young enough to receive the stamp of the national moral curriculum.[37]

The highly loaded debate on the appropriate form of placement for the moralement abandonnés emerged in the early 1880s at the very moment when republicans were celebrating the promulgation of the Ferry Laws. Although the ideology of the Third Republic clearly raised the stakes involved in shaping the minds and characters of the young, for officials charged with creating an effective regime of care for the enfants moralement abandonnés the republican valorization of education did not provide solutions to the problem of moralizing children above the age of thirteen. With the formal establishment of the new Service, moreover, the question of age was no longer abstract. In 1881, the first year of operation, roughly one-half of the young people admitted to the Service were thirteen or older. In subsequent years, the proportion of adolescents listed in the annual admission records declined, but their paucity was more than made up for by the number of children who passed the age of thirteen while still in the care of the Service.[38]

The advanced age of the children categorized as morally abandoned ensured that the administration could not count on the primary schools to provide an education in secular morals. In a larger sense, increasingly refined notions of instruction, education, and reform created more, not less, uncertainty about how to construct a regime of state care for the moralement abandonnés. On the one hand, as the innocent victims of parental negligence, these children seemed to need only what their parents had failed to provide: an education in personal conduct and values and the provision of good moral example. The role of the guardian state would thus be simply to fill a void, to substitute for the negligent parent by proxy. On the other hand, given their precocious exposure to their parents' vices and immoral example, these children also seemed to require an upbringing that would correct for early deformation, a *re*education.[39] The moral ambiguity first written into the very cate-

---

[37] See, for example, Ferdinand Buisson's lecture from 1883, "La Nouvelle éducation nationale," in *La Foi laïque: Extraits de discours et d'écrits (1878–1911)*, 2d ed. (Paris: Hachette, 1913). In 1879 Buisson was named head of primary education in Jules Ferry's Ministry of Public Instruction. He remained in that position for the next twenty years. On Jules Ferry and the question of education in the Third Republic, see François Furet, ed., *Jules Ferry: Fondateur de la République* (Paris: Ecole des Hautes Etudes en Sciences Sociales, 1985), and Jean-Michel Gaillard's biography, *Jules Ferry* (Paris: Fayard, 1989). On civic and moral education in the classrooms of the Third Republic, see Phyllis Stock-Morton's *Moral Education for a Secular Society: The Development of Morale Laïque in Nineteenth Century France* (Albany: SUNY Press, 1988).

[38] CGS, no. 15 (1889), 8.

[39] It is important to note that the adjective *éduquable* appears to have been coined in approximately 1845, during a period of widespread and harsh criticism of the penal system in France, particularly in its treatment of children. The word *rééducation* appeared in the late nineteenth

gory of the enfant moralement abandonné was thus mirrored in this double vision of the state's educational task. In the ideal, the regime of educative care provided by the parental state would produce both the lost moralizing inscription on the tabula rasa of childhood and the remoralizing erasure of what had previously been written in the degrading hand of the dangerous parent.

Officials' efforts to find the seam between more basic notions of education and a particularized regime of *re*education or reform of the moralement abandonnés had serious consequences beyond the arena of their own labors. Most important, perhaps, the problem posed by the moralement abandonnés complicated the republican vision of a generalized moral curriculum. In 1883 Senator Théophile Roussel, the sponsor and primary author of the 1889 law on abandon moral, stressed the limits of the classroom for any effective reeducation of the moralement abandonnés. "[W]e have just come under a regime of obligatory schooling," he reminded his fellow senators, "which will be a great boon for the country; but which, in regard to the class which is the nursery of young delinquents and criminals, will be altogether inadequate."[40]

The question of how the republican state should raise and educate the moralement abandonnés destabilized the ideal of a universal moral foundation for France so dear to liberal republicans. The pressure of suppressed class distinctions and the fear they generated in bourgeois administrators exploded the professed egalitarianism of republican educational ideology.[41] Educating the moralement abandonnés meant not only addressing a breakdown in individual and familial morals but admitting that republican France was deeply riven by class conflict and social fears. In this context, the project of educating the moralement abandonnés appeared to entail far more than directing the formation of the individual. It meant intervening in a socially distinct life course already removed from the curve of the normal. This life course, in the eyes of these republican reformers, was the route from childhood poverty to adult criminality.

Contemporary notions of criminality had been crucial when reformers first attempted to constitute the category of the enfant moralement abandonné.

---

century. On the chronology of and citations for these usages, see Paul Robert, *Dictionnaire alphabétique et analogique de la langue française* (Paris: Société du Nouveau Littré, 1963).

[40] *JOS*, 11 May 1883, 463.

[41] As Linda Clark and Françoise Mayeur have pointed out, however, the distinctions of gender were well-articulated in republican educational ideology. See Linda L. Clark, *Schooling the Daughters of Marianne: Textbooks and the Socialization of Girls in Modern French Primary Schools* (Albany: SUNY Press, 1984); Françoise Mayeur, *L'Enseignement sécondaire des jeunes filles sous la Troisième République* (Paris: A. Colin, 1977); and Mayeur, *L'Education des filles en France au XIXe siècle* (Paris: Hachette, 1979). See also Jo Burr Margadant, *Madame le professeur: Women Educators in the Third Republic* (Princeton: Princeton University Press, 1990).

They provided the ground of deviancy against which the morally endangered child could appear as both vulnerable and potentially culpable. In defining the particular educative task the state confronted in the enfants moralement abandonnés, officials once again ran headlong into the adjacent campaign to reform France's criminal justice and penitentiary systems, most of all where they addressed minors.

In the treatment of both adults and children, the trend of the second half of the century has often been described as the move away from punishment and toward a structure of "humane" rehabilitation. Working within this principle, officials and philanthropists concerned with the fate of minors in the penal system increasingly agitated to end the "promiscuity" of the general prison through the segregation and the specialized treatment of the young.[42]

The discourse of remoralization was a powerful element in their campaigns. In the case of adults, new schemes for rehabilitation turned on the incitement of conscious repentance and on the inculcation of modes of behavior that precluded recidivism. This was the principle behind Senator Bérenger's reform of the penal code, approved by the National Assembly in 1885. The new law stressed the potential for reform among first-time adult offenders. For repeat offenders, however, the tone shifted from rehabilitation to punishment.[43] In the criminal psychology of the day, there was little real hope that any adult character could be fully remade, but reformers clung fervently to the possibility that they could at least be taught to control their criminal impulses. In the case of minors, however, particularly those who were adjudged too young to bear responsibility for their crimes, the stakes in penal reform were set much higher. Authorities involved in penal reform suggested that by reaching young miscreants while they were still evolving they could effect profound and permanent transformations of character.

As reformers worked in the early decades of the Third Republic to distinguish juvenile offenders from irredeemable adult criminals by virtue of the formers' essential educability, so too they focused with ever greater intensity on defining the modes of moralizing reeducation or correction best suited for reshaping young characters. The Société générale des prisons, for example, in its comprehensive report of 1878, denounced the practice of incarcerating "impressionable" youths with a population of "hardened" adult criminals.

---

[42] On the move in the second half of the nineteenth century away from the punitive treatment of criminal adults and children and toward their reeducation or reform, see Patricia O'Brien, *The Promise of Punishment: Prisons in Nineteenth-Century France* (Princeton: Princeton University Press, 1982); Dupoux, *Sur les pas*; Perrot, "Sur la ségrégation de l'enfance au XIXe siécle"; Henri Gaillac, *Les Maisons de correction, 1830–1945* (Paris: Editions Cujas, 1971); Maurice Crubellier, *L'Enfance et la jeunesse dans la société française, 1800–1950* (Paris: Armand Colin, 1979); and Jacques Donzelot, *The Policing of Families*, trans. Robert Hurley (New York: Pantheon, 1979).

[43] O'Brien, *The Promise of Punishment*, 265–67, 287–96.

Instead, the society contended, the future of juvenile correction lay in moving away from demoralizing prison terms and toward a program of carefully engineered prevention and reeducation.[44] The society's report further tied the increasing differentiation among categories of delinquent minors to the growing need for differentiated regimes of reeducation. It too spun the logic of contagious vice, so central in the definition of the enfant moralement abandonné, from the articulations of categories to the institutional practices they inspired. A proper reeducation for the juvenile offender, in short, would both break the hold of vice and prevent any further exposure to it.

Of particular importance to the efforts to define an educational regime appropriate for the moralement abandonnés was the increasingly violent critique of the agricultural colony's utility in the moral correction of the young. In the decades that followed the enactment of the 1850 law on the treatment of minors who had committed crimes without discernment, the agricultural colony became one of the primary institutional destinations for boys who would later fall under the rubric of moralement abandonnés. As early as the mid-1850s, one-half of all juveniles in correction had been sent to such colonies, many of them established in direct response to the new law and run as private enterprises by individual entrepreneurs and religious institutions.[45]

Despite the confident declarations issued in the 1850s that the agricultural colony would be an institution of moral redemption rather than one of repression, the veneer of innovative humane correction had worn thin by the later 1870s. Critics charged that the colonies were no better than the brutal correctional institutions for adults, that the children were mistreated, that their living conditions were inadequate and demoralizing, and that their labor in the fields, rather than instilling obedience and virtue, was simply a form of exploitation. The agricultural colony of Mettray, in particular, once held up as a model of modern correctional methods, now stood as an example of corruption and failure. Plagued by revolts, escapes, and the embarrassing recidivism of its former charges, Mettray represented the bankruptcy of the colony as an institution of gentle reform.[46]

---

[44] See Martine Kaluszynski, "Les Juristes en action: La société générale des prisons (1877–1940) ou l'exercice politique d'une société savante" (Paris, 1989, photocopy), and Kaluszynski and Françoise Tetard, "Un Objet: L'enfant en 'danger moral.' Une expérience: La société de patronage" (Paris, 1989, photocopy).

[45] On the reform of juvenile correction and the organization of the agricultural colony, see O'Brien, The Promise of Punishment, esp. 131–38. Jean Lebrun provides an important case study of the agricultural colony as the intersection of monastic and correctional discipline in "Cloîtrer et guérir: La colonie pénitentiaire de la Trappe, 1854–1880," in L'Impossible prison: Recherches sur le système pénitentiaire au XIXe siècle, ed. Michelle Perrot (Paris: Editions du Seuil, 1980).

[46] According to Gaillac, many of the most important private colonies, founded in the 1840s and sharing Mettray's aspiration of total remoralization, were closed or ceded to the state by the early 1870s. On the critique of the agricultural colony, see Gaillac, Les Maisons de correction,

Like the revelation of primary schooling's limits in the constitution of moral subjects and citizens, the apparent failure of penal institutions, and especially the agricultural colony, to provide a properly moralizing experience and environment for the young placed the problem of educating the morally abandoned child against a ground of institutional limits. Both sets of reflections on institutional efficacy also tied the question of the moralement abandonnés into the wider late-nineteenth-century discussions of education and the formation of character. Despite the increasing emphasis on the deviant and the delinquent, the republican faith in education and the malleability of the young nevertheless seems at first glance to have stood firm in this period. The debate on how to place and educate the moralement abandonnés was articulated wholly within the frame of the belief that environment, along with the education derived from daily experience, was the primary force in shaping an individual's moral disposition. Again, these ideas were held with special reverence when it came to educating children and young adolescents. In contemporary discussions of domestic life, primary schooling, prisons, and the workplace, reformers saw the regulation of environment as one of the most effective paths to the moral protection and regeneration of the young.[47]

As always, however, the republic's enthusiasms also betrayed its anxieties. The early Third Republic's apparently soaring optimism about the power of education and a regulated environment also carried an uncomfortably heavy ballast of pessimism. In particular, reformers had to contend with science's warnings about the inherent and intransigent aspects of moral deviance. A moralizing environment, experience, and education, in other words, could not necessarily negate a child's "natural" taste for vice determined by his or her latent hereditary proclivities. In the main, doctors and scientists asserting theories of the biological transmission of vice tended to be Lamarckian rather than Darwinian in their understanding of heredity.[48] A moral decline catalyzed by poverty and degrading social experiences might thus be passed

86. O'Brien likewise notes that the colonies continued to exist after the initial phase of disillusionment, although control had shifted from mostly private to mostly public hands by the turn of the twentieth century (*The Promise of Punishment*, 135–39). On the place of Mettray in the development of disciplinary institutions, see also Foucault, *Discipline and Punish*, 293–96.

[47] On these later-nineteenth-century visions of youth and the influence of social environment, see, among others, Crubellier, *L'Enfance et la jeunesse*, esp. 207–23, and Renouard, *De l'enfant coupable*, 62–72.

[48] For an overview of the dominant views on this topic, see Robert B. Nye, *Crime, Madness, and Politics in Modern France: The Medical Concept of National Decline* (Princeton: Princeton University Press, 1984), esp. chap. 4, "Heredity or Milieu: The Born-Criminal Debate and the Foundations of Criminology." For an influential contemporary articulation of the relationship between heredity, "degeneration," environment, and mental disorders in children, see Paul Moreau de Tours, *La Folie chez les enfants* (Paris: Librairie J.-B. Baillière et fils, 1888), esp. 17–56.

biologically from parent to child. Again, no example better illustrates this principle than Emile Zola's Nana, whose descent into "debauchery" stemmed from the blood in her veins as much as it did from the degrading stimuli rampant in the Parisian worlds of labor and leisure.[49]

In the late-nineteenth-century scientific discourse on immorality and heredity, the boundaries between lived experience and ingrained biological traits were as fluid as they were in Zola's writings. Not all experts agreed on the proportional weight of the learned against the inherent, and not all believed that a deep-seated inherited criminal character could ever be reformed. Even among those in basic agreement, the importance of what had been learned and what was intrinsic was thought to vary by the gender, age, profession, and social class of the individual in question. The possibility of reform similarly was conditioned by these same factors.[50]

These darker reservations about the intransigence of vice—inherited and acquired—were thus woven through the more luminescent fabric of the early Third Republic's powerful belief in the essential constitutive power of education. Unlike their revolutionary forebears in the late eighteenth century, it was impossible for the reformers and theorists of the Third Republic to be completely utopian. Historical self-consciousness and the evolutionary epistemologies of science conspired to make them far more pessimistic about the possibility of overcoming the past than the authors of the French Revolution had been. In a nation ravaged by a century of social and political conflict, it no longer seemed possible to posit a condition of perfect collective or individual innocence.

If the abstract agenda and the stakes attached to it were clear to Parisian officials, the more concrete elements of providing public parental guidance for the enfants moralement abandonnés were not. How could Seine officials bring together a regime of state-supervised care tailored for the moralement abandonnés that would provide a proper moral formation, correct for a demoralizing past, and ensure the legitimacy of the state's claim to serve as protective guardian for these children?

The Seine's General Council and the Paris Bureau of Public Assistance first confronted the project of designing their new Service and finding appropriate, remoralizing placements for the moralement abandonnés in the early 1880s. In the sixteen years of its independent operation, the Service des Enfants Moralement Abandonnés brought nearly ten thousand children from the Paris region into the care of the state under the rubric of moralement

---

[49] See Emile Zola's *L'Assommoir* (Paris: Garnier Flammarion, 1969) for the sparking of young Nana's "vicious" nature, and *Nana* ([Paris]: Fasquelle, 1963) for the portrayal of her licentious adulthood. See also Zola's *Le Docteur Pascal* (Paris: Charpentier, 1893) for his meditations on science, vice, heredity, and environment.

[50] For a survey of these distinctions in nineteenth-century penology, see O'Brien, *The Promise of Punishment*, chap. 2, "Men and Women in Prison," and chap. 4, "Youth in Prison."

abandonné.[51] Responsibility for the Service was split between the Seine's General Council and the Paris Bureau of Public Assistance, whose administrators and staff carried out the everyday tasks of admitting and placing the moralement abandonnés. This division also followed an old pattern: both administrative bodies shared responsibility for the department's Service des Enfants Assistés. Similarly, the institutional headquarters for the Service des Enfants Moralement Abandonnés in Paris was also the heart of the Service des Enfants Assistés: the foundling hospital, or Hospice, also run by the Bureau of Public Assistance. With such a significant degree of institutional overlap, it is small wonder that the departmental council repeatedly used the Service des Enfants Assistés in the 1880s as its datum, even as members protested its appropriateness to the new undertaking.

The unstable category of enfant moralement abandonné did not in itself determine a rational regime of specialized care; neither did the formal constitution of the Service in 1880 in itself produce an answer to the problem that had inspired its creation. With the general goal of implementing a proper and effective form of state-supervised upbringing for the moralement abandonnés, the new Service nonetheless lacked a clear course of action, set of techniques, or even a definite sense of precisely which children fell within the new rubric of moralement abandonné. In short, the Service des Enfants Moralement Abandonnés began its life as a bureaucratic shell, its order structured only by the desire that the specific needs of this ill-defined category of children be addressed through equally specific administrative action.

As has always been the case in the development of bureaucracies and bureaucratic practice, the codification of the Service's policies for placing and raising the moralement abandonnés, along with its strategies for their implementation, did not emerge naturally or logically from the establishment of a new administrative body. Instead, it arose through administrators' active elaboration of the discourse on abandon moral, the morally endangered children, and their intertwined dangers.

No less important than developments on the ideological plane were the lessons learned from practical experience. Trial and error, experiments shaped and evaluated through the prism of late-nineteenth-century thought on morals, the family, urban experience, and agrarian life, played an essential role in the department's efforts to solidify the conceptual and practical substance of the new regime of care. At the same time, however, the department's experiments in institutionalizing an appropriate structure of place-

---

[51] That figure is based on the cumulative number of recorded admissions to the Service. It is not clear, however, that the total number of admissions did not include readmissions or even multiple readmissions to the Service. Indeed, the impressions recorded in departmental reports suggest that officials viewed repeated entry into the care of the Service a problem of both administrative and moral significance (CGS, *Rapports sur le service des enfants moralement abandonnés* [1881–1896]).

ment and education for the moralement abandonnés would put pressure on internal contradictions and ambiguities in the nascent category of vulnerable children. The suppression of some contradictions under these pressures and the explosion of others would play an important role in determining the department's evolving strategies. Ironically, these experiments, the strains they produced, and the ongoing effort to build an effective regime of care would end in destabilizing the category of enfant moralement abandonné, draining it of its conceptual specificity and ultimately destroying its administrative utility.

In 1889, in a moment of striking candor, Councillor Rousselle admitted that the Seine's first administrative actions on behalf of the enfants moralement abandonnés had indeed taken a paradoxical form. Founding the Service des Enfants Moralement Abandonné before the category, its juridical implications, and its administrative consequences had been fully worked out, he confessed, "complicated the question by resolving it in advance."[52] Small wonder, then, that determining exactly what constituted appropriate regimes of care for such an ambiguous and internally contradictory category of children could happen only by means of institutional and administrative improvisation. Only through its attempts to harmonize the variety of moral discourses and institutional practices that marked the new category of the enfant moralement abandonné could the new service even begin to chart a workable course of action.

Despite the frequent expression of uncertainty about the nature of the category and its implication, and despite equally frequent changes of policy in the 1880s and into the 1890s, Seine officials never doubted their duty or their capacity to provide for the morally endangered children. Nor did they ever question the fundamental assumption guiding their efforts: that providing morally educative placements comprised the means of reclaiming and reforming a young population teetering on the edge of deviance. Thus, at the outset, council members proclaimed with the utmost confidence that placements designed for the particular needs of the moralement abandonnés, whatever they turned out to be, would provide just the right mortar to fill what appeared to be mere cracks in an otherwise sound structure of child protection. Rousselle's simple "lacuna" in the department's assistance to children, however, like the category of enfant moralement abandonné, quickly proved both far too capacious and far too unstable to be covered over with such a simple patch.

[52] CGS, no. 15 (1889), 3.

CHAPTER 8

Experiments in Placement, 1881–1889

IN THE FIRST decade of its existence, the Service des Moralement Abandonnés tended to avoid using rural foster placement as its primary medium for rearing the moralement abandonnés. This position veered sharply away from the traditions of state-organized child rearing. For centuries rural foster placement had been the rule where the rearing of foundlings was concerned. Since the early nineteenth century, the Service des Enfants Assistés had followed this older pattern, which consistently favored placing abandoned infants in the countryside, and preferably with foster families.[1] Officials charged with the care of the moralement abandonnés, however, feared that these older children, apparently accustomed to the seductive pleasures of life in the streets of Paris, would not readily submit to the slower rhythms and stricter discipline of life as an agricultural laborer or domestic servant for a farm family. One legal commentator rearticulated this widespread concern in 1899 when he warned his readers that the children least suited for rural placements were "wards of urban origin, taken in at a relatively advanced age, whose nostalgia for the city cannot be overcome."[2] In a prescient and literalized echo of the American World War I song, Parisian officials in the 1880s continually asked themselves whether they would be able to keep these older, more experienced children down on the farm once they had seen Paris.

In certain respects, their fears may have been well grounded. Little evidence exists to testify to what the petits parisiens themselves thought of their experiences in placement. Nevertheless, we may speculate based on a letter from one boy placed by the Service des Enfants Assistés near Saint-Calais in the department of the Sarthe. This child, Charly C., proclaimed his particular

---

[1] On the history and organization of rural foster placement, see Albert Dupoux, *Sur les pas de Monsieur Vincent: Trois cent ans d'histoire parisienne de l'enfance abandonnée* (Paris: Revue de l'Assistance publique à Paris, 1958); Rachel G. Fuchs, *Abandoned Children: Foundlings and Child Welfare in Nineteenth-Century France* (Albany: SUNY Press, 1984); and Danielle Laplaige, *Sans famille à Paris: Orphelins et enfants abandonnés au XIXe siècle* (Paris: Centurion, 1989).

[2] Georges Gérard, *Régime actuel des enfants assistés de la Seine* (Paris: Edouard Duchomin, 1899), 45. Gérard's sentiments were echoed in V. Radenac's *Du rôle de l'Etat dans la protection des enfants maltraités ou moralement abandonnés: Commentaire de la loi du 24 juillet 1889 (Titre II)* (Paris: Arthur Rousseau, 1901). Radenac argued that industrial trades would be best for older children "habituated to the freedom and unhealthy pleasures of the big city" (64).

dissatisfaction with rural life in general and agricultural apprenticeship in particular in a letter to the local administrator written in July 1890.

I see that I won't be able to last the year at the Chrètiens, because there ain't even time to eat and they don't like my eating at all anyway. And farming don't suit me. I'd rather be a baker or coachman, because in the countryside they want you to do two days of work in one but that's impossible and they already seem like they're going to tell me to get lost, and I can't stand the fields. Always being [in the stinking sun?] really gets me.[3]

Charly's complaint about hard work and his assertion that agricultural labor simply did not "suit him" may perhaps provide the historian with a glimpse into the discontents of dozens, if not hundreds or even thousands, of other disaffected but silent state wards. It was not uncommon, moreover, for the state to lose track of its apprenticed wards when they ran away or simply found new situations on their own. The extensive rural exodus in late-nineteenth-century France suggests that even those who had never seen the city with their own eyes were affected by the allure of economic possibility and urban pleasures.[4]

At the same time, officials charged with the placement of the foundlings from the Service des Enfants Assistés had their own interest in excluding the moralement abandonnés from state-supervised placements with individual peasant families. Dependent on the regional networks of foster families they had been cultivating for decades for the exclusive use of the Service des Enfants Assistés, these administrators were concerned about maintaining a favorable image in their provincial outposts.[5] The departmental council, interested, like the Bureau of Public Assistance, in the smooth functioning of both services, took note of similar fears expressed by the provincial administrators (*directeurs d'agence*) working for the Service des Enfants Assistés. Those directors, Councillor Paul Strauss wrote in his report of 1889,

fear that the mixing in of some vicious children, who are found among the enfants moralement abandonnés in small number, would create a bad reputation for the entire Service, and would thus create real difficulties in the placement of

[3] AAP, Fosseyeux Liasse 647, Agence de Saint-Calais (Sarthe), Circulaires et Correspondance, 1872–1873.

[4] See Abel Châtelain, *Les Migrants temporaires en France de 1800 à 1914*, 2 vols. (Villeneuve d'Ascq: Université de Lille III, 1976); Leslie Page Moch, *Paths to the City: Rural Migration in Nineteenth-Century France* (Beverly Hills: Sage, 1983); and Philip E. Ogden and Paul E. White, eds., *Migrants in Modern France: Population Mobility in the Later Nineteenth and Twentieth Centuries* (London: Unwin Hyman, 1989).

[5] On the tensions surrounding the integration of the petits parisiens into rural communities, see Nancy Fitch's exemplary article " 'Les Petits Parisiens en province': The Silent Revolution of the Allier, 1860–1900," *Journal of Family History* 11, no. 2 (1986).

the older wards of the Enfants Assistés, with regard to which the farming population does not know how to draw distinctions.[6]

Parisian officials and regional administrators both contended that one "corrupt" child could throw the entire provincial project of the Bureau of Public Assistance into disfavor; fertile ground for the cultivation of foster families might easily be laid fallow by a single hostile family or village.

Instead of embracing the model of rural foster placement and agricultural apprenticeship, then, the new departmental agency experimented with several other kinds of placements and institutions thought to offer an appropriate moralizing environment for this special category of children. Councillor Rousselle defined the department's early objectives this way: "[T]wo things are necessary, the habits of work and the knowledge of a trade, on the one hand, and on the other hand the development of all the good sentiments budding within the child. It is necessary, in short, to train the hand and educate the heart."[7]

Although the Service initially avoided rural foster placement or apprenticeship with peasant families, officials nevertheless remained bound by a logic of state child rearing that associated effective moralization with familial forms. The department's experiments in alternative forms of placement— from group industrial apprenticeships to specialized vocational schools— were all cast within a language of familial relations, most of all, in the language of paternal benevolence and filial obedience. Only those alternatives that fit the metaphorical paradigm of proper, moralizing familial relations or substituted a literal family for the child's own could fulfill the state's educative demands.

While asserting the moral necessity of familial forms, the Service also framed its task in the terms of the industrial wage economy. Officials working in the early 1880s hoped that in providing morally sound wage-earning apprenticeships the Service would return the moralement abandonnés to a legitimate way of life before the habits of "criminal existence" had taken a permanent hold. In this context, industrial apprenticeships seemed to represent an especially promising form of placement. As Councillor Rousselle put it, group (industrial) placements were thought to be most efficacious because

---

[6] Seine, Conseil Général [CGS], no. 25, *Rapport présenté par M. Strauss au nom de la 3e commission sur le service des enfants assistés* (1889), 48. Curiously, the discourse on the enfants moralement abandonnés tended to efface the administration's enduring concerns about the "pariah" status of the enfants assistés placed in the countryside. On the persistence of this fear, particularly among provincial inspectors, see Ernest Gegout, *Les Parias: Vie anecdotique des enfants abandonnés placés sous la tutelle de l'Assistance publique* (Paris: Bureaux du journal *l'Attaque*, 1898), and Gilbert Dolanne, *Un Paria moderne: Le pupille de l'Assistance publique* (Saint-Dizier: A. Brulliard, 1929).

[7] CGS, no. 15, *Rapport présenté par M. Rousselle au nom de la 3e commission sur le budget du service des enfants moralement abandonnés* (1889), 47.

they "scatter the children less, which permits a stricter regime and more efficacious supervision, and which in the end are more productive for the young apprentices and more economical for the state purse."[8]

The Paris Bureau of Public Assistance, working in conjunction with the department in the operation of this new agency, voiced a parallel preference that the majority of the moralement abandonnés be placed in supervised apprenticeships with private industrialists. In its view, the moralement abandonnés needed placements where they could learn a trade and where supervision would be more vigilant. Fearful that older children might already be insubordinate by nature or as a result of their early experiences and upbringing, Public Assistance officials working at the hospice favored placements where the prospect for rebellion could be minimized.

To this end, Public Assistance authorities introduced a period of observation as the first step leading to placement. This two-week observation at the Paris Hospice gave officials "the leisure to study the character, the aptitudes, and the temperament of each one in order to be able to direct him effectively toward the placement that suits him best."[9] Belief in the intransigence of tastes formed in this early stage of life even led officials to formulate the principle that the children be placed "in an industry they have chosen for themselves as often as possible."[10]

If it expressed the administration's commitment to rationality and empirical notions of suitability, it seems unlikely that this principle informed the placement of the moralement abandonnés with any real frequency. Nevertheless, the Hospice observation policy suggests the degree to which Parisian administrators were saturated with the contemporary logic of reform. Rearing the morally endangered children left in the care of the state required the production of an increasingly fine spectrum of specialized treatments tailored to the individual. At the same time, however, the process of individuation produced through this kind of "scientific" observation contributed to the further elaboration of a new category of delinquency into which these individuals fell together as equivalent, but not interchangeable, representatives of the same type.[11]

The records of placement in the Service des Moralement Abandonnés testify strongly to the department's early preference for industrial apprenticeships over rural foster placements or agricultural apprenticeships. Between 1881 and 1883 only about 25 percent of the roughly two thousand morale-

---

[8] Ibid., 10.

[9] CGS, no. 18, *Rapport présenté par M. Curé au nom de la 3e commission sur le budget du service des enfants moralement abandonnés pour l'année 1888* (1887), 5.

[10] Ibid., 2. See also CGS, no. 15 (1889).

[11] On observation, classification, and the operation of normative discipline, see Michel Foucault, *Discipline and Punish: The Birth of the Prison*, trans. Alan Sheridan (New York: Vintage Books, 1979), 170–94.

ment abandonnés in the department's care were listed as having been placed *chez des cultivateurs*. By comparison, in 1880 roughly 90 percent of the nearly thirty thousand wards of the department's Service des Enfants Assistés had been placed in the countryside.[12] Instead, the department placed the majority of the first moralement abandonnés in industrial apprenticeships, usually in group placements. Not surprisingly, most of these children were apprenticed into industries that traditionally absorbed the better part of the nonagricultural child labor pool. By 1883 more than 300 moralement abandonnés had been placed in the clothing and needle trades, 255 in thread and cloth making, and 206 in glassmaking.[13] Although the report did not distinguish these placements by the sex of the children, it is likely that the girls in the Service were placed primarily in traditional feminine sectors such as cloth production, clothing manufacture, and other needlework occupations.[14] By 1887 more than forty industrial group placements had been organized throughout France for the Seine's enfants moralement abandonnés.

The early 1880s were years of optimism about the moralizing effects of closely supervised industrial labor. Departmental officials were especially taken with the idea that these placements might provide the best opportunity for the moralement abandonnés to earn regular wages and hence to be introduced to the economic stability that would become both the cause and the hallmark of successful social integration. An 1881 report issued by the Seine's General Council included among its first recommendations that the establishment of a savings account be a mandatory element in every apprenticeship agreement, a practice also endorsed at this time by the Service des Enfants Assistés. In the evidence of the passbook, the report argued, "[T]he

[12] This figure included infants placed with peasant wet nurses, children under twelve placed with peasant foster families (together about 14,000), and those between twelve and twenty-one placed as agricultural laborers and domestics (about 12,500). See CGS, no. 17, *Rapport fait par M. Thulié au nom de la 3e commission sur le service des enfants assistés* (1881), 9.

[13] According to the report, 502 children had been placed in agricultural apprenticeships; 255 in spinning, weaving, or silk making; 254 in dressmaking, fashion industries, or laundry; 206 in glass- or cup-making; 60 in the manufacture of faience; 49 in shoemaking; 48 in horticulture; 44 in the artifical flower industry; 43 in cabinetmaking; 32 with locksmiths; 32 in embroidery shops; 22 in the manufacture of hosiery; 22 in the manufacture of needles; 15 with bakers; 15 with farriers or blacksmiths; 11 in hat making; 9 in the manufacture of tinware; 8 in button making; 8 in carpentry; 6 in passementerie; 5 in lace making; 4 as turners or founders; and 4 in the manufacture of jewelry. In addition, the report lists 268 placed in "diverse trades" and 79 under observation or in treatment, presumably of a medical nature (CGS, no. 15 [1889], 11–12).

[14] Colin Heywood's *Childhood in Nineteenth-Century France: Work, Health, and Education among the "Classes Populaires"* (Cambridge: Cambridge University Press, 1988) provides a useful survey of children's work patterns in agriculture and industry. For girls in the industrial labor force, see especially pt. 2 of Heywood, "The Impact of Industrialization." For a detailed account of women's typical experiences in the needle trades during the late nineteenth century, see also R. Espinasse, *L'Ouvrière de l'aiguille à Toulouse: Etude d'économie sociale* (Toulouse: Edouard Privat, 1906).

child can watch his little fortune grow from week to week. Work thus is not a fruitless obligation for him, forced labor in which he discerns no end." The child thus "sees by way of his passbook that he feeds himself, that he owes his existence to his arms and his intelligence, and that his efforts are transformed into a nest egg the value of which he always knows." Better than any chapbook, the savings account passbook would serve as a record of individual moral accounting and as a personalized narrative of moral progress. Hard work and obedience appeared in the regular entry of wages. Thrift, or *prévoyance*, one of the most frequently invoked terms in the nineteenth-century discourse on moralizing the working class, was signified by the minimal expenditures in the opposing columns. And the child's general moral development could be measured in the balance. "Precious few speeches, and good ones at that," the departmental report contended, "would be worth this lesson of experience."[15] Where Marx had seen in wage labor the alienation of the worker from both his product and the "true" value of his work, the departmental council envisioned the happy reunion of spirit and body. In the ideology of moralization through work, particularly industrial work, wages signified nothing about the conditions of production and everything about the moral constitution of the worker.

Disillusionment with industry as a site for moral and professional education, however, and particularly disillusionment with group placements in private industry, was not long in coming. The demands of market production, particularly in the depressed economy of the 1880s, and the department's failure to protect its moral agenda forced a rapid collapse of these experiments in public-private cooperation. Mention of severed contracts began to enter the annual reports in 1886. In the next three years the Service found itself dismantling between eight and ten groups annually. The council was especially dismayed by conditions in the silk industry and in machine-embroidery shops. These particular group placements accounted for ten out of the twenty-six failures. By the end of 1889 the department had salvaged only fifteen of the forty industrial groups established over the decade.

Almost as soon as members of the General Council began to visit the workshops in which they had placed the moralement abandonnés, they began to denounce them. In the view of these delegated inspectors, the conditions found at these sites of industrial group placement were a far cry from the department's ideal marriage of concentrated vocational training and rigorous

---

[15] CGS, no. 18 (1881), 2. The annual inspection reports for the Seine's Service des Enfants Assistés reveal the centrality of the savings accounts in the inspectors' evaluation of the everyday operation of the Service (Commission des Enfants Assistés, procès-verbaux, ADS, D.1 X4). The moral significance of wages underscored the department's early association of the enfant moralement abandonné with the delinquent in its resonance with contemporary theories of criminal reform through wage-earning labor. On wages in the disciplinary order of the prison, see Foucault, *Discipline and Punish*, 243.

moral supervision. According to departmental reports, these industrialists were consistently more interested in profit than in altruistic ventures in trade education and moral supervision. Further, they rarely observed the conditions stipulated in the contracts. The council's list of reasons for ending relations with these private entrepreneurs included "excessive work," "inadequate food," "lack of supervision," the industrialist's general "noncooperation," "failure to train workers capable of earning a living," "neglect of primary school instruction," and "harassment" by overseers. Council members also mentioned low wages and generally unhealthy living and working conditions as common problems for children placed in industrial groups.[16]

The consequences of these revelations were serious, both for the children and the officials entrusted with their care. The Seine's departmental council, for example, feared that it had sentenced many of its wards to lives more desperate and morally degrading than those they had led before entering the ranks of the "protected" wards of the state. In the context of a project designed to extract children from morally dangerous environments, these charges proved especially humiliating for the department.

Also troubling to the departmental council was industry's failure to implant an ethic of obedience and self-discipline in these wards of state. Frequent escapes, rebellions, and mutinies were listed among the reasons for withdrawing approval for group placements. At one glassworks in the Allier, for example, twenty out of the fifty wards of the Service placed between 1881 and 1887 had run away. Rouselle's report of 1889 also noted the response of the moralement abandonnés to heavy work and inhumane treatment at a garden shears factory in the Jura; the children, he remarked, "rose up in mutiny. Many ran away."[17] The report included no details of this incident beyond this single cryptic observation.

The choice of flight over submission was not limited to the children placed in industrial groups. By the end of 1881, 37 of the 696 children accepted by the Service des Enfants Moralement Abandonnés in 1881— more than 5 percent—had been entered in its registers as "runaway, still at large." As the Service grew, the number of runaways each year continued to increase, averaging close to one hundred per year between 1883 and 1889.[18] Throughout this period, flight was second only to "returned to their families" as an explanatory note in the tables listing the reasons children left the care of the Service.[19] The numbers recorded in these tables usually included only those children who had not been found and returned to the Service by the

[16] CGS no. 15 (1889), 30–33.

[17] Ibid., 31.

[18] Ibid., 6. This average should not obscure the fluctuation of this figure over the years, from a low of 16 runaways in 1882 to a high of 143 in 1887. In general, however, the trend over the 1880s was toward higher numbers.

[19] Ibid., 6.

year's end. One report notes 134 total runaways for 1892, with 90 remaining "unlocated" on December 31 of that year.[20]

Once more, officials invoked early and prolonged engagement in the stimuli of urban life in their efforts to explain the penchant for escape. At the first international congress devoted to the problem of the enfant moralement abandonné, held in Belgium in 1891, Loys Brueyre, the longtime head of the Service des Enfants Assistés at the Bureau of Public Assistance, declared that the combination of advanced age and urban experience presented a serious and enduring obstacle to any form of provincial placement. By the age of ten, he argued, "[T]he child has been habituated to the turbulent city life, to the active existence of the workshop. To send him to the countryside would be to risk fixing in him a nostalgia for the city and forcing him to make his escape."[21] Although the provincial industrial group had failed to prove itself the ideal form of placement, then, officials remained skeptical that the moralement abandonnés could ever successfully be weaned from the urban "turbulence" that had bred them.

Despite the economic advantages it offered, despite its promise as an alternative placement for children deemed ill suited to familial living, industrial apprenticeship was widely opposed by departmental officials by the end of the decade. The report of 1889 rang with the departmental council's condemnation.

> [P]lacement in groups lends itself less than any other kind to this education of the heart. The work there is harsher; the industrialist is always obliged to weigh that which he gives out against that which he gets back. . . . Outside of the workshop and the few games by which he can amuse himself, the child is left to his painful memories, to his former inclinations; no affection, no sympathy helps him to catch a sight of and love a new existence. . . . [T]he worker can be molded, but not the man.[22]

With its apparent failure to provide the most minimal provisions for vocational training and moral supervision, private industry appeared by the late 1880s to offer no future for the moralement abandonnés. Even in the rare cases where the conditions of apprenticeship were deemed acceptable, the overall project of combining professional and moral training had been lost. Of particular concern, the group placements seemed to have failed to provide the familial frame on which proper moralization was presumed to rest. Even

---

[20] CGS, no. 1 (1894), 10. As the early cohorts of the moralement abandonnés aged, the phrase "reached majority" began to be entered as a reason for leaving the service in about equal numbers to the runaways beginning in 1888, with 84 escapees and 70 adults.

[21] Belgium, Ministère de la Justice, *Congrès international pour l'étude des questions relatives au patronage des détenus et à la protection des enfants moralement abandonnés. Anvers, 1890* (Brussels: E. Guyot, 1891), 143.

[22] CGS, no. 15 (1889), 47.

more important, perhaps, in neglecting his "paternal" obligation to educate the state's wards, the private industrialist failed to embody the state's own parental status, thus throwing its moral identity, as well as its right to claim the task of moralizing the young, into question.

Industry was not the only sector in which group placements with private entrepreneurs were tried and found wanting in the 1880s. Seine officials also experimented with agricultural labor, placing morally endangered boys in their care at private agricultural colonies. This effort, like the experiment with private industry, would also end in failure. One scandal, surrounding the private agricultural colony on the island of Porquerolles, near Toulon, where the department had been placing morally endangered boys since 1883, threatened the legitimacy of the new Service more than any other of its failed experiments. The "Porquerolles incident," as it was known in the council's reports, cast further doubt on the department's ability to carry out its moralizing metaparental role through strategies of extrafamilial placement.

The scandal began with the testimony of several boys who had fled the vineyards of Porquerolles in July 1886. Speaking before the magistrates of Toulon, the boys charged the director with serious abuses. As Seine officials launched an inquiry into the boys' complaints, they learned of a recent large-scale revolt at Porquerolles, apparently triggered by the prolonged cellular confinement of one of the boys who had dared to complain to the director about the quality of the food. The investigation, described with great enthusiasm by a local newspaper, *Le Var républicain*, exposed the desperate conditions at the colony: methods of discipline notable for their "excessive severity, often pushed to the edge of cruelty"; the indiscriminate mixing of boys sent for training in the art of viticulture and those sent for more serious correction; despotic rule by the director; inadequate food and clothing; irregular meals; and the mishandling of the boys' wages. Sexual assault also figured in the litany of horrors; the boys testified that one of the guards had repeatedly performed "immoral acts" on several of their peers.[23]

The scandalous stories surrounding Porquerolles badly damaged the reputation of the fledgling Service in Paris. Annual admissions fell in 1887 from a total of 689 the year before to a low of 183. Reluctance to send children to the Service appears to have affected both public officials and individual families. The number of children sent from the courts dropped to 15 from 45 the previous year; the police sent only 41 children compared with 166 in 1886; and parents and mayors, who together had been responsible for 478 admissions in 1886, brought only 127 children to the Service in 1887.[24] The espe-

---

[23] CGS, no. 34, *Rapport présenté par M. Navarre au nom de la 3e commission sur les événements de Porquerolles* (November 1886), 6–7.

[24] CGS, no. 15 (1889), 8.

cially high number of runaways still at large at the end of 1886 and 1887, 133 and 143 respectively, suggests as well that news of the events on the island may well have filtered back into the population of the moralement abandonnés themselves.[25] The debacle of Porquerolles provided clear evidence that leaving the education of the moralement abandonnés in the hands of private enterprise not only would ensure that the project of providing sound moral and professional education would never be achieved, but also that it seriously threatened the existence and moral identity of the Service as a whole.[26]

At the same time as they explored industrial apprenticeships and the use of private agricultural colonies, departmental officials pursued one other site of experimental placement in the 1880s: state-founded and state-run institutions designed exclusively for the moralement abandonnés. The Seine's Ecole d'horticulture de Villepreux (later the Ecole le Nôtre) in the Seine-et-Oise, a horticulture school for boys, and the Ecole d'Alembert in Montévrain in the department of the Seine-et-Marne, a school for woodworking and printing, also for boys, opened their doors in 1882.[27] A school for girls, the Ecole Ménagère d'Yzeure in the department of the Allier, accepting students from both the department's Service des Enfants Assistés and its Service des Moralement Abandonnés, opened in 1888.[28] And in 1889, in a venture designed to combine moral and vocational education with France's imperial agenda, the department sent the first boys from the Service des Moralement Abandonnés to its new agricultural school in Algeria, the Ecole Roudil.[29]

---

[25] Ibid., 6.

[26] In the course of the departmental investigation, members of the General Council charged the Bureau of Public Assistance with deliberately turning its back on the evidence turned up by its own inspectors, neither intervening in the way the colony was being run nor apprising the General Council of the bad conditions there. Chief among the accused was Loys Brueyre. "See nothing, hear nothing, and above all, say nothing: this is the system followed by the division chief [Brueyre] and the inspector of the Service des Enfants Assistés in regard to the school at Porquerolles," M. Navarre remarked bitterly in his report of 1886 (CGS, no. 34 [1886], 24).

[27] On the prewar development of these institutions, see the series of works published by the Administration Général de l'Assistance publique à Paris, including *Les Ecoles professionnelles du service des enfants assistés de la Seine: L'école d'Alembert (1882–1909) à Montévrain* (Paris: Berger-Levrault, 1909); *Notice historique et statistique sur l'école d'horticulture de Villepreux (Seine-et-Oise) de 1882 à 1894* (Montévrain: Imprimerie typographique de l'école d'Alembert, 1894); [L. Guillaume], *Rapports sur l'Exposition universelle de 1900: Les écoles professionnelles (agriculture, horticulture, etc.)* (Montévrain: Imprimerie typographique de l'école d'Alembert, 1900); and [J. Marcelin], *Rapports sur l'Exposition universelle de 1900: Les écoles professionnelles (typographie et ébénisterie)* (Montévrain: Imprimerie typographique de l'école d'Alembert, 1900).

[28] CGS, no. 34, *Rapport présenté par M. Navarre au nom de la 3e commission sur l'école professionnelle d'Yzeure et sur l'école de réforme de la Salpêtrière* (1892).

[29] AGAPP, *Notice sur l'école Roudil, établissement agricole des enfants assistés du département de la Seine à Ben-Chicao (Algérie)* (Montévrain: Imprimerie typographique de l'école d'Alembert, 1894). See also the proposal issued earlier by the Conseil Général of the AGAPP,

Several more schools, including a maritime academy on the shores of the English Channel, would be founded in the next decade.[30]

The department and the Bureau of Public Assistance advertised the virtues of the schools early on. In his report of 1889, Councillor Rousselle heartily endorsed the schools of horticulture and cabinetry. "If there is one necessary and moralizing occupation," he argued, "it must be horticulture." Rousselle commented further on the high level of technical skill imparted to the students, noting that students from le Nôtre had won numerous medals in agricultural competitions between 1882 and 1889. The councillor also had high praise for the Ecole d'Alembert. After gardening, Rousselle asserted, furniture making was the next best occupation, both "healthy and lucrative." Set in the provinces but enclosed and supervised, the Ecole d'Alembert offered the students the best advantages of provincial living. According to Rousselle, the school building was "a spacious and healthy establishment, full of air and light, situated on a hillside in a picturesque site."[31]

Even these apparently exemplary schools soon raised serious questions for departmental officials. In 1891, for example, the student population at the Ecole le Nôtre totaled only thirteen, with more than one hundred students expelled that year for "misconduct and refusal to learn the trade."[32] In 1894 the Paris Bureau of Public Assistance, here too a partner in the department's educational ventures, published a brief history of the school that included this rather surprising confession: "If the school has appeared to function normally up to this point, the students have been far from giving the desired satisfaction . . . we have seen already that the little Parisian is not easily habituated to the fields, that he prefers the workshop."[33] Discipline problems also seem to have plagued the Ecole d'Alembert. In 1886 one report revealed that "among the children sent to Montévrain, there are some who don't comprehend the benefits of their stay at the school. Heeding bizarre suggestions, they run away and go back to the hospice or to their parents, who often return them to the Administration [of Public Assistance] to be placed anew."[34]

Ever concerned about the cost-effectiveness of its investments in the moralement abandonnés, the General Council also raised questions about the expense of public institutional education. Although the Ecole d'Alembert

---

Rapport de la délégation chargée d'étudier un avant projet de colonisation agricole en Algérie pour les enfants assistés du département de la Seine (Paris: Imprimerie municipale, 1883).

[30] Dupoux, *Sur les pas*, 256–57.

[31] CGS, no. 15 (1889), 19.

[32] CGS, no. 59, *Rapport présenté par M. Georges Berry au nom de la 3e commission sur le budget de l'école d'horticulture de Villepreux* (1891), 1.

[33] AGAPP, *Notice historique et statistique sur l'école d'horticulture de Villepreux*, 7.

[34] CGS, no. 64, *Rapport présenté par M. Curé au nom de la 3e commission sur le service des enfants moralement abandonnés* (1886), 8–9.

earned a considerable amount of income from the furniture it produced in its workshops, and later from the books and forms produced in its print shop, costs ran high and the population of moralement abandonnés enrolled remained quite limited. Annual admissions in the 1880s averaged about thirty-five boys a year for a four-year program of training.[35] At the horticulture school, admissions averaged about twenty-seven new male students per year for a three-year stay.[36] The expenses per student at the Ecole le Nôtre were calculated at four francs per day in 1891, much higher than any other school under the Seine's aegis. That year, moreover, only thirteen students remained in residence.[37] By comparison, the monthly "pensions" for foundlings placed with foster families in the countryside ranged from twenty-five francs per month for infants under the age of one year down to thirteen francs for children between three and thirteen years of age.[38] Adolescents placed in agricultural or other forms of apprenticeship by the Service des Enfants Assistés and the Service des Enfants Moralement Abandonnés generally earned their full keep, representing no cost to the department beyond what it spent on inspection and basic administration. Such comparisons, although not always entered in the departmental reports, were nonetheless an omnipresent force in the council's quest to tailor a regime of care for the moralement abandonnés that would also satisfy the department's growing interest in rationalized and efficient administrative structures.

Ironically, despite the fact that many of these schools had been specifically opened with the enfants moralement abandonnés in mind, administrators did not ultimately see these children as the ideal candidates for admission. According to the General Council, the quality of the student body and the cost-effectiveness of the schools improved only when boys from the Service des Enfants Assistés were integrated into the pool of potential trainees. The council's 1892 report on the horticulture school noted the department's resolution in the previous year to open a school for boys from the Enfants Assistés as well. The new policy swelled the student population from thirteen in 1891 to fifty in 1892 and brought an infusion of apparently more appropriate pupils as well. A report from that year favorably compared the enfants assistés with their more troublesome peers from the Service des Enfants Moralement Abandonnés. The enfants assistés, "reared in the countryside in honest surroundings," the report contended, "have adapted perfectly to institutional life, sticking to their studies instead of seeking only to escape, like

---

[35] CGS, no. 17, *Rapport présenté par M. Boll au nom de la 3e commission sur l'école professionelle d'Alembert* (1890), 10. Most of the school's furniture and printed materials were commissioned by the Bureau of Public Assistance itself, making the school a form of in-house workshop.

[36] AGAPP, *Notice historique et statistique sur l'école d'horticulture de Villepreux*, 17.

[37] CGS, no. 59 (1891).

[38] Dupoux, *Sur les pas*, 238.

their predecessors, from a place they consider a veritable prison."[39] In short, the vocational schools ultimately did little to answer the specific needs of the moralement abandonnés. Discipline and efficiency manifested themselves only when the population of moralement abandonnés had been sufficiently diluted by apparently more malleable children from the Enfants Assistés.

Despite the high cost of maintaining them, the Ecole d'Alembert and the Ecole le Nôtre remained the showpieces in the department's array of institutions for assisted children well into the twentieth century. Other schools fell under far more serious critical fire. Most troubling to the General Council and the Bureau of Public Assistance was the Ecole d'Yzeure, the domestic arts and needlework school for girls. In the particular problems posed by an institution devoted to morally endangered girls, problems shot through with the contradictions of gendered identities, departmental officials were forced to view the moral dilemmas posed by the state care of the enfants moralement abandonnés in especially sharp focus.[40]

When the Ecole d'Yzeure opened its doors in 1887, it housed two services: a reform ward and a professional school. As in the other schools, vocational pupils were at first drawn exclusively from the Service des Moralement Abandonnés, whereas the reform school served both the Moralement Abandonnés and the Enfants Assistés. In 1891 the reform school was transferred to the Salpêtrière in Paris, leaving Yzeure with the sole function of vocational training. In that year, the school's ateliers were opened to older girls from the Service des Enfants Assistés as well. The total school population climbed from the first class of ninety-three to an annual average of almost three hundred students in the mid-1890s.

No sooner was this function of intensive vocational education established, however, than doubt about the viability of the school's aims appeared in the departmental record. Had the school proved successful in its quest to transform girls of fragile physical and moral constitutions into highly skilled workers? What happened to them once they left Yzeure? Faith in the creative powers of education broke down as newly gathered information fed departmental anxieties that no amount of training could dispel the clouds of misfortune and vice threatening the unmarried women workers in the streets and ateliers of Paris. Returning the trained petite parisienne to the city, that is, to the primal scene of her supposed infection by vice, seemed to many to be the deliberate and inevitable undercutting of her years of reeducation.

---

[39] CGS, no. 25 *Rapport présenté par M. Georges Berry au nom de la 3e commission sur le budget de l'école d'horticulture de Villepreux* (1892), 1.

[40] For a closer examination of the practical and conceptual problems posed by the Ecole d'Yzeure, see my article "When the Child Is the Father of the Man: Work, Sexual Difference, and the Guardian-State in Third Republic France," *History and Theory* (1992) *beiheft* 31: History and Feminist Theory, reprinted in *Feminists Revision History*, ed. Ann-Louise Shapiro (New Brunswick: Rutgers University Press, 1994).

Early investigations carried out by inspectors assigned to Paris revealed, moreover, that very few of the girls trained in the needlework ateliers at Yzeure found jobs that made good use of their new skills. The General Council's 1892 report on the school showed that of the 29 students who left Yzeure that year, not 1 had been placed as a seamstress or needleworker. Instead, 14 had been returned to the hospice in Paris, 2 had been sent back to their families, 4 had been sent to foster placements in the provinces, and 2 had left "without authorization." Only 7 students had found any work, all as nurses, still primarily an unskilled and low-status occupation in nineteenth-century France.[41]

The difficulty of finding relevant employment for girls trained at the Ecole d'Yzeure gradually abated, but concern about their future did not. Figures from later years showed a clear increase in the number of girls who found their way to the professions for which they had been prepared. A 1910 departmental report, for example, noted that the girls trained at Yzeure had finally gained a good reputation in Paris. Finding positions for them in Parisian workshops now required little effort on the part of administrators, particularly in linen, embroidery, and corsetry workshops.[42]

If the graduates of Yzeure increasingly found work in the needle trades, their apparent professional success did not dispel all the department's fears. Moral issues, rather than basic questions of employment, increasingly took pride of place in the reports on the school and its students. As inspectors and departmental administrators developed their policy of follow-up investigation, they began to attend not only to the types of work available to their young wards in Paris but also to the conditions of the workplace and urban experience more generally. Interestingly, criticism of the effects of professional needlework on the bodies of the *filles pupilles* also refracted onto the school's own workshops. Departmental reports frequently mentioned the school's poor hygienic conditions and taxing workloads, claiming that they aggravated the "unhealthy appearance" of many of the students.[43] This mechanism of refraction reveals the ways in which the department's policies, embedded in its grid of moral concerns, once again threw its own status as legitimate protective guardian into question. How could an administration that endangered its wards in its own institutions be seen as properly enacting its parental obligations? How had it come to pass that the strategies for protecting and training these girls seemed to produce the very dangerous or

---

[41] CGS, no. 34 (1892), 2. On social class and the professionalization of nursing, see Yvonne Knibiehler et al., *Cornettes et blouses blanches: Les infirmières dans la société française (1880–1980)* (Paris: Hachette, 1984).

[42] CGS, no. 38, *Rapport au nom de la 3e commission sur le projet de budget pour 1911 . . . : Ecole Henri Mathé à Iseure présenté par M. E. Chausse* (1910), 5.

[43] CGS, no. 36, *Rapport au nom de la 3e Commission sur l'inspection de l'école d'Yzeure par M. Chérot* (1901), 3–5.

demoralizing circumstances they were designed to avoid? These questions were serious ones for the Service des Enfants Moralement Abandonnés and the department of the Seine.

That laboring in the Parisian needle and clothing trades was a formula for despair and degradation had been well established in the social literature of the nineteenth century.[44] Nevertheless, Seine officials seemed to have suffered a curious, if temporary, myopia when they opened the Ecole d'Yzeure in the 1880s. With the growing interest in life after vocational training, however, came the realization that these female wards of the Seine, no matter how expert in their craft, would be subject to the same low wages and miserable work experience that defined professional sewing for most women in late-nineteenth-century Paris. One inspector for the Enfants Assistés, after tracking the fate of former Yzeure students for several years around the turn of the century, concluded that Paris promised no future to these girls, and that there was little point in continuing a program that endangered their physical and moral health. Another inspector railed against "the impossibility for the pupils to save or to earn their living . . . under suitable conditions."[45] Although sewing might be the most feminine of activities, as a source of income it threatened to destroy the twin foundations of a young woman's "true" femininity: her delicate body and her moral purity.

Although they complained about the lack of employment opportunities and the prevalence of low wages, Seine officials placed an even greater weight on the moral and sexual "dangers" the girls faced after their departure from Yzeure. Even in flush years, only a few girls could be placed in establishments such as the House of Minier, which was particularly valued by department officials for its "familylike environment."[46] Other former students worked in less desirable circumstances but were lodged in pensions certified by the Bureau of Public Assistance for their high level of moral supervision. For most of the graduates of Yzeure, however, the department seemed to be able to provide little guarantee of "suitable" moral supervision, in or out of the workplace. Once in Paris, the majority of these girls were far beyond the reach of school administrators, more than three hundred kilometers away from Yzeure. Hidden in workshops, boardinghouses, and, for those who went into domestic service, private households, many also lived beyond the reach of the Paris Bureau of Public Assistance, and it is not hard to speculate that most of them may have been eager to do so.

[44] On women in the needle trades in nineteenth-century Paris, see especially Judith G. Coffin, *The Politics of Women's Work: The Paris Garment Trades, 1750–1915* (Princeton: Princeton University Press, 1996).

[45] ADS, D.1 X4:19, Commission des Enfants Assistés, procès-verbaux, 16 December 1908 and 21 December 1909.

[46] CGS, no. 27, *Rapport par M. Astier au nom de la 3e commission sur l'école profession-nelle et ménagère d'Yzeure* (1896), 3.

Those girls who had come to the Ecole d'Yzeure as wards of the Service des Moralement Abandonnés inspired the bleakest prognoses of all. Once again, the coordinates of age and degree of demoralizing experience located these girls in a space apart from the "ordinary" state ward. The themes are familiar. In the official view, these older girls from Paris had already suffered the effects of "demoralization" at an age when the spectacle of vice could make a deep impression.

When wards from the Service des Enfants Assistés were introduced into the population at the Ecole d'Yzeure, the question of moral contagion appeared again. In their report from 1893, departmental inspectors doubted the wisdom of mixing girls from the Enfants Assistés, who had spent their childhood in the provincial agencies, with the older and more corrupt girls sent from Paris by the Moralement Abandonnés. "There is good reason," the inspectors' report concluded, "to stop sending older girls from Paris [to Yzeure] who can stir up trouble among their peers."[47] At the same time, in the view of the General Council, returning the moralement abandonnées to Paris constituted a "genuine danger" to what little remained of their innocence and decency.[48] Once again, the morally endangered girl, a figure at odds with the essential abstract conceptualization of the enfant moralement abandonné, revealed the intrinsic moral ambiguity of the category in its most acute form. In the administration's lexicon, *abandon moral* stood for the very set of urban experiences that threatened the graduate of Yzeure, most of all those experiences that appeared to take place at the gendered and highly charged intersection of poverty and sexual depravity.

In the first decades of the twentieth century, evidence against the school continued to accumulate, and the criticisms leveled by the inspectors grew louder and more militant. Gradually, the departmental council came to accept that training young women as expert needleworkers in an era of ever-increasing mechanization, pieceworking, and overall deskilling could not guarantee them a reliable living. Equally important, authorities recognized that the school, both as a source of professional skills and a site of moral supervision, could not in the end guarantee the moral safety of the female moralement abandonnées.

By 1914 the Ecole d'Yzeure loomed large in the vision of its departmental officials as an unnerving monument to their conceptual and practical failure. During World War I the school suspended its apprenticeship programs altogether, and the buildings were used as army hospitals. In 1918 a much abridged version of the school was transferred to a site closer to Paris. Among the reasons given for abandoning Yzeure, officials of the Seine included material damage sustained during the war and the hope that moving

---

[47] ADS, D.1 X4:17, Commission des Enfants Assistés, procès-verbaux, 29 December 1893.
[48] CGS, no. 27 (1896), 4.

the school closer to the city might improve postplacement contact. The reports on the school after the war also introduced a new strain into the department's discourse on moral contagion: the strain of racial difference. While they stressed the ravages of war and the demands of efficient administration, the reports implied that since black troops had been treated at the temporary hospital, most likely in a second segregated ward—thus the reference in the report to *two* hospitals at Yzeure—the locale had been rendered unfit for further occupation by the vulnerable girls in the care of the state.[49]

The fate of the Ecole d'Yzeure magnified the stakes in articulating new policies and founding new institutions for the care and rearing of morally endangered children. That a school run by the state should spend public monies preparing endangered young women for what would amount to a life of destitution and probable prostitution shocked the world of reformers and made the department seem complicit in the very process of "moral degeneration" it was trying to arrest. By throwing the status of the department as moral guardian into question, moreover, the establishment of the school ultimately threatened the moralizing mission of the Service des Moralement Abandonnés far more than it contributed to it.

Overall, the department's efforts to create specialized institutions for the moralement abandonnés did not provide a satisfying answer to the problems posed by this new category of state-assisted children. The questions of urban vice and advanced age plagued administrators across the range of their placement experiments. The moralement abandonnés from Paris disrupted the General Council's vision of providing advanced professional training far from the temptations of the city and under the watchful eye of benevolent private entrepreneurs or agents of the state. A few of the vocational schools nevertheless survived into the twentieth century despite the criticism of their narrow recruitment and high cost. These schools, the horticulture and furniture schools among them, became the destinations of an elite group of male enfants moralement abandonnés and assistés. The Ecole d'Yzeure, however, simply disappeared from departmental records.

Even by the end of the 1880s, Parisian authorities found that it was impossible to create and maintain institutions designed to address the specific educative problems posed by such an unstable administrative category. There was, in short, no way of establishing a regime of care that mirrored the distinctiveness of a group defined primarily as a negation of extant categories of state-protected children and structures of public care. The ambiguities embedded in the category of moralement abandonné, the internal contradictions produced through its location in some nether zone between innocence and culpability, endangered past and dangerous future, childhood and adult-

---

[49] CGS, no. 28, *Rapport au nom de la 3e commission tendant à la liquidation de l'école Henri Mathé à Yzeure . . . présenté par M. Henri Sellier* (1918), 2.

hood, stymied authorities' efforts to construct policies and institutions that met its particular needs.

The only route left at the end of the decade was to allow the category to dissolve under the combined strain of its own internal contradictions and the increased external pressure produced by the department's series of failed experiments in placements. Through further differentiation among the children once grouped together as moralement abandonnés and the enlargement of the more general category of the state ward, authorities gradually erased the distinctiveness of the enfants moralement abandonnés. With it went the troubling imperative to build a regime of care tailored to their apparently special needs. Nevertheless, the category of the enfant moralement abandonné would leave important traces on both the French state's understanding of all children in its care and the structure of its policies and institutions in the next century.

CHAPTER 9

The Assimilation of the
Enfants Moralement Abandonnés

THE FAILURE of the industrial groups and the high cost of the exclusive professional schools forced the General Council to rethink the conceptual and practical problems posed by the enfants moralement abandonnés. Perhaps, the General Council's third commission began to suggest toward the end of the 1880s, these children were not as ill suited for placement with peasant families or for agricultural labor as council members had first believed.

Reversing the department's policy on placing the moralement abandonnés, although of clear economic advantage, would not be a simple matter. The earlier strategies of placement, the determination of appropriate forms of education and supervision, and the development of particular institutions such as the vocational schools had all stood on the foundation of a particular conceptualization of the morally endangered child. In the early discourse and practices of the Seine administration, the enfant moralement abandonné had been defined as a category of children damaged by the immorality of their own families and fundamentally dangerous to the moral order of all families. Suitable placement for the moralement abandonnés in the early years of the service tended above all to mean nonfamilial placement. Instead, "family" in these first experiments took only its most metaphorical form; it described the department's ideal of stringent moral supervision and paternalistic craft training for wards placed in the care of private industrialists, in reform colonies, or in departmental vocational schools.

How, then, did the council circumvent the obstacle of its own vigorous arguments against rural foster placement and agricultural apprenticeship for the moralement abandonnés? How did it reconcile its earlier vision of the morally endangered child as antithetical to rural family life and agrarian labor?

The stakes in reversing the department's position were high. Reconceptualizing the contours of an appropriate educative experience for the moralement abandonnés would affect more than the basic organization of placement. It would restructure the very category on which those policies had originally been founded; in aligning the enfant moralement abandonné with the tradition of rural foster placement, authorities would efface the distinctive indeterminacy of the category and hence, ironically, its conceptual and administrative specificity. The practical consequences of such a conceptual revision would be profound as well.

As early as 1887 the third commission began to exhort other council members to reconsider the possibilities of agricultural labor as a form of moral education not only available but particularly suited to the moralement abandonnés. The use of farming by reform schools under the penal administration, they argued, demonstrated that farming was in fact "one of the most moralizing occupations," and it might prove effective in the education of even the least disciplined of the moralement abandonnés. "In the labors of the field," the report declared, "man almost always becomes serious and reflective; constantly engaged in battle with the elements, he knows very well that he has no power, neither over drought, nor rain, nor ice, nor over hail." The agricultural laborer, the report continued, thus "does not rebel, he submits, becomes philosophical, and forms an upright and healthy faculty of judgment."[1]

Inspired by the possibility of the moralizing experiences apparently intrinsic to agriculture, the third commission nevertheless carefully distinguished its understanding of the educative potential of farming from its prior use in the correction of delinquent boys. In the hands of the Service des Enfants Moralement Abandonnés, the commission's report contended, agricultural labor would not be used as a form of punishment or criminal correction. Instead, it would be exploited for its essential moral curriculum. In place of industrial wage labor, with its moralization of the body through satiated appetite and the character through the balance of the savings account, the 1887 report recommended the moralizing lesson of humility in the face of the unpredictable forces of nature. Finally, the report concluded, even if it shifted toward agriculture as a medium of moral education, the Service should not lose sight of the principle of individuation in the care of the moralement abandonnés; farmwork could be an effective means of moral education only if it found some favor in the preferences (*le goût*) of the children.

In reconceiving the moral influences of agricultural labor and rural life, Seine officials also began to tie rural placement to the perceived needs of the nation as a whole. As the alarm sounding over rural depopulation grew increasingly shrill in the last decades of the nineteenth century, the moralement abandonnés, like the children in the Service des Enfants Assistés, came to be seen as an important reserve of transplantable bodies.[2] In replenishing the

[1] Seine, Conseil Général [CGS], no. 18, *Rapport présenté par M. Curé au nom de la 3e commission sur le budget du service des enfants moralement abandonnés pour l'année 1888* (1887), 6.

[2] On rural depopulation in the late nineteenth century, see Maurice Agulhon, "Les Transformations du monde paysan," in *Histoire de la France rurale*, ed. Georges Duby and Armand Wallon, vol. 3, *Apogé et crise de la civilisation paysanne, 1789–1914*, ed. Etienne Juillard

population of hearty French peasants, children placed in the countryside—not to mention the department of the Seine itself—would realize their fundamental moral duty to the nation.[3]

Rehabilitating agriculture as appropriate to the task of rearing and remoralizing the enfants moralement abandonnés was only one piece in the department's reconceptualization of its strategies. Officials also embraced the notion that truly effective moral education required integration into a stable family setting. Affection and paternal discipline, along with the moral training intrinsic in the experience of the field, became the new cornerstones of the Service's educational ideology.

Councillor Rousselle described the department's change of heart by placing this tableau of rustic familial bonding at the center of his report of 1889. "[I]ndividualized placements," he claimed, ensure that the child "lives in brotherhood among the children of the house, sits at the same table, by the same hearth." Furthermore, "[I]f he is not unmanageable, [he] soon comes to be loved and, as it were, adopted by the family where he participates in both its sorrows and its delights."[4] Whereas early in the decade departmental officials had initially deemed morally endangered children categorically unsuitable for placement with individual families, they now lauded foster placement with peasant families as the ideal site of their moralization. Not only would the child be exposed to the influences of the virtuous and loving peasant family, he or she would be assimilated into it as virtually equivalent to the biological offspring of the peasant couple.

This new interest in the specific quality of moralizing experiences offered by farm labor and rural foster placement destabilized the department's earlier celebration of the wage as a primary route to moralization. Too great a stress on the discipline of wage earning alone would take a serious toll on the child's developing character and moral sensibilities. "Some will object in

---

(Paris: Editions du Seuil, 1976). See also Michael Burns's excellent introduction to his book on rural political life under the Third Republic, *Rural Society and French Politics: Boulangism and the Dreyfus Affair, 1886–1900* (Princeton: Princeton University Press, 1984), 3–16.

[3] This interest became especially acute after the war, when Seine officials began to look for ways to settle their wards in the countryside once they attained the age of majority. In the 1920s the department experimented by giving its female wards plots of land as dowries in the hope that they would become more desirable marriage partners for young men in the provinces. Thus established in a rural marriage, they would stay in the countryside and, in reproducing, contribute toward the larger repopulation of rural France. See CGS, no. 25, *Proposition relative à l'établissement à la campagne des enfants assistés au nom de la comité du retour à la terre présenté par M. Ambroise* (1925).

[4] CGS, no. 15, *Rapport présenté par M. Rousselle, au nom de la 3e commission sur le service des enfants moralement abandonnés* (1889), 48. See also V. Radenac, *Du rôle de l'Etat dans la protection des enfants maltraités ou moralement abandonnés: Commentaire de la loi du 24 juillet 1889 (Titre II)* (Paris: Arthur Rousseau, 1901), 64–67. The jurist was slightly more circumspect in his support of rural placement but agreed that it would greatly benefit those children suited for it.

vain that the child should work and save earlier," Rouselle observed in 1889. "[T]he reckoning is incorrect, it is above all for [the child's] sake that the family must be chosen over the bankbook."[5] To be sure, the department continued to place a high premium on the moralizing value of wages and continued to stress the evidence of thrift as proof of a successful moral education. Nonetheless, by the end of the 1880s, the quality and context of the child's wage-earning experience appear to have won out over the bankbook as the primary site of moral education.

To complete this gesture of reversal, Rousselle's 1889 report concluded that extrafamilial placement was a necessary but less desirable complement to rural foster care or agricultural apprenticeship. Group industrial placement should be recommended only for that minority of the irrevocably "habituated to the noise and fever of the city."[6] Those qualities that had originally defined the norm for the category—infection with the vices and "fever of the city"—now defined only its margins and its misfits. This discursive move, displacing the earlier, more morally charged definitions of the category to its edges, played a critical role in the department's efforts to reconceive its placement strategies. Ultimately, it would also contribute to the conceptual dismantling of the very category of enfant moralement abandonné.

By the end of the decade, the familial structuring of moral education deemed appropriate for the enfant moralement abandonné no longer took a strictly metaphorical form. By recasting the moral effects of familial placement as directly beneficial to the moralement abandonné, and by isolating the child irreducibly saturated with urban experience as extrinsic to the essence of the category, the familial aspects of moralizing experience could now be rendered literal.

Transforming the administrative practices developed around the enfant moralement abandonné thus also required—and helped produce—a profound revision of the meanings and implications affixed to the category in its earlier incarnation. One crucial aspect of the effort to recast the moral quality of the moralement abandonné centered on the move away from the ambivalent vision of these children as both innocent victim and potentially dangerous social menace. By the close of the 1880s, officials increasingly described the enfant moralement abandonné as a virtual innocent, the martyr of delinquent parents and an uncaring social order. As Rousselle put it in 1894, the enfant moralement abandonné was one "who lacks the basics often and supervision and good counsel always, who in his family engages neither a mother's tenderness nor a father's watchfulness, who did not know, who never knew, affection." Although Rousselle continued to warn that the moralement abandonnés would always constitute a potential threat to social

[5] CGS, no. 15 (1889), 48.
[6] Ibid., 47.

stability, he nevertheless transferred the burden of moral culpability from the child to the parent, and from the parent to society as a whole. "Who then is the guilty party, the main culprit," he asked, "if not, I repeat, that society which devours its own children?"[7]

Rousselle's reasoning, which negated a good part of the category's earlier criminal connotations, typified the rhetorical transformations of the late 1880s and the 1890s. The use of the language of victimization in the definition of the enfant moralement abandonné was a far cry from the discursive constructs of the late 1870s and early 1880s in which the morally endangered child first appeared as the dangerous, even criminal, street urchin. Both the fear of the child as oversaturated by his experiences in a degenerate family and demoralizing urban arena and the fear that he would contaminate the "innocent" peasant home with his immoral education were thus displaced in a grounding vision of the category as essentially determined by the experience of deprivation, that is, as suffering, in a state of relative innocence, from moral underdevelopment caused by a lack of proper familial education. Most important, then, the move to reconceive the enfant moralement abandonné as a relatively innocent victim of familial and social neglect allowed administrators to integrate these children into a system of care designed to provide precisely what they were presumed to have lacked before: an intact and morally sound family.

Even the boundaries imposed by the ideologies of age fell before this new definition of the problem. Rousselle described the decision in the later 1880s to admit young people over the age of sixteen—as well as children under ten—this way: "[T]oday one crosses these boundaries, and when it is a matter of saving a child or a young man, we do not get locked into questions of age."[8] The upper limit of sixteen in particular failed to accommodate the new vision of the enfant moralement abandonneé emphasizing the child's needs rather than his degree of educability and level of moral culpability. "Today," Rousselle claimed in his report of 1889, "every minor under 21 years of age for whom an appropriate education seems likely to produce results from the occupational and moralizing standpoint is admitted." By 1889 more than 900 of the 5,619 children and youths who had passed through the Service had been admitted between the ages of sixteen and twenty-one.[9]

This change in attitude toward older children and the possibility of their moral rehabilitation was echoed in a parallel drive to raise the age of penal minority from sixteen to eighteen. A law to this effect was eventually passed in 1906 and reinforced by the legislation of 1912 establishing a separate

---

[7] CGS, no. 1, *Rapport général présenté par M. Rousselle au nom de la 3e commission sur le service des enfants moralement abandonnés* (1894), 3.

[8] CGS, no. 15 (1889), 8.

[9] Ibid., 9.

juvenile court. The formation of character and habit, it seemed, depended less and less on educative intervention at a particularly early point in the child's life.

As always, budgetary concerns also shaped the department's assessment of its policies. Like the private industrialist who had figured so prominently in the schemes of the early 1880s, the department had to weigh its expenses against its return. Nonetheless, the decision to assimilate the enfants moralement abandonnés into a regime of rural foster care was not wholly determined by its fiscal benefits. Well aware of the economic advantages of rural foster placement even before the founding of the Service des Enfants Moralement Abandonnés, departmental authorities never dissociated the task of moral (re)education from their concern for the departmental budget. When the enfant moralement abandonné was conceptualized as ill suited for and dangerous to peasant families, officials deliberately chose more costly forms of state child rearing. And only the discursive reconfiguration of the category and its implications for policy would permit the department to follow the course apparently laid by economic rationality.[10]

As the structure of its discourse shifted, so too did the department's practice. By the end of the decade, the Service's placement records began to reflect its reorientation toward the foster family and agricultural apprenticeship. In 1883, 502 out of 1,999, or about 25 percent of the department's enfants moralement abandonnés, had been listed as placed with farmers. By contrast, in 1890, 2,813 out of 3,408 placements, more than 82 percent, were entered under the heading "with families" (*chez des familles*), a category that seems to have replaced the earlier "farmers" in the rubrics employed in the annual reports.[11] Although some of these familial placements may not have been with peasant or farming families, the enthusiasm expressed for placing these children with individual peasant families dominates the reports in which these undifferentiated figures appear. This change in terminology may also be read as underscoring the newfound importance of establishing solid family ties for the moralement abandonnés; the importance of the peasant family thus may have shifted from the form of work it supplied to the type of domestic experience it represented.

The annual reports also document a correlate decline in industrial placements. Six hundred eighty, or 34 percent of the children placed in 1883, had

---

[10] Michel Foucault's remarks on rationality, the implementation of "programmes," and their hidden or unexpected outcome pertain here. Above all, Foucault suggests, institutional rationalities lie beyond the realm of "straightforward calculation of immediate interest," in the intersection of "diverse practices and strategies" (Foucault, "Questions of Method," in *The Foucault Effect: Studies in Governmentality*, ed. Graham Burchell, Colin Gordon, and Peter Miller [Chicago: University of Chicago Press, 1991], 80–81).

[11] CGS, no. 93, *Rapport général présenté par M. Rousselle au nom de la 3e commission sur le service des enfants moralement abandonnés* (1891), 7–8.

been apprenticed to industry in groups, and another 20 percent had been placed in individual apprenticeships.[12] In 1890 only 198, or about 6 percent, of the moralement abandonnés had been sent to similar placements. Almost all the industrial apprentices counted in 1890 were boys whom the department had distributed among six workshops and factories. Four of those six were glassworks. The forty-two girls included in these figures were divided as apprentices among four industrial shops: an artificial-flower workshop where nearly half of the girls had been placed; a gold and silver embroidery workshop; a clothing workshop; and a noodle factory.[13]

Officials and social critics would continue to issue warnings against the indiscriminate mixing of urban vice and rural purity well into the twentieth century. Nonetheless, by the end of the nineteenth century, those fears had ceased to influence the formation of practical policy where the majority of the children classified as moralement abandonné were concerned. The integration of the enfants moralement abandonnés into the Bureau of Public Assistance's larger network of individual placements with peasant families proved so successful that inspectors for the Service des Enfants Assistés began to complain. In some regions, the added population was putting a dangerous strain on the already limited supply of familial placements and agricultural apprenticeships that met departmental standards.[14]

Larger institutional changes also played their part in reshaping the category of the moralement abandonné and its administrative consequences. In 1896, the year of Councillor Rousselle's death, the General Council took its first concrete steps toward the formal erasure of the distinctions between its two sets of wards when it unified the department's budgets for the Service des Enfants Assistés and the Service des Moralement Abandonnés. Henceforth, the third commission recommended, children admitted to the care of the department by virtue of their status as enfants moralement abandonné should be known, like the enfants assistés, simply as "wards of the Seine" (*pupilles de la Seine*).

Interestingly, the faith in the wisdom of such an administrative merger was not entirely unshakable. A strong sense of trepidation about eradicating the distinctiveness of the enfant moralement abandonné colored the annual report of that year. Paul Strauss, the new *rapporteur* for the third commission, assured his colleagues on the council that all administrative changes would be effected "without . . . the two categories getting confused." Al-

---

[12] The heading "apprentis isolés," like the heading "chez des cultivateurs," had disappeared by 1890, but again, we may assume that some more individualized craft apprenticeship was incorporated under the less specific category of placements "chez des familles."

[13] CGS, no. 93 (1891), 7–8.

[14] This was the complaint of the inspectors in the Service des Enfants Assistés in regard to the area around Avallon in the department of the Yonne. ADS, D.1 X4:18, Commission des Enfants Assistés, procès-verbaux, 5 December 1905.

though the children might bear the generic title of *pupille*, he argued, the category of moralement abandonné "must necessarily keep its own physiognomy, its distinct recruitment, and its special form of supervision."[15] Strauss's promises appear to have made their mark primarily on the statistics of the Bureau of Public Assistance, where children continued to be categorized by the cause of their admission, including abandon moral. In most other respects, the enfant moralement abandonné did indeed disappear into the more general rubric of "pupille de l'Assistance."

Overall, changes in the department's placement practices over the course of the 1880s could be effected only by exploiting the essential indeterminacy of the category of the moralement abandonné. At the same time, later changes also led to the rationalization and eventual erasure of those very ambiguities both from the abstract categories and theories of public assistance to children and from the policies and institutions through which those abstractions took concrete form. The turn to placement with individual peasant foster families also allowed the department of the Seine, the most important source of enfants moralement abandonnés in France, to bring its administrative practices into alignment with the discourse on morality, parenthood, and state action that gave the law of 1889 its cultural and ideological foundation.

The department's transformation of the administrative practices surrounding and defining the enfants moralement abandonnés thus also rested on—and supported—a concurrent reorganization of the Bureau of Public Assistance and its agencies devoted to the protection and rearing of all abandoned or endangered children. In particular, the turn to rural foster placement in the Service des Enfants Moralement Abandonnés facilitated its administrative assimilation with the Service des Enfants Assistés in 1896.

Finally, there was law. In the 1880s the department of the Seine had struggled to define this new category of state-protected children and to develop an administrative regime appropriate to them without formal legal guidance. After the enactment of the 1889 law on abandon moral, however, national legislation became a new and critical site for working out the conceptual and practical problems posed by the category of the enfant moralement abandonné. For its part, the law of 1889 formally shifted most of the burden of moral culpability from the shoulders of the child found wandering in the street to the child's parents; the child's status as moralement abandonné spoke less and less to a self-contained potential for delinquency and appeared increasingly as the symptom of parental inadequacy.

Between 1889 and 1914, a grid of new and more finely textured legal

---

[15] CGS, no. 12, *Rapport général présenté par M. P. Strauss au nom de la 3e commission sur le service des enfants secourus, des enfants assistés et des enfants moralement abandonnés* (1896), 114, 116.

definitions began to efface the presumed uniqueness of the enfants moralement abandonnés. The more lawmakers articulated new categories of delinquent or abused children in need of state protection, the less distinctive—or useful—the category of the enfant moralement abandonné appeared to be. The passage of the law of 19 April 1898, addressing the treatment of "children who committed or were the victims of crime," was especially critical in this turn of events. Although this law contained its own highly ambiguous conflation of "authors" and "victims" of crime, it served to eliminate the delinquent connotations attached to the moralement abandonné by constructing a new, more precisely defined median category between innocent victimization and juvenile criminality. In this case, the evidence of criminal action—either the acts of violence committed on minors by their parents or the crimes the children committed themselves—was a far more accessible standard for judging the child's status than the opaque condition of abandon moral and the potential criminality embodied in the moralement abandonné.

The conceptual and administrative distinctions articulated by the laws of 1889 and 1898 also had an institutional analog. After 1889 most of the children described as enfants moralement abandonné were formally produced by justices in the civil courts through the divestiture of parental authority. Their status was determined through the regulatory actions of civil law, rather than by the norms of criminal justice. By contrast, the *enfants victimes ou auteurs de crimes* were so designated in criminal court.[16]

Even with these legislative formalizations, however, the essential indeterminacy of the category of enfant moralement abandonné persisted. At the turn of the century, for example, the Ministry of the Interior published a table recording the distribution of moralement abandonnés across France. Next to two headings designating children as moralement abandonnés through the respective application of title 1 and title 2 of the 1889 law, the ministry's table placed a third heading: "[Number of children] with regard to which judgments determined by the law of 24 July 1889 have not occurred and who are classified as *moralement abandonné because they do not belong to any of the categories delineated by the decree of 19 January 1811* [the decree organizing the Service des Enfants Assistés]." In subsequent pages, the table substituted the shorthand "included [as enfants moralement abandonnés] for lack of other classification." In the department of the Seine, 1,734 out of the 2,483 children in the care of the state as moralement abandonné, or nearly 70 percent, fell under this indeterminate heading in 1899. Although the proportion of the Seine's population was not typical of the country as a whole, six other departments were also recorded as having more than half of their moralement abandonnés produced at the interstices of other administrative categories rather than in the courtroom. Altogether, children

---

[16] Emile Alcindor, *Les Enfants assistés* (Paris: Emile Paul, 1912), 222.

designated moralement abandonnés by administrative default in 1899 constituted nearly one-quarter of the roughly twenty thousand morally endangered children in departmental care across the country.[17]

In the arena of criminal law, the transformations of categories also inflected the status of the enfant moralement abandonné. Although it introduced a more stable category of incipient juvenile criminality into the legislative canon, the law of 1898 also showed the influence of changing approaches to minors in the logic of criminal law. By allowing the same law to cover children who were victims and authors of crimes, legislators suggested that crimes committed by children might easily be interpreted as symptoms of their own victimization. The major portion of the law's text, introduced in the *Journal Officiel* as "the law on the repression of violence, assaults, acts of cruelty and outrages committed against children," addressed not the child's actions but the abusive acts of which he or she might be the object. In addition, the law provided that the court might entrust these children, both victims and authors of crimes, to the care of the Bureau of Public Assistance if no other responsible individual guardian could be found. The law did not, however, give full legal guardianship to the Bureau of Public Assistance, as the law of 1889 allowed. The new guardian was to exercise only the *droit de garde*, or custodial rights, while parents retained their civil rights. Overall, the law of 1898 made juvenile criminality both evidence of parental mistreatment and, at least in some cases, a problem solved through the institutions of public assistance rather than those of the penal administration. With the development of new categories and institutional practices, and drawing on both material and psychological trauma in articulating its central explanatory models, twentieth-century juvenile criminology was to produce accounts of child delinquency that increasingly displaced responsibility from the child.[18] A law thesis of 1908 announced the triumph of this new approach to juvenile crime and to the public protection of the young: "The day has come when, in the place of the old battle cry 'Let us chastise the guilty child' a cry of mercy has been substituted: Let us aid the unhappy child."[19]

Such a shift in thinking could not help but defuse the fears surrounding the potential criminality of the moralement abandonnés and to make their

[17] France, Ministère de l'Intérieur, Direction de l'Assistance et de l'Hygiène publiques, Bureau des services de l'enfance, *Statistique de la mortalité des enfants assistés (année 1899)* (Melun: Imprimerie administrative, 1901). The other departments include the Allier, the Ariège, the Aude, the Bouches-du-Rhône, the Puy-de-Dôme, and the Saône.

[18] On twentieth-century theories and institutions surrounding juvenile delinquency in France, see Jean-Marie Renouard, *De l'enfant coupable à l'enfant inadapté: Le traitement social et politique de la déviance* (Paris: Centurion, 1990). For the later twentieth century, see also Michel Chauvière, *Enfance inadaptée: L'héritage de Vichy* (Paris: Editions ouvrières, 1980).

[19] Charles Simon, *De la création d'écoles professionelles pour les pupilles difficiles de l'Assistance publique (loi du 28 juillet 1904)* (Paris: Arthur Rousseau, 1908), 3.

assimilation into the regime of the Enfants Assistés appear an ever more natural development. Ironically, by designating the Bureau of Public Assistance and its Service des Enfants Assistés as a possible destination for the enfants victimes ou auteurs de crimes, the law also permitted the displacement of the concern about moral contagion and social disruption from the moralement abandonnés to this newer category of children in state care.

Thus Councillor Rebeillard, in his report of 1912 on the Service des Enfants Assistés de la Seine (now responsible for both the enfants assistés and the moralement abandonnés), reflected on the "ill consequences" of the fourteen-year-old law, particularly dangerous to the Service's policy of rural foster placement. The law of 1898, he argued, "conferred into the care of the Bureau of Public Assistance a relatively large number of wards, already mature, and more often than not morally contaminated, who have begun to spread unrest and disrepute in our provincial agencies."[20] The threat once incarnated in the moralement abandonnés, and, indeed, the very language once used to describe it, settled easily on this new, more "obviously" dangerous category of children, leaving administrators and reformers the freedom to move the enfant moralement abandonné closer still to the status of pure victim protected by the benevolent state.

If the fear of delinquent children was still clearly in evidence, by the turn of the twentieth century the fear of the enfant moralement abandonné as a category of moral ambiguity and potential social danger had largely dissipated. With the disappearance of that anxiety also went the distinctiveness of the category as a whole. Where once the new category of the enfant moralement abandonné had militated for specialized institutions and regimes that could correct for its particular moral indeterminacy, the very existence and structure of that indeterminacy ultimately made it impossible to develop a rationalized regime of care specific to those children.

The gradual draining of meaning from the category of the enfant moralement abandonné was completed in 1904. That year the legislature enacted an "organic law" rationalizing the assortment of laws on assistance to children that had accrued over the course of the nineteenth century. Most important in determining the fate of the category, the new law incorporated abandon moral into its list of equally weighted justifications for taking a child into the care of the Bureau of Public Assistance and the Service des Enfants Assistés.[21] Al-

<hr>

[20] CGS, no. 19, *Rapport général présenté par M. Rebeillard au nom de la 3e commission sur le service des enfants assistés (budget de 1913)* (1912), 12.

[21] Included among the wards of the Bureau of Public Assistance would be

1. the child who, born of unknown father and mother, was found in any place or taken to a depository (the foundling); 2. the child who, born of known father or mother, is abandoned by them without means of recourse to them or their relatives (the abandoned child); 3. the child who, having neither father nor mother, nor relatives to whom there is recourse, has no

though the provisions and language of the law of 1889 ensured that the category of enfant moralement abandonné remained intact as a juridical designation, the law of 1904 codified the loss of its administrative and educative specificity. In particular, this legal assimilation of the enfant moralement abandonné to the general category of *pupille de l'Assistance Publique* laid to rest earlier demands, such as those of Paul Strauss, that the category remain distinct.

One last early-twentieth-century law contributed to the reconfiguration of the enfant moralement abandonné in relation to the institutions of public assistance for children: the law of 28 June 1904, on "difficult or vicious wards" (*pupilles difficiles ou vicieux*). Enacted just one day after the "organic law" on the Service des Enfants Assistés, this law addressed the treatment of those children already under the protection of the Bureau of Public Assistance who appeared to be recalcitrant, rebellious, or overly drawn to vice. One official defined the origins of the new population this way: "[D]ifficult and vicious pupils are recruited principally among criminal children, acquitted as having acted without discernment and conferred into the care of the Bureau of Public Assistance." The role of the Bureau of Public Assistance, the author specified, was to give these children the chance to "unlearn the habits of vagrancy or indiscipline."[22] Another high-ranking figure in the Bureau of Public Assistance described the law of 1904 as splitting the wards of the state into two distinct categories, each with its unique educational demands. "First," he argued, "there are the children who are simply difficult, the lazy ones for whom, in reality, family placement is not suitable; they are the boys who like to rove; they are the girls who are led to recklessness by the spring breeze, as the law of nature would have it." Although these girls and boys could not be classified as truly "wicked," the state was still bound to provide an education that would "protect the boy against the idea of vagrancy, the girl against the notion of emancipation." The second group, he continued, comprised "children with vicious instincts. . . . It is for them that a second category has been created, one for children who, being recognized as vicious through and through, will be confided to the care of the penitentiary administration."[23]

---

means of support (the poor orphan); 4. the child whose parents were divested of parental authority by virtue of the first title of the law of 24 July 1889 (the mistreated, neglected, or morally abandoned child); 5. the child admitted to the Service des Enfants Assistés by virtue of title 2 of the law of 24 July 1889.

The text of the law of 27 June 1904 appears in Albert Dupoux, *Sur les pas de Monsieur Vincent: Trois cent ans d'histoire parisienne de l'enfance abandonnée* (Paris: Revue de l'Assistance publique à Paris, 1958), 330.

[22] Léon Mirman, *Rapport sur le projet de règlement d'administration publique pour l'exécution de la loi du 28 juin 1904 sur les pupilles difficiles*, CSAP, fasc. 105, *Documents* 2 (Melun: Imprimerie administrative, 1906), 4 and 8.

[23] Loys Brueyre, *Rapport sur le projet de règlement d'administration publique pour l'exécution de la loi du 28 juin 1904 sur les pupilles difficiles*, CSAP, fasc. 105, *Documents* 2, 18.

The new law thus refined still further the separation of the qualities that had once been clustered together under the more capacious rubric of moralement abandonné. It shifted the concern about entrenched habits and tastes to a new site of intervention. In specifying a new troublesome population of children under the care of the state, the new law also redirected the anxiety about mixing urban vice with rural virtue. Now it was the pupille vicieux, isolated from the general mixture of assistés and moralement abandonnés, who was to be kept from individual rural placements with uncorrupted peasant families, who required a specialized education and more rigorous forms of supervision.

Redeploying the language and the educational vision once used to explain the best strategy to take with the moralement abandonnés, another administrator described the best means of moralizing the pupille difficile ou vicieux.

[T]he education to provide for these children should not be a collective, theory-ridden training, but an individualized one and one which comes from the facts of everyday life. Before teaching these children the value of abstract principles, it is important to get to know them individually and to know the points to which the work of moral reeducation should be addressed. To show them that one takes an interest in them, to teach them the basics, to give them the taste for labor, and, through a solid apprenticeship, to provide them with a trade which will later assure them of a steady and rather high income . . .[24]

Once more, skillful observation and practical indoctrination were seen as essential building blocks in the reeducation and professional training of the socially dangerous child. In questions of professional education as well as in questions of placement, the stigma once firmly affixed to the moralement abandonnés had shifted to a category whose boundaries had been drawn with far greater precision. Because the category of enfant vicieux also provided an outlet for those enfants moralement abandonnés who demonstrated the symptoms of moral corruption after they had been accepted into the Service, it served as both a conceptual and an institutional vent for the fear they had formerly inspired as an abstract group.

The fear of the enfants moralement abandonnés thus radically diminished as increasingly specialized types of marginal children came to be defined, although suspicion of them never entirely disappeared. In fact, the ambivalence about the endangered child, under whatever rubric he or she might happen to fall, remained an important factor in the determination of policies in the twentieth century, and it continued to lend a tinge of hostility to the reception of such children in the world beyond the institutions of public assistance. Despite these diffused traces of concern, however, the category of the enfant moralement abandonné had been almost completely denuded of its former overabundance of determining features a mere thirty years after it

---

[24] Mirman, *Rapport sur le projet de règlement*, 5.

had been introduced into the language of social reform. The competing definitions that had once met in the efforts to identify and treat a specific population had one by one been excised, and many of them had been developed as categories of their own. The fate of the category, and by extension the fate of efforts to construct correlating structures of education and placement, was sealed by 1906, when Emile Ogier, a member of the executive council of the Bureau of Public Assistance proclaimed, "This term no longer designates a special category."[25]

The turn to rural foster placement and the eventual assimilation of the enfant moralement abandonné into the broader regime of public assistance to children should perhaps also be read as the climax of another, more abstract, but far more powerful narrative about the Third Republic's developing relationship to its "parentless" wards. With the passage of the law of 1889, the moralement abandonnés were formally and doubly classified as parentless: first, in the discovery of the negligence or demoralizing conduct that rendered them, in the eyes of the state and private philanthropy, without the care of "proper" parents; and second, through the civil court's pronouncement that legal guardianship, and the "parental" rights attached to it, would pass from the child's "denatured" parents to either a family guardian or to the state. Even when the guardian was to be a family member, however, only through a process of state investigation and approval would legal tutelle pass from parent to guardian. The state, in other words, substituted itself for the deficient parent as the party charged with the protection of the child's best interests even in those cases where it did not in fact transfer legal guardianship to its own designated agent, the administration of the Bureau of Public Assistance.

It was not only the text of the law of 1889 that dictated the state's parental status in relation to the moralement abandonnés. The debates that had surrounded the law when it was still a proposal in the 1880s centered in large part on the state's power and obligation to substitute its own parental presence for the delinquent parents whose actions produced the moralement abandonnés. How better to ensure the full substitution of a healthy family for a dangerous one than to place the enfant moralement abandonné in foster care with a "virtuous" peasant family? How better to realize the state's commitment to serving as the metaphorical metaparent to all French children than to ensure that the forms of care and education it provided took the literal form of the family?

The significance of rural foster placement in making an almost seamless alignment between the state as parent and the enfant moralement abandonné as parentless was crystallized in Denise Bouchet's *Le Rôle de l'Assistance publique dans l'application de la loi du 24 juillet 1889 "sur la protection des enfants maltraités ou moralement abandonnés"* of 1938. Rural foster placement, Bouchet wrote,

---

[25] *Session ordinaire de 1906*, CSAP, fasc. 105, *Documents* 2 (1906), 118.

is the best way to create a new family for the child whose natural family has failed; moreover, in this way the ward is put into direct contact with the normal course of life. Of course the State cannot altogether replace the child's true family, one can't get perfect results, but it really seems that familial placement as it is currently practiced nears the ideal. . . . [T]he enfant moralement abandonné[,] . . . more than any other, must be embraced and given a moral upbringing, since he has been deprived of all these attentions during the time he spent with his family of origin. These children, devoted to vice and corruption, if they are reared in the bosom of an honest and hardworking family, would likely become excellent laborers and vigorous workers.[26]

The move to embrace the peasant foster family as the best solution for the problem posed by the category of the moralement abandonnés thus affirmed the Third Republic's original commitment to the language of family in the expression of its position and its policies in the care of morally endangered children. In providing surrogate parents, the practice of rural foster placement instantiated the state's parental role, a role cemented earlier—both discursively and legally—by the law of 1889 on abandon moral.

Cast at first as a simple extension of the Service des Enfants Assistés, defined in the 1880s as a wholly alternative system, the Service des Enfants Moralement Abandonnés was ultimately consumed by contradictions that officials could not overcome. The notion of the enfant moralement abandonné, once a critical element in the web of concerns and anxieties articulated around "marginal" children, also lost its conceptual specificity in this period. The introduction of increasingly refined categories of juvenile delinquency around the turn of the century split the category along its most troublesome internal fault lines: although all children from "delinquent" families remained suspect in the eyes of the state, by 1914 it began to seem possible to separate innocent victims of parental abuse from more clearly corrupted juveniles. No longer did every enfant moralement abandonné appear to embody both the endangered *and* the dangerous child.

Simultaneously, new typologies restructuring the penal administration allowed administrators to segregate the more "dangerous" moralement abandonnés and to place them in institutions of reform that had been reconceived on parallel lines. The early concern that all enfants moralement abandonnés required both a basic upbringing or education and corrective training, or reeducation, was thus eliminated by the practice of increasingly fine differentiation between the children. The establishment of a separate juvenile court system in 1912 and the growing use of social workers and psychologists as adjuncts to the court testify to the depth of the epistemological and

[26] Denise Bouchet, *Le Rôle de l'Assistance publique dans l'application de la loi du 24 juillet 1889 "sur la protection des enfants maltraités ou moralement abandonnés"* (Lyons: Imprimerie Grosjean-Fourgerat, 1938), 87–88.

institutional transformations wrought around the question of criminality among the young.[27]

Even as it was drained of any specific content and stripped of any particular administrative implications, the category of the enfant moralement abandonné lived on in the jurisprudence of the civil court, as well as that of the new juvenile court system. After the war, moreover, social critics and jurists continued to wrestle with the meaning of this social type for a state expanding the net of public assistance and basic welfare at an increasingly rapid pace. Well into the 1930s, graduates of French law schools such as Bouchet continued to produce theses on the legal and practical question of abandon moral and the enfant moralement abandonné.[28]

The Service des Enfants Moralement Abandonnés, groundbreaking in the 1880s, ultimately had only an ephemeral life in Paris's agencies devoted to assisting and protecting children. For the historian, however, the institutional life and death of the service and the category around which it was built provide a critical window onto the ways in which law, administrative practice, and the conceptual frames underlying them intersect. In the end, the founding and later dismantling of the Service des Enfants Moralement Abandonnés revealed the difficulties inherent in inventing public policies and institutions in response to newly perceived social problems. To borrow the words of Councillor Rousselle, the experience of the Service des Moralement Abandonnés demonstrated the practical and conceptual complications of "solving a problem in advance"—in fact, the ground zero of every effort to formalize institutions, their conceptual foundations, and their practices.[29] In articulating for the first time a category of children for public protection who were defined by their compromised past, their unstable present, and their potentially dangerous incarnation in the future, the Service des Enfants Moralement Abandonnés and the category of the enfant moralement abandonné would profoundly shape the French state's approach to "children at risk" in the twentieth century.

[27] On the creation of the juvenile court and its apparatus, see Renouard, *De l'enfant coupable.* For a more controversial analysis of these developments, see Jacques Donzelot, *The Policing of Families,* trans. Robert Hurley (New York: Pantheon, 1979), esp. 96–168.

[28] In addition to Bouchet, see Geneviève Azèma, *L'Etat et les enfants abandonnés* (Bordeaux: Imprimerie de l'Université, 1930), and Madeleine Léonard, *Les Enfants assistés en droit comparé* (Melun: Imprimerie administrative, 1938). That the authors of these three works on assistance to children, the law, and the state were women suggests intriguing paths of research on gender and legal specialization in the early twentieth century.

[29] Rousselle's words resonate particularly strongly with Foucault's remarks on transforming institutions and rationalities: "[R]ational schemas . . . don't take effect in the institutions in an integral manner; they are simplified, or some are chosen and not others; and things never work out as planned" (Foucault, "Questions of Method," 80).

Conclusion

THE PROBLEM of abandon moral and the category of the enfant moralement abandonné, originally embedded in the deepest fears and the strongest hopes of the early Third Republic, appeared to have lost much of their distinctive signifying power by the eve of the Great War. Particularly in the arena of administration, the conceptual resonance of abandon moral and the integrity of the category of the enfant moralement abandonné were broken down by ever more differentiated accounts of juvenile deviancy and the moral order of the family. The category's place in the juridical apparatus of protection was similarly redefined through the creation of specialized juvenile courts in 1912. At the same time, moreover, new forms of professional expertise emerging at the intersection of social science and justice, most notably professionalized social work and the subspecialty of child psychiatry, began the work of refashioning danger in the family. From this point forward, the language of morals began to be displaced by more explicitly social and psychological terms. The "best interests" of the child would increasingly be defined for the court by these new disciplines and their practitioners in the twentieth century.[1]

The gradual evisceration of the category of the enfant moralement abandonné is an especially striking feature of the twentieth-century rereading of "dangerous" families and their consequences. To be sure, through the application of the 1889 law on abandon moral the twentieth-century juvenile court continued to classify children as moralement abandonné. Even with this sustained usage, however, and even despite the "scientific" efforts of social workers and psychologists to rationalize their new domains, the category continued to resist precise definition; its contours, as unstable in the twentieth century as in the 1880s, emerged only through the play of opposition and negation. Thus a pamphlet for French social workers published in 1954 explained that children correctly categorized as moralement abandonné were "neither delinquents nor vagabonds, neither victims of penal infractions nor the object of paternal correction proceedings."[2] This account of the oper-

---

[1] In the 1950s the author of a pamphlet written to educate social workers attached to the juvenile court noted that in the current application of the 1889 law on abandon moral the courts were ever more influenced by "the sciences of psychology and pedagogy." The "interests of the child," she added approvingly, were increasingly conceived in terms of their "affective needs," rather than strictly in terms of "food, hygiene, and education" (Anne-Marie Fournié, "La Protection judiciaire de l'enfance en danger: Loi du 24 juillet 1889," *Textes de droit familial* [July–Sept. 1954]: 63).

[2] Ibid., 1.

ations of justice and the exercise of professional expertise similarly testifies to the enduring elasticity of the law and the essential ambiguity of these categories of familial danger, even when appropriated by new types of professionals and deployed in new institutional and historical contexts.

The twin imperatives to segregate children exposed to dangerous familial influences and to provide them with a program of reform and reeducation tailored precisely to their condition also lost their urgent quality in the twentieth century. Yet concern about children in moral danger did not disappear. Instead, with the interwar modifications to the law, that concern took the family rather than the individual child as its primary object. To this end, the courts and the professionals attached to it created new regimes of segregation and reeducation shaped by contemporary readings of the 1889 law on moral danger. These programs focused on individual families and the inculcation of "parenting" skills under the supervision of social workers attached to the court. These midcentury programs of managed familial reeducation continue to resonate with French family policy today, policy increasingly focused on regulating the practices of "dangerous" immigrant families, that is, families whose ethnicity, religion, race, or cultural practices threaten dominant visions of proper family order.

With the new juridical-administrative order of the twentieth century, the category of the child in moral danger realized its full potential as a pure symptom of familial disorder, and the family, rather than the child, became the object of state tutelage and state programs of managed, individualized reform. The all-or-nothing conditions written into the law of 1889 by the stringent legislative reformers of the 1880s ensured that decisions of déchéance would sever all connections between children and their families of origin. Only then, in the logic of these early reformers, could endangered and possibly dangerous children be rid of the effects of their earlier exposure to demoralizing influences and their still-malleable characters be recast. By 1940 this unconditional regime, centered on the entwined futures of child and nation, had ceded to policies that appeared to visit less violent measures on dangerous families. Yet these new policies, supplanting the principle of segregation with that of surveillance, have perhaps constituted the foundation of a far more coercive order of familial normalization and governance.

This book concludes, then, not with the disappearance of abandon moral as a social problem or juridical category but with its detachment from the particular political, moral, and social concerns that structured the founding of the republican republic and, simultaneously, gave the problem its original contours. As an issue first articulated at a particular historical juncture in France, abandon moral and the categories and institutions it generated were endowed with historically specific—and historically powerful—meanings, resonances, ellipses, and contradictions. The gradual erosion of abandon moral's signifying power and the concurrent deterioration of the specificity of the enfant moralement abandonné can be attributed both to the pressures exerted by those very historically bounded sets of meanings and to the institutional effects they generated. If the terms and the categories lived on in the twentieth century's languages and practices of child protection, it was largely due to massive conceptual and institutional regrounding as well as to the formal recontouring of the 1889 law, its field of application, and its range of possible consequences.

What is to be gained by insisting on the particular historicity of such issues as abandon moral? Why should the historian locate breaks in a narrative of social policy that appears to demand the assertion of continuity? I would argue that only in interrupting—or at least challenging—the flow of such chronologies can the historian take up particular legislative reforms, administrative experiments, or institutional restructurings as the object of a wider, more synthetic historical analysis. At the same time, exploring the degree to which certain social "crises" or policy changes were embedded in particular historical conjunctures disrupts efforts to place all nineteenth-century state activity related to the social at the "origin" of the modern welfare state. Releasing these questions from the grip of monolithic social policy or welfare state narratives makes them available as points of access into other questions about the state and its own historicity.

The appearance of abandon moral as a critical affair for state and nation in the 1880s reveals the intensity of the early Third Republic's investment in fashioning its own moral identity and in embedding that new identity in the fabric of its laws and administrative practices. In this sense, the discursive and institutional articulation of abandon moral in the first decades of the new regime provides a critical window onto the centrality of a secular, or secularized, moral order in the imaginaire d'état of the early Third Republic. The new problem and its moral implications stood at the crossroads of the republic's particular reading of France's past and its particular efforts to found a political, cultural, and social base for the future. The crisis of abandon moral, as articulated between the late 1870s and 1914, in short, challenged the new regime to read the moral history of particular families as versions of the national history it took as its own political—and moral—point of departure.

In tying the moral status and "private" histories of the French family to the moral status of the state and the history of the nation, the issue of abandon moral thus suggests the complexity of the Third Republic's intersecting frames of reference. It points to the multiplicity of desires and fears at work in this relatively late moment of modern state building, most of all in the Third Republic's efforts to make the regulation of the family a cornerstone of both its own moral identity and its methods of governance under the sign of republican democracy.

The question of governance and the family has become a critical and much debated issue for both historians and analysts of the politics of the family working in a variety of other disciplines. The history of abandon moral in late-nineteenth-century France raises certain questions about the ways scholars of the later twentieth century have been reading family regulation and its effects. Above all, I would argue, the history of abandon moral suggests that scholars, particularly those interested in questions of power, governance, and social regulation in a "liberal" setting, might enrich their studies by embracing ambivalence as a legitimate and revealing category of analysis, both contemporary and historical. Despite the expansion and much-vaunted "rationalization" of the republic's administrative apparatus, the reformers of the Third Republic did not relish the prospect of creating permanent forces or strategies for intervening in family affairs. Nor did they celebrate the state's potential to settle itself as a permanent inhabitant of the terrain of family relations or the possibility of displacing in perpetuity the private exercise of domestic authority with its own powers of normalization and adjudication. Instead, they consistently framed their reforms in a language and within a conceptual universe haunted by the fear of excess, by the possibility of misstep, a language and a universe laced as much with anxiety and regret as it was with the optimism and confidence inherited with their positivist creed.

Nowhere is this ambivalence more visible to the historian's eye than in the Third Republic's uncertainty about the effects of recasting the boundaries between public and private life. In their efforts to address the crisis of abandon moral, particularly through the enactment of new legislation, reformers were clearly engaged in refashioning—and politicizing—the social, a space of governance one scholar has recently defined as a "hybrid of public/private differentiations."[3] The 1889 law and the discourse surrounding it turned on a logic of continual differentiation between public and private. At the same time, paradoxically, they also depended on the blurring of those differentiations, engaging a logic of analogy, rather than difference, that likened the state to parent and nation to family. In their debates, French legislators of the late nineteenth century insisted on the "natural" integrity of private family life, and in their metaphorical elaborations they rendered the boundaries between public and private ever more permeable. Even for the critics of the 1889 law, the issue was not the total destruction of family privacy and autonomy but the undesirable effects of empowering the state to trespass on an

[3] The phrase comes from Jeffrey Minson, *Genealogies of Morals: Nietzsche, Foucault, Donzelot, and the Eccentricity of Ethics* (London: Macmillan, 1985), 182. See also Jacques Donzelot, *The Policing of Families*, trans. Robert Hurley (New York: Pantheon, 1979), and esp. Denise Riley, *"Am I That Name?" Feminism and the Category of "Women" in History* (Minneapolis: University of Minnesota Press, 1988), for their discussions of the social and the regulation of domestic life.

intact private life, of allowing the state to enmesh itself in the "natural" exercise of paternal authority in the home.

Ambiguity similarly inflected reformers' recognition of the epistemological limits of their project. Providing state functionaries with transparent knowledge of a family's moral interior seemed both impossible and morally undesirable. Protective action remained strictly contingent on readings of the visible—that is, "public"—face of familial breakdown. Regulating the family, particularly through the application of the law of 1889 on abandon moral, demanded that legislators, police, magistrates, family members, and their acquaintances all participate in a complex process of narration, interpretation, and negotiation which centered on the essential opacity of "private" family relations. Here, too, the historian finds clear traces of the regime's reverence for the private, its devotion to the essential definition of the private as a naturally self-regulating moral space, even as it created legislation permitting agents of the state to evaluate and transform that order as they saw fit.

How, then, did the liberal republic dream of escaping the condition of paralysis so often engendered by ambivalence? How was it possible for reformers to have acted in any way on their desire to protect the morally endangered child and the morally endangered nation? For the public authorities who forged the first generation of solutions to the crisis of abandon moral, the object was to draw, and then to walk, the thin line of supplementarity. In this imagined universe of moral and moralizing government, the distinction between public and private life, although recast, would remain intact. The state would intervene only where the family failed; it would negotiate the closed, interior space of familial moral order only where "unnatural" conditions rendered that space permeable, where denatured parents and dangerous domestic relations invited state action. In casting the state as a parental figure best equipped to determine and protect children's best interests, the reformers of the Third Republic drew on the power of metaphor, perhaps the rhetorical figure most suited to the fear of usurpation, in order to stabilize their uncertainties and ground their quite concrete transformations in the world of law and in the institutions of public assistance. The imaginaire d'état that produced the formalized problem of abandon moral consistently cast the state's actions in the form of urgent protective measures, marked by the liberal faith that the state's place in the family was a matter of temporary readjustment. Public regulation of the family would become unnecessary as the French family and the nation recuperated their moral foundation and their internal moral stability. Yet as the history of family policy in twentieth-century France reveals, the anxious institutionalization of "emergency" measures often left those temporary and internally unstable measures deeply entrenched in the state's more enduring apparatus of social government.

Accepting and analyzing ambivalence as a mode of discursive or institutional action in the past, rather than pushing it aside as a symptom of confusion, inefficacy, or rhetorical camouflage for more clearly articulated but nefarious intentions, might allow historians to pose different kinds of questions about the history and politics of government. This approach might yield new kinds of insights about historically defined possibilities for conceptual, cultural, and political order. It also calls for the use of a variety of methods and theoretical insights. For the historical analysis of ambivalence, the close reading of language, particularly the metaphorical articulations of difference, becomes essential. For it is precisely in the figuration of these distinctions, boundaries, and oppositions that ambivalence and its real historical effects become most visible.

To place this kind of emphasis on ambivalence, on the imaginaire d'état, and on language is also to suggest that the problem of effective governance under the Third Republic was in many respects a problem situated in the realm of representation. Historians of the French Revolution have recently given much play to these questions in their analyses of symbolic order and revolutionary language, a critical approach for which the Revolution has seemed especially ripe.[4] But the question of representation, in its deeply discursive sense, also pertains to regimes of governance less apparently endowed with symbolic wealth than those comprising France's revolutionary tradition. This is perhaps particularly true for the first few decades of the Third Republic, where the problem of governing the social, that "hybrid" terrain of "of public/private differentiations," was moved to the forefront of national politics and state action. For it was precisely the question of differentiation—differentiation between political regimes, historical eras, generations, sexes, individuals, and collectivities, as well as between public and private—that fundamentally structured the early Third Republic's effort to establish its political identity and practices.

The Third Republic's efforts to regulate moral danger in the family also raise the question of the relationship between representation and efficacious government. As I have suggested, the text of the 1889 law allowed a great deal of latitude both in its interpretation and its application. It provided, moreover, a space in which moral norms and familial behaviors became a subject of dialogue between ordinary individuals and agents of the state seeking the representational coherence necessary to pursue a judgment of déchéance de la puissance paternelle. Particularly in the arena of juridical practices, the difficulty of establishing and maintaining representational order suggests that there could be no simple application of the law without the

---

[4] See, for example, the work of Lynn Hunt, *Politics, Culture, and Class in the French Revolution* (Berkeley: University of California Press, 1984), and more recently, *The Family Romance of the French Revolution* (Berkeley: University of California Press, 1992).

effacement of contradiction, without the construction of a representational frame sturdy enough to contain an actionable case of moral danger.

While the justice system produced the image of efficient and efficacious government through its cautious selection of cases and its pursuit of representational consistency, legislators emphasized the possibility, if not always the desirability, of effective state regulation of the family. Proponents of the 1889 law thus posited the state, and particularly the liberal republican state, as a rational and benevolent regulatory force, frequently drawing on the identity of the bon père de famille to underscore this combination of reason and emotion. Together, the authors of the law and those authorities charged with its implementation generated a representation of the state and its powers that tended to eliminate its quite real frailties and uncertainties from view. The ambivalence roused by the regulation of the family thus reappeared in the guise of conscience.

The law of 1889 undeniably increased the state's power to transform families. Yet the "policing of the family," which some historians have taken as evidence of expanding and increasing totalizing systems of social control, may in fact have been something more like a "social control effect," produced at the intersection of discourses and practices allied in an effort to obscure ambivalence and efface the ragged edges of inefficacy.[5]

This may not seem surprising to some readers, who might ask what regime has not attempted to represent itself in the best possible light. Yet, the best light, the visible aspect of "good" government, differs over time and between places. The political paradox of the Third Republic, to produce a regime that was both liberal and strongly statist, lay deeply embedded in the particular political history of the French nation-state. That paradox produced especially difficult representational problems as well. Producing the state for public consumption in this era required new frames of reference, new languages of government: secular, democratic, and republican but untainted by the radicalism of those earlier republican experiments produced in the crucible of revolution. It was under this pressure, perhaps, that the discourses of science and secularized morality found such strong purchase in the last decades of the nineteenth century.

The representational aspect of governance, and especially the representation of the state by its constituent actors, institutions, and practices, as well as those representations forged by those outside the hierarchies of state office, invites further historical analysis. The example of the Third Republic's invocation of and response to a crisis of abandon moral suggests that the

---

[5] This literal reading of representation, it seems to me, is one of the chief faults of Donzelot's *The Policing of Families*. Indeed, in this misreading Donzelot produces the relentless and increasingly all-powerful machine of social control from an analysis that tends in other places toward a much more nuanced understanding of child protection in French history and social politics.

representational qualities of government cannot be reduced to what some might see as mere rhetoric or political propaganda. Instead, this book suggests that representational practices comprising the regime's particular imaginaire d'état made social governance possible. Those same elements were equally critical in the creation of the juridical and administration terrains in which the relations between government and the governed have been the object of continual negotiation, interpretation, and representation in the past.

"[M]aybe, after all," Michel Foucault suggested in one of his later essays, "the state is no more than a composite reality and a mythicized abstraction, whose importance is a lot more limited than many of us think."[6] Taken literally, as Foucault so often has been taken by historians, it is debatable whether the state is truly less important than we think, especially in the modern era. But Foucault's remarks can also be read as an invitation to push aside unexamined truths about the state, to stop bracketing the state as a fully formed entity or set of forces. Instead, Foucault may be suggesting that historians and others concerned with the history of government should address themselves directly to the operation of mythification around and through the state. Examining the state as a "mythicized abstraction" thus means discarding reified notions of state in order to analyze the changing processes and terrains of reification in the past. It is precisely the reality of these processes that calls for rigorous historical location and analysis. If the abstraction of the state is less important than we think, the means by which the state comes into being, the sites in which it attributes an identity to itself, the moments when it seems to become more visible as a coherent entity endowed with particular attributes, and the exchanges or challenges through which the contours of its power are articulated and rearticulated, that is, the historical reality of governance, are perhaps more important than we have realized. It is to this end, to complicating our understanding of the state and historicizing the practices of government, that I have addressed this history of abandon moral and the enfant moralement abandonné.

[6] Michel Foucault, "Governmentality," in *The Foucault Effect: Studies in Governmentality*, ed. Graham Burchell, Colin Gordon, and Peter Miller (Chicago: University of Chicago Press, 1991), 103.

Select Bibliography

Archival Sources

Archives de l'Assistance Publique (AAP)

M. Fosseyeux, ed. *Catalogue des manuscrits*, 1913.

Liasse 647   Assistance à l'enfance, Agence de Saint-Calais (Sarthe). Circulaires et Correspondance, 1872–1883.

Liasse 688   Enfants Assistés. Circulaires, Rapports, Statistiques.

Archives de la Ville de Paris et du Département de la Seine (ADS)

Series D.1 U5   Première Chambre de Conseil, Parquet de la Seine, Tribunal de Première Instance.

D.3 U7   Parquet de la Seine.

D.1 X4   Procès-verbaux de la Commission des Enfants Assistés, 1879–1934 (13–20).

Archives de la Préfecture de Police de Paris (APP)

Series DB   Enfants abandonnés (61–76).

Bibliothèque Marguerite Durand

Dossier AP   Assistance Publique.

Public Documents

Belgium, Ministère de la Justice. *Congrès international pour l'étude des questions relatives au patronage des détenus et à la protection des enfants moralement abandonnés. Anvers, 1890*. Brussels: E. Guyot, 1891.

Carpentier, Etienne, ed. *Les Cinq codes*. Paris: Sirey, 1938.

Les Cinq codes de l'empire français. Paris: F. Guitel, 1812.

Codes Napoléon. 7th ed. Paris: Auguste Durand, 1852.

Commission spéciale de l'Exposition universelle en 1889. *Catalogue de l'exposition spéciale de la ville de Paris et du département de la Seine*. Paris: Imprimerie et librairies centrales des Chemins de Fer/A. Chaix, 1878.

———. *Notice sur les objets et documents exposés par les divers services de la ville de Paris et du département de la Seine*. Paris: Imprimerie et librairies centrales des Chemins de Fer/A. Chaix, n.d. [1889].

Commission spéciale de l'Exposition universelle en 1900. *Catalogue de l'exposition spéciale de la ville de Paris et du département de la Seine*. Paris: Imprimerie et librairies centrales des Chemins de Fer/A. Chaix, 1900.

Duvergier, Jean-Baptiste, et al., eds. *Collection complète des lois, décrets, ordonnances, règlements et avis du conseil d'état*. Paris: Editions du Recueil Sirey, 1834–1909.

Ecole Pratique d'Administration. *L'Assistance publique à Paris et les enfants assistés de la Seine.* Paris: Marcel Rivière, 1909.

France, Assemblée nationale. *Journal officiel.*

————, Assemblée nationale, Sénat. *Rapport fait au nom de la commission chargée d'examiner: 1° La Proposition de loi ayant pour objet la protection des enfants abandonnés, délaissés ou maltraités, présenté par MM. Théophile Roussel, Bérenger, Dufaure, l'amiral Fourichon, Schoelcher et Jules Simon. 2° Le Projet de loi sur la protection de l'enfance présenté par M. Cazot, Garde de Sceaux, Ministre de Justice.* Sénat session 1882. No. 451. Annexe au procès-verbal de la séance du 25 juillet 1882. Paris: Imprimerie du Sénat, 1882.

————. Conseil supérieur de l'Assistance publique. *Documents.* Melun: Imprimerie administrative, 1904–1908.

————. Conseil supérieur de l'Assistance publique. *Rapports.* Melun: Imprimerie administrative, 1901–1922.

————, Ministère de l'Intérieur. Direction de l'Assistance et de l'Hygiène publiques. Bureau des services de l'enfance. *Statistique de la mortalité des enfants assistés (année 1899).* Melun: Imprimerie administrative, 1901.

Paris. Conseil Municipal. *Rapports, 1880–1892.*

Seine (Département de la). Administration Général de l'Assistance publique à Paris. *Les écoles professionnelles du service des enfants assistés de la Seine: L'école d'Alembert (1882–1909) à Montévrain.* Paris: Berger-Levrault, 1909.

————. Service des enfants assistés, pupilles du département de la Seine. *L'Adoption.* Montévrain: l'école d'Alembert, [1930?].

————. *Exposition universelle de 1889: Catalogue.* N.p., 1889.

———— [L. Guillaume]. *Rapports sur l'Exposition universelle de 1900: Les écoles professionnelles (agriculture, horticulture, etc.).* Montévrain: Imprimerie typographique de l'école d'Alembert, 1900.

———— [J. Marcelin]. *Rapports sur l'Exposition universelle de 1900: Les écoles professionnelles (typographie et ébénisterie).* Montévrain: Imprimerie typographique de l'école d'Alembert, 1900.

————. Conseil Général. *Rapport de la délégation chargée d'étudier un avant projet de colonisation agricole en Algérie pour les enfants assistés du département de la Seine.* Paris: Imprimerie municipale, 1883.

————. Conseil Général. *Rapports sur le service des enfants assistés.* In Conseil Général, *Rapports, 1876–1930.*

————. Conseil Général. *Rapports sur le service des enfants moralement abandonnés.* In Conseil Général, *Rapports, 1881–1896.*

————. Conseil Général. *Le Service des enfants assistés pendant la guerre.* Paris: Imprimerie municipale, 1915.

————. *Les Enfants assistés, pupilles du département de la Seine.* Montévrain: L'école d'Alembert, 1939.

————. *Notice historique et statistique sur l'école d'horticulture de Villepreux (Seine-et-Oise) de 1882 à 1894.* Montévrain: Imprimerie typographique de l'école d'Alembert, 1894.

————. *Notice sur l'école Roudil, établissement agricole des enfants assistés du département de la Seine à Ben-Chicao (Algérie).* Montévrain: Imprimerie typographique de l'école d'Alembert, 1894.

————. Service des enfants moralement abandonnés. *Souvenir de l'Exposition ouvrière 1886.* N.p., n.d. [1882].

Printed Primary Sources

Alcindor, Emile. *Les Enfants assistés.* Paris: Emile Paul, 1912.

Azèma, Geneviève. *L'Etat et les enfants abandonnés.* Bordeaux: Imprimerie de l'Université, 1930.

Berthélemy, Henri, and Jean Rivero. *Cinq ans de réformes administratives, 1933–1938: Législation, réglementation, jurisprudence.* Paris: Librairie Arthur Rousseau, 1938.

Blin, Ernest. *Ce que coûte un pupille du département de la Seine* (extracted from *Bulletin des sciences économiques et sociales du Comité des travaux historique et scientifique,* 1934). Paris: Imprimerie nationale, 1935.

————. "Les Enfants assistés de la Seine dans l'Avallonais, 1819–1906: Etudes statistiques." typescript [1907].

Bonzon, Jacques. *La Réforme du service des enfants assistés.* Paris: Berger-Levrault, 1901.

Bouchet, Denise. *Le Rôle de l'Assistance publique dans l'application de la loi du 24 juillet 1889 "sur la protection des enfants maltraités ou moralement abandonnés."* Lyons: Imprimerie Grosjean-Fourgerat, 1938.

Bourgeois, Léon. *Discours en faveur de l'assistance à l'enfance.* Albi: Imprimerie Pezous, 1897.

Brueyre, Loys. "Comité de défense des enfants traduits en justice," *Revue philanthropique* 1 (1897).

————. "L'Ecole algérienne de Ben-Chicao fondée pour les enfants assistés de la Seine," *Revue philanthropique* (1899–1900).

————. "Projet de loi sur le service des enfants assistés, dispositions financières," *Revue philanthropique* 14 (1903–1904).

Buisson, Ferdinand. *La Foi laïque: Extraits de discours et d'écrits (1878–1911).* 2d ed. Paris: Hachette, 1913.

Bureau, Paul. *La Crise moral des temps nouveau.* Paris: Bloud et Cie, 1907.

Chevallier, Pierre, and B. Grosperrin, eds. *l'Enseignement français de la Révolution à nos jours.* Vol. 2, *Documents.* Paris: Mouton et Cie, 1971.

Congrès international de la protection de l'enfance (Bordeaux, 1895). Bordeaux: Librairie Bourlange, n.d.

Congrès international de la protection de l'enfance (Bruxelles). Brussels: Imprimerie du Moniteur Belge, 1913.

Congrès international de la protection de l'enfance (Palais du Trocadero, 15–23 juin 1883). Paris: Pédone-Lauriel, 1885.

David, Edouard. *La Fille Bazentin: Pièce social en quatre actes sur l'Assistance publique.* Amien: Imprimerie du Progrès de la Somme, 1908.

Delzons, Louis. *La Famille française et son évolution.* Paris: Armand Colin, 1913.

Dolanne, Gilbert. *Un Paria moderne: Le pupille de l'Assistance publique.* Saint-Dizier: A. Brulliard, 1929.

Droz, Gustave. *Monsieur, madame et bébé.* Paris: V. Havard, 1878.

Durkheim, Emile. *Durkheim and the Law*. Edited by Steven Lukes and Andrew Scull. New York: St. Martin's Press, 1983.

————. *Moral Education: A Study in the Theory and Application of the Sociology of Education*. Translated by Everett K. Wilson and Herman Schnurer. New York: Free Press of Glencoe, 1961.

————. *Textes*. Edited by Victor Karady. 3 vols. Paris: Editions de Minuit, 1975.

Engels, Friedrich. *The Origins of the Family, Private Property, and the State*. New York: International Publishers, 1972.

Espinasse, R. *L'Ouvrière de l'aiguille à Toulouse: Etude d'économie sociale*. Toulouse: Edouard Privat, 1906.

Fouillée, Alfred. *La Conception morale et civique de l'enseignement*. Paris: Editions de la Revue Bleue, n.d.

————. *La France au point de vue morale*. 2d ed. Paris: Félix Alcan, 1900.

Gegout, Ernest. *Les Parias: Vie anecdotique des enfants abandonnés placés sous la tutelle de l'Assistance publique*. Paris: Bureaux du journal *l'Attaque*, 1898.

Gérard, Georges. *Régime actuel des enfants assistés de la Seine*. Paris: Edouard Duchomin, 1899.

Guyot, Yves. *La Prostitution*. Paris: G. Charpentier, 1882.

Haussonville, Othenin d'. "L'Enfance à Paris," *Revue des deux mondes* 17 (1876).

Janet, Paul. *La Famille: Leçons de philosophie morale*. Paris, 1873.

Lallemand, Léon. *La Question des enfants abandonnés et delaissés au XIXe siècle*. Paris: Alphonse Picard/Guillaumin et Cie, 1885.

[Landrin, Amélie]. *Assistance publique à l'Exposition universelle de 1900 à Paris: Rapport du comité d'installation*. N.p., [1900].

Lefebvre, Charles. *La Famille en France dans le droit et dans les moeurs*. Paris: Marcel Giard et Cie, 1920.

Legouvé, Ernest. *Histoire morale des femmes*. 7th ed. Paris: Didier, 1882.

————. *Les Pères et les enfants au XIXe siècle: La jeunesse*. 3d ed. Paris, n.d.

Léonard, Madeleine. *Les Enfants assistés en droit comparé*. Melun: Imprimerie administrative, 1938.

Le Play, Frédéric. *L'Organisation de la famille selon le vrai modèle signalé par l'histoire de toutes les races et de tous les temps*. Paris: Saint Michel, 1871.

Littré, Emile. *Dictionnaire de la langue française*. 4 vols. Paris: Librairie Hachette et Cie, 1877.

————. *Dictionnaire de la langue française*. Paris: Hachette et Cie, 1889.

Mayeur, Alexandre. *De la mortalité excessive du premier âge considérée comme cause de dépopulation et des moyens d'y remédier*. Paris: J.-B. Baillière et fils, 1873.

Melin, Gabriel. *Droit romain: Essai sur la clientèle. Droit français: De la protection légale des enfants légitimes contre les abus de la puissance paternelle*. Nancy: E. Desté, 1889.

Monod, Henri. *L'Assistance publique en France en 1889*. Paris: Imprimerie nationale, 1900.

————. *L'Assistance publique en France en 1900*. Paris: Imprimerie nationale, n.d.

————. *Les Enfants assistés de France*. Melun: Imprimerie administrative, 1898.

Montesquieu. *Persian Letters*. Translated by C. J. Betts. Harmondsworth, England: Penguin Books, 1973.

Moreau de Tours, Paul. *La Folie chez les enfants*. Paris: Librairie J.-B. Baillière et fils, 1888.

Napias, Dr. Henri. "L'Assistance publique à l'Exposition universelle de 1900," *Revue philanthropique* (1897).

Radenac, V. *Du rôle de l'Etat dans la protection des enfants maltraités ou moralement abandonnés: Commentaire de la loi du 24 juillet 1889 (Titre II)*. Paris: Arthur Rousseau, 1901.

Ravon, Dr. E. *Guide du médecin examinateur de l'assistance aux viellards, infirmes et incurables et du médecin inspecteur des enfants protegés et assistés et des écoles*. Paris: Berger Levrault, 1911.

Rebeillard, E. *Les Enfants assistés: Historique-règlementation, lois des 27 et 28 juin 1904, règlement du département de la Seine*. Paris: H. Dunod et E. Pinat, 1908.

Rey, Emile. *Assistance aux enfants des familles indigentes*. N.p., [1900].

Rigaud, Louis. *L'Evolution du droit de la femme de Rome à nos jours*. Paris: Spes, 1930.

Rivet, Auguste. *Législation sur les pupilles de la nation: Textes législatifs et administratifs (27 juillet 1917–1er décembre 1920) et commentaire pratique*. Paris: Editions de la "Documentation Catholique," 1921.

Rousseau, Jean-Jacques. *Emile, ou de l'éducation*. Edited by Marcel Launay. Paris: Flammarion, 1966.

———. *Emile, or On Education*. Translated by Allan Bloom. New York: Basic Books, 1979.

Simon, Charles. *De la création d'écoles professionelles pour les pupiles difficiles de l'Assistance publique (loi du 28 juillet 1904)*. Paris: Arthur Rousseau, 1908.

Simon, Jules. *L'Ouvrier de huit ans*. Paris: A. Lacroix, Verboeckhoven et Cie, 1867.

Strauss, Paul. *L'Enfance malheureuse*. Paris: Bibliothèque Charpentier, 1896.

Thabaut, Jules. *L'Evolution de la législation sur la famille depuis 1804*. Toulouse: Edouard Privat, 1913.

Tocqueville, Alexis de. *The Old Regime and the French Revolution*. Translated by Stuart Gilbert. Garden City, N.Y.: Doubleday, 1955.

Tolstoy, Leo. *Anna Karenina*. Translated by David Magarshack. New York: Signet, 1961.

Tourtel, Roger, and Jean Favard. *Cent ans d'assistance publique à Paris, 1849–1949*. Paris: Imprimerie de Bobigny, 1949.

Vallès, Jules. *L'Enfant*. Paris: Flammarion, 1968.

Vidocq, Eugène-François. *Mémoires de Vidocq, chef de la police de Sûreté, jusqu'en 1827*. Paris: Tenon, 1828–29.

Vingtrinier, [Arthus-Barthélemy]. *Des prisons et des prisonniers*. Versailles: Klefer, 1840.

Weber, Max. *Max Weber*. Edited by S. M. Miller. New York: Thomas Y. Crowell, 1963.

Zola, Emile. *L'Assommoir*. Paris: Garnier Flammarion, 1969.

———. *L'Assommoir*. Translated by Leonard Tancock. Harmondsworth, England: Penguin Books, 1970.

———. *Le Docteur Pascal*. Paris: Charpentier, 1893.

———. *Nana*. [Paris]: Fasquelle, 1963.

Secondary Sources

Agulhon, Maurice. *La République: De Jules Ferry à François Mitterrand, 1880 à nos jours*. Paris: Hachette, 1990.

Aisenberg, Andrew R. "Contagious Disease and the Government of Paris in the Age of Pasteur." Ph.D. diss., Yale University, 1993.

Alaimo, Kathleen. "Adolescence in the Popular Milieu in France during the Early Third Republic: Efforts to Define and Shape a Stage of Life." Ph.D. diss., University of Wisconsin, Madison, 1988.

————. "Shaping Adolescence in the Popular Milieu: Social Policy, Reformers, and French Youth, 1870–1920," *Journal of Family History* 17, no. 4 (1992).

Allain, Ernest. *l'Oeuvre scolaire de la Révolution, 1789–1802*. New York: Burt Frank, 1969.

Allen, James Smith. *In the Public Eye: A History of Reading in Modern France, 1800–1940*. Princeton: Princeton University Press, 1991.

Amussen, Susan Dwyer. *An Ordered Society: Gender and Class in Early Modern England*. Oxford: Basil Blackwell, 1988.

Ariès, Philippe. *Centuries of Childhood: A Social History of Family Life*. Translated by Robert Baldick. New York: Vintage, 1962.

Arnaud, André-Jean. *Les Juristes face à la société du XIXe siècle à nos jours*. Paris: Presses Universitaires de France, 1975.

Aron, Jean-Paul, ed. *Misérables et glorieuses: La femme au XIXe siècle*. Brussels: Editions Complexes, 1984.

Baczko, Bronislaw. *Les Imaginaires sociaux: Mémoires et espoirs collectifs*. Paris: Payot, 1984.

Barrows, Susanna. "After the Commune: Alcoholism, Temperance, and Literature in the Early Third Republic." In *Consciousness and Class Experience in Nineteenth-Century Europe*, edited by John M. Merriman. New York: Holmes and Meier, 1979.

————. *Distorting Mirrors: Visions of the Crowd in Late Nineteenth-Century France*. New Haven: Yale University Press, 1981.

Barthes, Roland. "Structure du fait divers." In *Essais Critiques*. Paris: Editions du Seuil, 1964.

Beecher, Jonathan. *Charles Fourier: The Visionary and His World*. Berkeley: University of California, 1987.

————, ed. and trans. *The Utopian Vision of Charles Fourier: Selected Texts on Work, Love, and Passionate Attraction*. Boston: Beacon Press, 1971.

Behlmer, George K. *Child Abuse and Moral Reform in England, 1870–1918*. Stanford: Stanford University Press, 1982.

Benabou, Erica-Marie. *La Prostitution et la police des moeurs au XVIIIe siècle*. Paris: Librairie Académique Perrin, 1987.

Berenson, Edward. *The Trial of Madame Caillaux*. Berkeley: University of California Press, 1992.

Bergeron, Louis. *France under Napoleon*. Translated by R. R. Palmer. Princeton: Princeton University Press, 1981.

Berlanstein, Lenard R. "Vagrants, Beggars, and Thieves: Delinquent Boys in Mid-Nineteenth Century Paris," *Journal of Social History* 12, no. 4 (summer 1979).

Bezucha, Robert J. "The Moralization of Society: The Enemies of Popular Culture in the Nineteenth Century" In *The Wolf and the Lamb: Popular Culture in France from the Old Regime to the Twentieth Century*, edited by Jacques Beauroy, Marc Bertrand, and Edward T. Gargan. Saratoga: ANMA Libri, 1976.

Black, Mindie Lazarus, and Susan F. Hirsch, eds. *Contested States: Law, Hegemony, and Resistance*. London: Routledge, 1994.

Boisbourdain, Marie-Claude. *Comment la violence vient aux enfants*. Paris: Casterman, 1983.

Borie, Jean. *Mythologies de l'hérédité au XIXe siècle*. Paris: Editions Galilée, 1981.

Burchell, Graham, Colin Gordon, and Peter Miller, eds. *The Foucault Effect: Studies in Governmentality*. Chicago: University of Chicago Press, 1991.

Burdeau, Georges. *L'Etat*. Paris: Editions du Seuil, 1970.

Burney, Ian. "The Obscene in Legislative Language: A Case of Moral Censorship in Late Nineteenth-Century France." University of California, Berkeley, 1985. Photocopy.

Burns, Michael. *Rural Society and French Politics: Boulangism and the Dreyfus Affair, 1886–1900*. Princeton: Princeton University Press, 1984.

Cattelona, Georg'Ann. "Control and Collaboration: The Role of Women in Regulating Female Sexual Behavior in Early Modern Marseille," *French Historical Studies* 18, no. 1 (spring 1993).

Chadwick, Owen. *The Secularization of the European Mind in the Nineteenth Century*. Cambridge: Cambridge University Press, 1975.

Chartier, Roger, ed. *La Correspondance: Usages de la lettre au XIXe siècle*. Paris: Fayard, 1991.

Chastenet, Jacques. *Histoire de la Troisième République*. 7 vols. Paris: Hachette, 1954.

Châtelain, Abel. *Les Migrants temporaires en France de 1800 à 1914*. 2 vols. Villeneuve d'Ascq: Université de Lille III, 1976.

Chauvière, Michel. *Enfance inadaptée: L'héritage de Vichy*. Paris: Editions ouvrières, 1980.

Chevalier, Louis. *Laboring Classes and Dangerous Classes in Paris during the First Half of the Nineteenth Century*. Translated by Frank Jellinek. Princeton: Princeton University Press, 1973.

Cholvy, Gérard, and Yves-Marie Hilaire. *Histoire religieuse de la France contemporaine, 1800/1880*. Paris: Bibliothèque historique Privat, 1990.

Cipolla, Carlo M. *Literacy and Development in the West*. Baltimore: Penguin Books, 1969.

Clark, Linda L. *Schooling the Daughters of Marianne: Textbooks and the Socialization of Girls in Modern French Primary Schools*. Albany: SUNY Press, 1984.

Coffin, Judith G. *The Politics of Women's Work: The Paris Garment Trades, 1750–1915*. Princeton: Princeton University Press, 1996.

Cole, Joshua. "The Power of Large Numbers: Population and Politics in Nineteenth-Century France." Ph.D. diss., University of California, Berkeley, 1991.

Coleman, William. *Death Is a Social Disease: Public Health and Political Economy in Early Industrial France*. Madison: University of Wisconsin Press, 1982.

Connelly, Owen. *Napoleon's Satellite Kingdoms*. New York: Free Press, 1965.

Corbin, Alain. *Les Filles de noce: Misère sexuelle et prostitution aux 19e et 20e siècles.* Paris: Aubier, 1978. Translated by Alan Sheridan as *Women for Hire: Prostitution and Sexuality in France after 1850.* Cambridge: Harvard University Press, 1990.

Cottereau, Alain. "The Distinctiveness of Working-Class Cultures in France, 1848–1900." In *Working Class Formation: Nineteenth-Century Patterns in Western Europe and the United States,* edited by Ira Katznelson and Aristide R. Zolberg. Princeton: Princeton University Press, 1986.

———. "Méconnu, la vie des enfants ouvriers au XIXe siècle," *Autrement* 10 (1977).

Crubellier, Maurice. *L'Enfance et la jeunesse dans la société française, 1800–1950.* Paris: Armand Colin, 1979.

Darnton, Robert. *The Great Cat Massacre and Other Episodes in French Cultural History.* New York: Basic Books, 1984.

Darrow, Margaret H. *Revolution in the House: Family, Class, and Inheritance in Southern France, 1775–1825.* Princeton: Princeton University Press, 1989.

Davidoff, Leonore, and Catherine Hall. *Family Fortunes: Men and Women of the English Middle Class, 1780–1850.* Chicago: University of Chicago Press, 1987.

Davis, Natalie Zemon. *Fiction in the Archives: Pardon Tales and Their Tellers in Sixteenth-Century France.* Stanford: Stanford University Press, 1987.

———. *Society and Culture in Early Modern France.* Stanford: Stanford University Press, 1975.

Degler, Carl. *At Odds: Women and the Family in America from the Revolution to the Present.* New York: Oxford University Press, 1980.

Delasselle, Claude. "Abandoned Children in Eighteenth-Century Paris." In *Deviants and the Abandoned in French Society,* edited by Robert Forster and Orest Ranum. Translated by Elborg Forster and Patricia M. Ranum. Baltimore: Johns Hopkins University Press, 1978.

Deniel, Raymond. *Une Image de la famille et de la société sous la Restauration.* Paris: Editions ouvrières, 1965.

Dessertine, Domenique. *La Société lyonnaise pour le sauvetage de l'enfance (1890–1960): Face à l'enfance en danger, un siècle d'expérience de l'internat et du placement familial.* Toulouse: Erès, 1990.

Dijksdtra, Bram. *Idols of Perversity: Fantasies of Feminine Evil in Fin-de-Siècle Culture.* New York: Oxford University Press, 1986.

Donzelot, Jacques. *The Policing of Families.* Translated by Robert Hurley. New York: Pantheon, 1979.

Duché, Jacques Didier. *L'Enfant au risque de la famille.* Paris: le Centurion, 1983.

Dupoux, Albert. *Sur les pas de Monsieur Vincent: Trois cent ans d'histoire parisienne de l'enfance abandonnée.* Paris: Revue de l'Assistance publique à Paris, 1958.

Dupuy, Micheline. *Le Petit Parisien. İLe plus fort tirage des journaux du monde entier*M. Paris: Plon, 1989.

Elias, Norbert. *The Civilizing Process: The History of Manners.* Translated by Edmund Jephcott. New York: Pantheon, 1982.

Ellis, Jack D. *The Physician-Legislators of France: Medicine and Politics in the Early Third Republic, 1870–1914.* Cambridge: Cambridge University Press, 1990.

Elwitt, Sanford. *The Third Republic Defended: Bourgeois Reform in France, 1880–1914.* Baton Rouge: Louisiana State University Press, 1986.

Emsley, Clive. "Policing the Streets of Early Nineteenth-Century Paris," *French History* 1, no. 2 (1987).

Ewald, François. *L'Etat providence.* Paris: Grasset, 1986.

————, ed. *Naissance du Code civil: La raison du législateur.* Paris: Flammarion, 1989.

Farge, Arlette. *La Vie fragile: Violences, pouvoirs et solidarités à Paris au XVIIIe siècle.* Paris: Hachette, 1986. Translated by Carol Shelton as *Fragile Lives: Violence, Power, and Solidarity in Eighteenth-Century Paris.* Cambridge: Harvard University Press, 1993.

————, ed. *Vivons dans la rue à Paris au XVIIIe siècle.* Paris: Gallimard/Julliard, 1979.

Farge, Arlette, and Michel Foucault, eds. *Le Désordre des familles: Lettres de cachet des Archives de la Bastille au XVIIIe siècle.* Paris: Gallimard, 1982.

Faure, Alain. "Enfance ouvrière, enfance coupable," *Les Révoltes logiques* 13 (winter 1980–81).

Feldbauer, Peter. *Kinderelend in Wien: Von der Armenkinderpflege zur Jugendfürsorge, 17.–19. Jahrhundert.* Vienna: Gesellschaftskritik, 1980.

Fildes, Valerie, et al., eds. *Women and Children First: International Maternal and Infant Welfare, 1870–1945.* New York: Routledge, 1993.

Fitch, Nancy. " 'Les Petits Parisiens en province': The Silent Revolution of the Allier, 1860–1900," *Journal of Family History* 11, no. 2 (1986).

Foucault, Michel. *Discipline and Punish: The Birth of the Prison.* Translated by Alan Sheridan. New York: Vintage Books, 1979.

————. *Language, Counter-Memory, Practice: Selected Essays and Interviews.* Edited by Donald F. Bouchard. Translated by Donald F. Bouchard and Sherry Simon. Ithaca: Cornell University Press, 1977.

————. *Politics, Philosophy, Culture: Interviews and Other Writings, 1977–1984.* Edited by Lawrence D. Kritzman. Translated by Alan Sheridan et al. New York: Routledge, 1988.

————. *Power/Knowledge: Selected Interviews and Other Writings, 1972–1977.* Edited by Colin Gordon. Translated by Colin Gordon et al. New York: Pantheon, 1980.

————, ed. *I, Pierre Rivière, Having Slaughtered My Mother, My Sister, and My Brother. . . .* Translated by Frank Jellinek. New York: Random House, 1975; Lincoln: University of Nebraska Press, 1982.

Fournié, Anne-Marie. "La Protection judiciaire de l'enfance en danger: Loi du 24 juillet 1889," *Textes de droit familial* (July–Sept. 1954).

Fraisse, Geneviève, and Michelle Perrot, eds. *Emerging Feminism from Revolution to World War.* Vol. 4 of *A History of Women in the West,* edited by Georges Duby and Michelle Perrot. Cambridge: Belknap Press of Harvard University Press, 1993.

Fuchs, Rachel G. *Abandoned Children: Foundlings and Child Welfare in Nineteenth-Century France.* Albany: SUNY Press, 1984.

————. "Crimes against Children in Nineteenth-Century France," *Law and Human Behavior* 6, no. 3/4 (1982).

————. "Legislation, Poverty, and Child Abandonment in Nineteenth-Century Paris," *Journal of Interdisciplinary History* 18, no. 1 (summer 1987): 55–80.

————. *Poor and Pregnant in Paris: Strategies for Survival in the Nineteenth Century*. New Brunswick: Rutgers University Press, 1992.

Furet, François, and Jacques Ozouf. *Lire et écrire: L'alphabétisation des Français de Calvin à Jules Ferry*. 2 vols. Paris: Editions de Minuit, 1977.

Furet, François, ed. *Jules Ferry: Fondateur de la République*. Paris: Ecole des Hautes Etudes en Sciences Sociales, 1985.

Gaillac, Henri. *Les Maisons de correction, 1830–1945*. Paris: Editions Cujas, 1971.

Gaillard, Jean-Michel. *Jules Ferry*. Paris: Fayard, 1989.

Gallagher, Catherine. "The Body versus the Social Body in the Works of Thomas Malthus and Henry Mayhew," *Representations* 14 (spring 1986).

Garçon, Maurice. *Histoire de la justice sous la IIIe République*. 3 vols. Paris: Arthème Fayard, 1957.

Garrioch, David. *Neighborhood and Community in Paris, 1740–1790*. Cambridge: Cambridge University Press, 1986.

Gaudemet, Yves-Henri. *Les Juristes et la vie politique de la IIIe République*. Paris: Presses Universitaires de France, 1970.

Gilissen, John. *Introduction historique au droit*. Brussels: Bruylant, 1979.

Gillis, John R. *Youth and History: Tradition and Change in European Age Relations, 1770–Present*. New York: Academic Press, 1974.

Goldstein, Jan. *Console and Classify: The French Psychiatric Profession in the Nineteenth Century*. Cambridge: Cambridge University Press, 1987.

————, ed. *Foucault and the Writing of History*. Oxford: Basil Blackwell, 1994.

Goodman, Dena. "Public Sphere and Private Life: Toward a Synthesis of Current Historiographical Approaches to the Old Regime," *History and Theory* 31, no. 1 (1992).

Gordon, Linda. *Heroes of Their Own Lives: The Politics and History of Family Violence, Boston, 1880–1960*. New York: Penguin Books, 1988.

Greenblatt, Stephen. *Renaissance Self-Fashioning: From More to Shakespeare*. Chicago: University of Chicago Press, 1980.

Grossberg, Michael. *Governing the Hearth: Law and the Family in Nineteenth-Century America*. Chapel Hill: University of North Carolina Press, 1985.

Guillais-Maury, Joëlle. *La Chair de l'autre: Le crime passionnel au XIXe siècle*. Paris: Olivier Orban, 1986.

Hacking, Ian. "The Making and Molding of Child Abuse," *Critical Inquiry* 17 (winter 1991).

Halévy, Daniel. *The End of the Notables*. Translated by Alain Silvera and June Guicharnaud. Middletown, Conn.: Wesleyan University Press, 1974.

Hanley, Sarah. "Engendering the State: Family Formation and State Building in Early Modern France," *French Historical Studies* 16, no. 1 (1989).

————. "The Monarchic State in Early Modern France: Marital Regime Government and Male Right." In *Politics, Ideology, and the Law in Early Modern Europe*, edited by Adrianna E. Bakos. Rochester: University of Rochester Press, 1994.

————. "Social Sites of Political Practice in France: Lawsuits, Civil Rights, and the Separation of Powers in Domestic and State Government," *American Historical Review* 102, no. 1 (February 1997).

Harris, Ruth. *Murders and Madness: Medicine, Law, and Society in the Fin de Siècle*. Oxford: Clarendon Press, 1989.

Harsin, Jill. *Policing Prostitution in Nineteenth-Century Paris*. Princeton: Princeton University Press, 1985.

Hartmann, Mary S. *Victorian Murderesses: A True History of Thirteen Respectable French and English Women Accused of Unspeakable Crimes*. New York: Schocken Books, 1977.

Hatzfeld, Henri. *Du paupérisme à la sécurité sociale, 1850–1940*. Paris, Armand Colin, 1971.

Hause, Steven C., with Anne R. Kenney. *Women's Suffrage and Social Politics in the French Third Republic*. Princeton: Princeton University Press, 1984.

Heywood, Colin. *Childhood in Nineteenth-Century France: Work, Health, and Education among the "Classes Populaires"*. Cambridge: Cambridge University Press, 1988.

Hildreth, Martha. *Doctors, Bureaucrats, and Public Health in France, 1888–1902*. New York: Garland, 1987.

Hunt, David. *Parents and Children in History: The Psychology of Family Life in Early Modern France*. New York: Basic Books, 1970.

Hunt, Lynn. *The Family Romance of the French Revolution*. Berkeley: University of California Press, 1992.

———. *Politics, Culture, and Class in the French Revolution*. Berkeley: University of California Press, 1984.

Hunter, John. "The Problem of the French Birth Rate on the Eve of World War I," *French Historical Studies* 11 (1962).

Irigaray, Luce. *Ethique de la différence sexuelle*. Paris: Editions de Minuit, 1984.

Johnson, Barbara. *A World of Difference*. Baltimore: Johns Hopkins University Press, 1987.

Jolly, Jean, ed. *Dictionnaire des parlementaires français: Notices biographiques sur les ministres, députés et sénateurs français de 1889 à 1940*. 8 vols. Paris: Presses Universitaires de France, 1960–77.

Jonas, Raymond A. "Monument as Ex-Voto, Monument as Historiosophy: The Basilica of the Sacré-Coeur," *French Historical Studies* 18, no. 2 (fall 1993).

Jones, H. S. *The French State in Question: Public Law and Political Argument in the Third Republic*. Cambridge: Cambridge University Press, 1993.

Joseph, Isaac, Philippe Fritsch, and Alain Battegay. "Disciplines à domicile: L'édification de la famille," *Recherches* 28 (28 November 1977).

Juillard, Etienne, ed. *Apogé et crise de la civilisation paysanne, 1789–1914*. Vol. 3 of *Histoire de la France rurale*, edited by Georges Duby and Armand Wallon. Paris: Editions du Seuil, 1976.

Kaluszynski, Martine. "Les Juristes en action: La Société générale des prisons (1877–1940) ou l'exercice politique d'une société savante." 1989. Photocopy.

Kaluszynski, Martine, and Françoise Tetard. "Un Objet: L'enfant en 'danger moral.' Une expérience: La société de patronage." 1989. Photocopy.

Kanipe, Esther Sue. "The Family, Private Property, and the State in France, 1870–1914." Ph.D. diss., University of Wisconsin, Madison, 1976.

Klinck, Dennis R. *The Word of Law*. Ottawa: Carleton University Press, 1992.

Knibiehler, Yvonne. *Les Pères aussi ont une histoire*. Paris: Hachette, 1987.

Knibiehler, Yvonne, et al. *Cornettes et blouses blanches: Les infirmières dans la société française (1880–1980)*. Paris: Hachette, 1984.

Knibiehler, Yvonne, ed. *Nous les assistantes sociales: Naissance d'une profession.* Paris: Aubier Montaigne, 1980.

Kok-Escalle, Marie Christine. *Instaurer une culture par l'enseignement de l'histoire: France, 1876–1912.* Berne: Peter Lang, 1988.

Kselman, Claudia Scheck. "The Modernization of Family Law: The Politics and Ideology of Family Reform in Third Republic France." Ph.D. diss., University of Michigan, 1980.

Landes, Joan B. *Women and the Public Sphere in the Age of the French Revolution.* Ithaca: Cornell University Press, 1988.

Laplaige, Danielle. *Sans famille à Paris: Orphelins et enfants abandonnés de la Seine au XIXe siècle.* Paris: Centurion, 1989.

Lasch, Christopher. *Haven in a Heartless World: The Family Besieged.* New York: Basic Books, 1977.

Legrand, Louis. *L'Influence du positivisme dans l'oeuvre scolaire de Jules Ferry: Les origines de la laïcité.* Paris: Librairie Marcel Rivière, 1966.

Lequin, Yves, ed. *La Société.* Vol. 2 of *Histoire des Français XIXe–XXe siècles.* Paris: Armand Colin, 1983.

Lévy, Marie-Françoise. *De mères en filles: L'éducation des Françaises, 1850–1880.* Paris: Calmann-Lévy, 1984.

———, ed. *L'Enfant, la famille et la Révolution française.* Paris: Olivier Orban, 1990.

Lewis, Jane. *The Politics of Motherhood: Child and Maternal Welfare in England, 1900–1939.* London: Croom Helm; Montreal: McGill-Queen's University Press, 1980.

Locke, Robert R. *French Legitimists and the Politics of Moral Order in the Early Third Republic.* Princeton: Princeton University Press, 1974.

Lougee, Carolyn C. *Le Paradis des femmes: Women, Salons, and Social Stratification in Seventeenth-Century France.* Princeton: Princeton University Press, 1976.

Lynch, Katherine A. *Family, Class, and Ideology in Early Industrial France: Social Policy and the Working-Class Family, 1825–1848.* Madison: University of Wisconsin Press, 1988.

MacMillan, James C. *Housewife or Harlot: The Place of Women in French Society, 1870–1940.* New York: St. Martin's Press, 1981.

Mandler, Peter, ed. *The Uses of Charity: The Poor on Relief in the Nineteenth-Century Metropolis.* Philadelphia: University of Pennsylvania Press, 1990.

Margadant, Jo Burr. *Madame le professeur: Women Educators in the Third Republic.* Princeton: Princeton University Press, 1990.

Martin, Benjamin F. *Crime and Criminal Justice under the Third Republic: The Shame of Marianne.* Baton Rouge: Louisiana State University Press, 1990.

Matlock, Jann. *Scenes of Seduction: Prostitution, Hysteria, and Reading Difference in Nineteenth-Century France.* New York: Columbia University Press, 1994.

Maugue, Annelise. *L'Identité masculine en crise au tournant du siècle, 1871–1914.* Paris: Rivages, 1987.

Mayeur, Françoise. *L'Education des filles en France au XIXe siècle.* Paris: Hachette, 1979.

———. *L'Enseignement sécondaire des jeunes filles sous la Troisième République.* Paris: A. Colin, 1977.

Mayeur, Jean-Marie. *Les Débuts de la IIIe République, 1871–1898*. Paris: Editions du Seuil, 1973.

Mayeur, Jean-Marie, and Madeleine Rebérioux. *The Third Republic from Its Origins to the Great War, 1871–1914*. Translated by J. R. Foster. Cambridge: Maison des Sciences de l'Homme and Cambridge University Press, 1984.

Maza, Sarah. *Private Lives and Public Affairs: The Causes Célèbres of Prerevolutionary France*. Berkeley: University of California Press, 1993.

McDougall, Mary Lynn. "Protecting Infants: The French Campaign for Maternity Leaves, 1890's–1913," *French Historical Studies* 13 (1983).

McLaren, Angus. *Sexuality and Social Order: The Debate over the Fertility of Women and Workers in France, 1770–1920*. New York: Holmes and Meier, 1983.

Merrick, Jeffrey. "Fathers and Kings: Patriarchalism and Absolutism in Eighteenth-Century French Politics," *Studies on Voltaire and the Eighteenth Century* 308 (1993).

Merriman, John Henry. *The Civil Law Tradition: An Introduction to the Legal Systems of Western Europe and Latin America*. 2d ed. Stanford: Stanford University Press, 1985.

Meyer, Philippe. *L'Enfant et la raison d'état*. Paris: Editions du Seuil, 1977.

Miller, D. A. *The Novel and the Police*. Berkeley: University of California Press, 1988.

Minson, Jeffrey. *Genealogies of Morals: Nietzsche, Foucault, Donzelot, and the Eccentricity of Ethics*. London: Macmillan, 1985.

Miquet, Pierre. *La Troisième République*. Paris: Fayard, 1989.

Moch, Leslie Page. *Paths to the City: Rural Migration in Nineteenth-Century France*. Beverly Hills: Sage, 1983.

Monestier, Alain, ed. *Le Fait divers*, catalog, Musée national des arts et traditions populaires. Paris: Editions de la Réunion des musées nationaux, 1982.

Moses, Claire Goldberg. *French Feminism in the Nineteenth Century*. Albany: SUNY Press, 1984.

Moses, Claire Goldberg, and Leslie Wahl Rabine, eds. *Feminism, Socialism, and French Romanticism*. Bloomington: Indiana University Press, 1993.

Le Mouvement social 144. Special issue: "Paternalismes d'hier et d'aujourd'hui." Edited by Marianne Debouzy (July–September 1988).

Murard, Léon, and Patrick Zylberman. *Le Petit travailleur infatigable: Villes-usines, habitat et intimités au XIXe siècle*. Paris: Recherches, 1976.

Nardinelli, Clark. *Child Labor and the Industrial Revolution*. Bloomington: Indiana University Press, 1990.

Nash, Suzanne, ed. *Home and Its Dislocations in Nineteenth-Century France*. Albany: SUNY Press, 1993.

Neirinck, Claire. *La Protection de la personne de l'enfant contre ses parents*. Paris: Librairie générale de droit et de jurisprudence, 1984.

Nord, Philip. "The Welfare State in France, 1870–1914," *French Historical Studies* 18, no. 3 (spring 1994).

Nye, Robert A. *Crime, Madness, and Politics in Modern France: The Medical Concept of National Decline*. Princeton: Princeton University Press, 1984.

O'Brien, Patricia. *The Promise of Punishment: Prisons in Nineteenth-Century France*. Princeton: Princeton University Press, 1982.

Offen, Karen. "Depopulation, Nationalism, and Feminism in *Fin-de-Siècle* France," *American Historical Review* 89 (June 1984).

Ogden, Philip E., and Paul E. White, eds. *Migrants in Modern France: Population Mobility in the Later Nineteenth and Twentieth Centuries*. London: Unwin Hyman, 1989.

Orecchioni, Pierre. "Eugène Sue: Mesure d'un succès," *Europe* (1982).

Pedersen, Susan. *Family, Dependence, and the Origins of the Welfare State: Britain and France, 1914–1945*. New York: Cambridge University Press, 1994.

Pelletier, André. *La Femme dans la société gallo-romaine*. Paris: Picard, 1984.

Perrot, Michelle. "On the Formation of the French Working Class." In *Working Class Formation: Nineteenth-Century Patterns in Western Europe and the United States*, edited by Ira Katznelson and Aristide R. Zolberg. Princeton: Princeton University Press, 1986.

———. "Quand la société prend peur de sa jeunesse en France, au 19e siècle." In *Les Jeunes et les autres*, edited by Michelle Perrot. Vol. 1 of 2. Paris: CRIV, 1986.

———. "Sur la ségrégation de l'enfance au XIXe siècle," *La Psychiatrie de l'enfant* 25, fasc. 1 (1982).

———. "The Three Ages of Industrial Discipline in Nineteenth-Century France." In *Consciousness and Class Experience in Nineteenth-Century Europe*, edited by John Merriman. New York: Holmes and Meier, 1979.

———, ed. *From the Fires of Revolution to the Great War*. Translated by Arthur Goldhammer. Vol. 4 of *A History of Private Life*, edited by Philippe Ariès and Georges Duby. Cambridge: Belknap Press of Harvard University Press, 1990.

———, ed. *L'Impossible prison: Recherches sur le système pénitentiaire au XIXe siècle*. Paris: Editions du Seuil, 1980.

Phillips, Roderick. *Untying the Knot: A Short History of Divorce*. Cambridge: Cambridge University Press, 1991.

Pisani-Ferry, Fresnette. *Le Coup d'état manquée du 16 mai 1877*. Paris: Robert Laffont, 1965.

Pollock, Linda. *Forgotten Children: Parent-Child Relations from 1500–1900*. Cambridge: Cambridge University Press, 1983.

Procacci, Giovanna. *Gouverner la misère: La question sociale en France, 1789–1848*. Paris: Editions du Seuil, 1993.

Rancière, Danielle. "Le Philanthrope et sa famille," *Les Révoltes logiques* 8/9 (winter 1979).

Reid, Donald. "Industrial Paternalism: Discourse and Practice in Nineteenth-Century Mining and Metallurgy," *Comparative Studies in Society and History* 24, no. 4 (October 1985): 579–607.

———. "Schools and the Paternalist Project at Le Creusot, 1850–1914," *Journal of Social History* 27, no. 1 (fall 1993): 129–43.

Reid, Roddy. *Death of the Family: Discourse, Fiction, and Desire in France*. Stanford: Stanford University Press, 1994.

Rémond, René. *L'Anticléricalisme*. Paris: Fayard, 1977.

Renouard, Jean-Marie. *De l'enfant coupable à l'enfant inadapté: Le traitement social et politique de la déviance*. Paris: Centurion, 1990.

Riley, Denise. *"Am I That Name?" Feminism and the Category of "Women" in History*. Minneapolis: University of Minnesota Press, 1988.

Robert, Paul. *Dictionnaire alphabétique et analogique de la langue française*. Paris: Société du Nouveau Littré, 1963.

Roberts, Mary Louise. *Civilization without Sexes: Reconstructing Gender in Postwar France, 1917–1927*. Chicago: University of Chicago Press, 1994.

Rollet-Echalier, Catherine. *La Politique à l'égard de la petite enfance sous la IIIe République*. Paris: Editions de l'INED/Presses Universitaires de France, 1990.

Rosanvallon, Pierre. *L'Etat en France de 1789 à nos jours*. Paris: Editions du Seuil, 1990.

Roumajon, Yves. *Enfants perdus, enfants punis: Histoire de la jeunesse délinquante en France*. Paris: Editions Robert Laffont, 1989.

Sandrin, Jean. *Enfants trouvés, enfants ouvriers, 17e–19e siècle*. Paris: Aubier, 1982.

Schafer, Sylvia. "Law, Labor, and the Spectacle of the Body: Protecting Child Street Performers in Nineteenth-Century France," *The International Journal of Children's Rights* 4 (1996). Reprinted with slight changes in *Governing Childhood*, edited by Anne McGillivray. Aldershot, England: Dartmouth, 1997.

———. "When the Child Is the Father of the Man: Work, Sexual Difference, and the Guardian-State in Third Republic France," *History and Theory* (1992) *beiheft* 31: History and Feminist Theory. Reprinted in *Feminists Revision History*, edited by Ann-Louise Shapiro. New Brunswick: Rutgers University Press, 1994.

Schnapper, Bernard. "La Correction paternelle et le mouvement des idées au dix-neuvième siècle (1789–1935)," *Revue historique* 263 (1980).

Scott, Joan Wallach, *Gender and the Politics of History*. New York: Columbia University Press, 1988.

Shapiro, Ann-Louise. *Breaking the Codes: Female Criminality in Fin-de-Siècle Paris*. Stanford: Stanford University Press, 1996.

———. *Housing the Poor of Paris, 1850–1902*. Madison: University of Wisconsin Press, 1985.

Shengold, Leonard. *Soul Murder: The Effects of Childhood Abuse and Deprivation*. New Haven: Yale University Press, 1989.

Shorter, Edward. *The Making of the Modern Family*. New York: Basic Books, 1977.

Smith, Bonnie G. *Confessions of a Concierge: Madame Lucie's History of Twentieth-Century France*. New Haven: Yale University Press, 1985.

———. *Ladies of the Leisure Class: The Bourgeoises of Northern France in the Nineteenth Century*. Princeton: Princeton University Press, 1981.

Sohn, Anne-Marie. "The Golden Age of Male Adultery: The Third Republic," *Journal of Social History* 28, no. 3 (spring 1995).

———. "Les Rôles féminins dans la vie privée à l'époque de la 3ème République." Thèse d'Etat, Université de Paris I, 1993.

Sonenscher, Michael. *The Hatters of Eighteenth-Century France*. Berkeley: University of California Press, 1987.

———. *Work and Wages: Natural Law, Politics, and the Eighteenth-Century French Trades*. Cambridge: Cambridge University Press, 1989.

Sorlin, Pierre. *La Société française*. Vol. 1, *1840–1914*. Paris: Arthaud, 1969.

Stansell, Christine. *City of Women: Sex and Class in New York, 1789–1860*. New York: Alfred A. Knopf, 1986.

Stewart, Mary Lynn. *Women, Work, and the French State: Labour, Protection, and Social Patriarchy, 1879–1919*. Kingston: McGill-Queen's University Press, 1989.

Stock-Morton, Phyllis. *Moral Education for a Secular Society: The Development of "Morale Laïque" in Nineteenth Century France*. Albany: SUNY Press, 1988.

Stone, Lawrence. *The Family, Sex, and Marriage in England, 1500–1800*. New York: Harper and Row, 1977.

Stora-Lamarre, Annie. *L'Enfer de la Troisième République: Censeurs et pornographes (1881–1914)*. Paris: Editions Imago, 1990.

Sussman, George D. *Selling Mothers' Milk: The Wet-Nursing Business in France, 1715–1914*. Urbana: University of Illinois, 1982.

Swart, Keonraad W. *The Sense of Decadence in Nineteenth-Century France*. The Hague: Martinus Nijhoff, 1964.

Teitelbaum, Michael S., and Jay M. Winter. *The Fear of Population Decline*. Orlando: Academic Press, 1985.

Théry, Irène, and Christian Biet, eds. *La Famille, la loi, l'état: De la Révolution au Code civil*. Paris: Editions du Centre Georges Pompidou/Imprimerie nationale, 1989.

Thiesse, A.-M. "Mutations et permanences de la culture populaire: La lecture à la Belle Epoque," *Annales: Economies, Société, Civilisations* 39, no. 1 (1984).

Thomson, David. *Democracy in France Since 1870*. London: Oxford University Press, 1969.

Tilly, Louise A. "Women and Family Strategies in French Proletarian Families," *Michigan Occasional Paper* no. 4 (fall 1978).

Tilly, Louise A., and Joan W. Scott. *Women, Work, and Family*. 2d ed. London: Methuen, 1987.

Traer, James F. *Marriage and Family in Eighteenth-Century France*. Ithaca: Cornell University Press, 1980.

Troyansky, David G. "Generational Discourse in the French Revolution." In *The French Revolution in Culture and Society*, edited by David G. Troyansky, Alfred Cismaru, and Norwood Andrews Jr. Westport, Conn.: Greenwood Press, 1991.

Untrau, Martine. "J'avais dix ans, j'habitais le 20e, c'était 1900," *Autrement* 10 (1977).

Vann, Richard T. "The Youth of *Centuries of Childhood*," *History and Theory* 21, no. 2 (1982).

Vigier, Philippe, et al., eds. *Maintien de l'ordre en France et en Europe au XIXe siècle*. Paris: Créaphis, 1987.

Walkowitz, Judith R. *Prostitution and Victorian Society: Women, Class, and the State*. Cambridge: Cambridge University Press, 1980.

Weber, Eugen. *Peasants into Frenchmen: The Modernization of Rural France, 1870–1914*. Stanford: Stanford University Press, 1976.

Weber, Samuel. *Institution and Interpretation*. Theory and History of Literature, vol. 31. Minneapolis: University of Minnesota Press, 1987.

Weissbach, Lee Shai. *Child Labor Reform in Nineteenth-Century France: Assuring the Future Harvest*. Baton Rouge: Louisiana State University Press, 1989.

———. "*Oeuvre Industrielle, Oeuvre Morale*: The *Sociétés de Patronage* of Nineteenth-Century France," *French Historical Studies* 15, no. 1 (spring 1987).

Williams, Alan. "Patterns of Conflict in Eighteenth-Century Parisian Families," *Journal of Family History* 18, no. 1 (1993).

Zeldin, Theodore, ed. *Conflicts in French Society: Anticlericalism, Education, and Morals in the Nineteenth Century.* London: George Allen and Unwin, 1970.

————. *France, 1848–1945: Ambition and Love.* Oxford: Oxford University Press, 1979.

Zucchi, John E. *The Little Slaves of the Harp: Italian Child Street Musicians in Nineteenth-Century Paris, London, and New York.* Montreal: McGill-Queen's University Press, 1992.

About the Author

SYLVIA SCHAFER is Assistant Professor of History at the University of Wisconsin–Milwaukee.

The History of Everyday Life: Reconstructing Historical Experiences and
Ways of Life *edited by Alf Ludtke*

The Savage Freud and Other Essays on Possible and Retrievable Selves
by Ashis Nandy

Children and the Politics of Culture *edited by Sharon Stephens*

Intimacy and Exclusion: Religious Politics in Pre-Revolutionary Baden
by Dagmar Herzog

What Was Socialism, and What Comes Next? *by Katherine Verdery*

Citizen and Subject: Contemporary Africa and the Legacy of Late Colonialism
by Mahmood Mamdani

Colonialism and Its Forms of Knowledge: The British in India
by Bernard S. Cohn

Charred Lullabies: Chapters in an Anthropology of Violence
by E. Valentine Daniel

Theft of an Idol: Text and Context in the Representation of Collective Violence
by Paul R. Brass

Essays on the Anthropology of Reason
by Paul Rabinow

Vision, Race, and Modernity: A Visual Economy of the Andean Image World
by Deborah Poole

Children in Moral Danger and the Problem of Government in
Third Republic France *by Sylvia Schafer*